EFFECTIVE METHODS
FOR BUILDING
THE HIGH SCHOOL BAND

EFFECTIVE METHODS
FOR BUILDING
THE HIGH SCHOOL BAND

Richard A. Otto

Parker Publishing Company, Inc.
West Nyack, New York

PRINTED IN THE UNITED STATES OF AMERICA
ISBN−0-13-244269-8
B&P

Dedication

To my wife, Margaret, and to
Richard, Robert, John, and Catherine
for their forbearance and assistance.

Why I Wrote This Book

The purpose of this book is to serve as a source of information and guidance for directors of school bands as they endeavor to meet the responsibilities and challenges of an increasingly demanding profession. Furthermore, it is hoped that the ideas, suggestions, and techniques contained in this volume will be of practical value to all who read it.

The material included in the book is based upon many years of varied experience in teaching and directing both instrumental and choral music at the senior high school level and in supervising music at all levels. While it is written primarily as an aid to active band directors, it should prove to be an invaluable source of information for those preparing to enter the field of school music.

Since the development of the senior high school band is dependent upon the establishment of a program of instrumental instruction, suggestions for organizing such a program are offered. In addition, a number of plans under which such a program can function are described and materials that are appropriate to use in each case are included. The advantages and disadvantages of various methods of scheduling the instrumental instructional program are weighed, as are those pertaining to the band itself.

In these days of building new schools to meet the needs of an expanding population, the band director may be confronted with problems relating to the planning for new facilities or the renovation of an existing area. In view of this possibility and its bearing upon the growth and success of the band program, the author, who has designed several music areas, has included information and advice regarding the location, size, and makeup of the various kinds of rooms found in the high school music area. Beyond this, equipment and furnishings felt to be necessary to the implementation of the band program are included, together with suggestions concerning their use, care, and storage.

Guidelines for the procurement of instruments and for the development of complete and balanced instrumentations are provided, with specific recommendations as to the number of each type of instrument needed in bands of different sizes. Furthermore, because of the importance attached to the organization and administration of the band, matters concerning the seating of the band, taking attendance, caring for music, holding elections, appointing section leaders, developing a handbook, and creating an awards system are discussed at some length.

Since one of the primary keys to success in the development of a fine high school band is that of the director's know-how when it comes to dealing with rehearsal problems, a number of approaches to rehearsing are outlined in some detail. Rehearsal techniques that have proven to be effective in achieving the desired results are amply provided.

The all important subject of public relations is also brought into focus, especially as it concerns the appearance of the high school band in events which occur in the school, the community, and beyond. A set of policies governing such performances is put forth to guide school band directors and administrators in reaching a decision regarding the educational, musical, and social implications and values inherent in these appearances.

Richard A. Otto

Acknowledgments

My grateful thanks for assistance in connection with the writing of this book go to: Alan J. Wallace, a member of the Wallingford Public School music faculty, who served as a critic reader; Don H. Razey, Educational Director, and Richard E. Thorne of the Educational Division of J.W. Pepper & Sons Inc., of Philadelphia, Pennsylvania, for materials relating to the care and filing of music and other information relevant to certain sections of the book; Earl A. Fortin of Holyoke, Massachusetts, an agent for the Century Custom Recording Service, for guidance in the techniques of using a tape recorder; John F. Marriott, Director of Audio-Visual Education in the Wallingford, Connecticut, Public Schools, for aid in connection with the use of motion picture and video recording equipment.

TABLE OF CONTENTS

EFFECTIVE METHODS
FOR BUILDING
THE HIGH SCHOOL BAND

chapter 1

Developing a Feeder
System for the Band

While the specific avenues of approach used in developing a high school band may vary in a number of ways, all school band directors should employ certain common practices during this process.

The truly successful high school band program has a solid foundation of instrumental instruction established in the early elementary grades and carried on with planned continuity through the middle and upper grades and including the senior high school. This program should involve a certain amount of exploratory experience in the playing of pre-band instruments. The length of time allotted to this activity would necessarily be influenced by several factors, foremost among which would be the need to determine whether this activity is to be carried on by the classroom teacher or by a music specialist. Once this has been established, other factors including the frequency and length of class meetings and the number and size of these classes may be determined. The ultimate decision regarding the nature of the program would depend upon the importance attached to this work as it relates to the total curriculum, and the availability of qualified personnel to implement the program.

The prevailing educational philosophy of the individual school system will determine whether this activity is to be shared by entire class units at a specific grade level or whether it is to be implemented on a more selective basis. While it is easier to choose potential instrumental candidates from a selected group, much can be said in favor of instituting a program of this type on the basis of broad involvement. Because of obvious individual differences, some pupils readily display their musical potential while others need to be discovered. Beyond this, participation by the entire class as a unit is of value in promoting music reading skills, increasing an awareness of the elements of music, and in general, fostering a greater interest in music on the part of the many.

PROMOTING INTEREST

The well organized approach to building a band program should include scheduled opportunities for music educators to visit the classroom of the grade level selected as the beginning level for the pre-band instrument training program throughout the school system. In this way, the staff member or members will be afforded a direct means of communication and a "stage" for demonstrating the instrument to be used in this training program. The alert music educator will seize upon this opportunity to stimulate interest in this activity and to explain further the many advantages of participation. In school systems where this program is established, pupils of similar age levels should be brought into the demonstration process, since their performance will have a more influential effect upon those in the immediate audience. If such a program does not exist, it may fall to the music specialist to demonstrate the basic techniques involved in playing this type of instrument. This would require a simple explanation of blowing, tonguing, and fingering as related to the chosen instrument, and at the same time should indicate that other basic music knowledge and skills attained up to that particular grade level would apply.

In school systems where an established pre-band instrument program exists, the best salesmen for the program are the youngsters themselves. Their interest and enthusiasm will exert a positive influence on those who are about to begin this kind of learning experience.

CHOOSING THE PRE-BAND TRAINING INSTRUMENT

The selection of an instrument to be used in the pre-band training program is an important one, with the responsibility for the proper choice falling within the province of the music teacher in charge. Whether the instrument selected is a recorder or one of a number of plastic types on the market designed for this purpose, the person making the decision should be aware of its blowing qualities, realizing, for example, that it will be used by children of nine, ten, or eleven years of age. The matter of its blowing qualities concerns itself not only with the ease of blowing and the amount of air required, but also with the kind of tone that can be produced. Closely allied to these features would be the matter of intonation; that is, the reliability of pitch within the instrument itself as well as the consistency of pitch among a group of instruments of the same kind. Another factor influencing the choice of instrument is the location of the finger holes as related to the size of a child's hand and the length of his fingers.

Also important, yet easily overlooked, is the matter of durability. Children at this age level are not inclined to exert great care in the use of this instrument, especially after the novelty stage has passed. Some manufacturers supply covers or cases to protect the instrument, at least from minor damage. Care should also be taken to see that there are no sharp edges, particularly on the mouthpiece section, as there might be in a molded type of instrument. Additional items to be noted include the size of the mouthpiece aperture, which if too large could make sustaining of tones very difficult; the location of the air vent on the top of the mouthpiece, which if too close to the end of the mouthpiece may lead to covering by the upper lip, resulting in a "smothered" tone; and the general size and contour of the mouthpiece, which if improperly designed could lead to discomfort and fatigue. In recent years manufacturers of these instruments have initiated a number of improvements which have eliminated some of the defects found in earlier models.

LINES OF COMMUNICATION

During the whole process of organizing the exploratory stages of a program of instrumental music, it is necessary to establish and maintain various lines of communication. This could be initiated by obtaining permission from the Superintendent of Schools for such a program and securing his cooperation in facilitating certain organizational matters. The assistance of elementary school principals should also be sought, as well as that of the classroom teacher, assuming they are to be involved in one way or another. Certainly, if it is felt by school authorities that this exploratory experience should be shared, for example, by all fourth grade pupils, then the classroom teacher's role will be a most significant one. If, on the other hand, this activity is established along highly selective lines with separate schedule provisions, it is likely to be implemented by members of the music staff only, thus limiting the active role of the classroom teacher.

Through the judicious use of announcements, written notices, letters to the parents, and other news media, the general public can be made aware of this phase of the school curriculum and be kept informed of its activity and progress. This effort to keep all individuals concerned in any way with the program fully informed will augur well in the direction of promoting a sympathetic understanding and support for the endeavor. (See Illustrations 1-1 and 1-2).

ILLUSTRATION 1-1

WALLINGFORD PUBLIC SCHOOLS
Wallingford, Connecticut
September 15, 1967

Dear Parent:

Instrumental music lessons will again be offered in the Wallingford Public Schools from Grades 5 through 12.

This year a somewhat different approach will be used in relation to the "beginner" stage of the program. Pupils termed "beginners," whether Grade 5 or 6, will be required to participate in a "pre-band" (orchestra) instrument training program of approximately ten weeks duration under the tutelage of a member of the school music faculty. Those who successfully meet the requirements of this program will qualify to enroll in the regular instrumental program. These requirements include: attendance at all group lessons, music reading aptitude, sense of rhythm, sense of pitch, ability to control breath, ability to articulate clearly, manipulative skills, and ensemble aptitude.

The purpose of this program is to upgrade and improve the results of the regular instrumental program in the schools, to avoid having parents expend unnecessary amounts of money for the purchase of an instrument, to promote better use of the pupil's time, to eliminate waste of time in scheduling, and to promote more efficient use of the teacher's time.

The instrument to be used in this training program will be a soprano recorder to be selected and ordered in bulk quantity by members of the music faculty. These will be purchased at a nominal fee and thus become the pupil's possession.

Upon completion of this training period, arrangements will be made by school authorities in cooperation with area music dealers for the eventual purchase of legitimate instruments of the band and orchestra by parents of pupils who successfully meet all of the aforementioned requirements.

Very sincerely yours,

Richard A. Otto
Supervisor of Music

ILLUSTRATION 1-2

WALLINGFORD PUBLIC SCHOOLS
Wallingford, Connecticut
Department of Music Education

December 4, 1967

Dear Parents:

The first step of our school-wide program of instrumental music for beginning pupils of the fifth grade is about ready to terminate and we are about to begin phase two of the program. As you know, since September we have been conducting classes in the playing of a pre-band (orchestra) instrument in an effort to better prepare pupils interested in furthering their education along the lines of instrumental music and for the purpose of discovering those pupils who it is felt would benefit from participation in the advanced phases of the program.

This program has been undertaken on a somewhat experimental basis with a view to promoting more positive results in connection with the instrumental offerings of the schools and to avoid having parents expend unnecessary amounts of money on the purchase of a regular band or orchestral instrument.

The initial program, conducted by members of the elementary instrumental music faculty, has involved the teaching of some of the most basic techniques of instrumental music performance. These have included such factors as: note reading, musical terminology, breath control, fingering skill, tongue control, pitch recognition, tone management, and learning to follow directions in the midst of an atmosphere of sound.

Obviously, as in any phase of learning, some pupils have proven aptitudes in music which would warrant their continuing to the next and more advanced step in the program. It is with these things in mind that we therefore recommend that your son or daughter: _____ continue further.

Arrangements have been made with music dealers in the area to provide a display of instruments which parents may purchase in connection with the instrumental instruction offerings. These may be rented from the dealer with the rental cost being later applicable to the cost of the instrument.

Members of the music faculty will be on hand to offer suggestions and guidance in the selection of an instrument best suited to an individual. Classes will be offered in small groups of like instruments on a weekly basis in the schools without charge. This instruction will be given by members of the instrumental music faculty of the schools.

The meeting scheduled for Tuesday evening, December 12 will be held at the Highland school for parents of pupils attending schools on the west side of town; namely, Moran Junior High, Highland, Parker Farms, Cook Hill and Washington. The meeting scheduled for Wednesday evening, December 13 will be held at the Simpson school for pupils attending schools on the east side of town; namely, Robert H. Earley Jr. High, Hammarskjold Junior High, Simpson, Whittelsey, Moses Y. Beach, and Rock Hill.

Parents planning to attend one of these meetings to arrange for an instrument are requested to be present at 7:30. The first part of the meeting will be devoted to an explanation of the program and some guidance will be offered to assist those in attendance. Parents are urged to make every effort to be on time with their musical aspirants.

If it is not possible to make the meeting on the designated side of town according to school attended, you may attend the alternate meeting on the opposite side of town.

Sincerely yours,

Richard A. Otto
Supervisor of Music

Fill out the form below and return to your classroom teacher by_____ .

Name_____Grade_____
Address_____Telephone_____
School_____Teacher_____
Choice of instrument desired: 1st choice_____
2nd choice_____ 3rd choice_____
Selection should be made from among the following: Violin, Cello, Flute, Clarinet, Saxophone, Cornet, Trombone, Horn, and Bass.
Have you had any previous instrumental instruction:____Please indicate instrument and length of study._____

Parent Signature:_____

ORIENTATION MEETINGS

In order to enlighten parents as to their role during the pre-band training period, one or more evening meetings should be held. The attendance of both fathers and mothers of participants should be solicited since the time would be devoted to stressing the aims and purposes of such a program, the function of the pre-band instrument, the benefits to be derived from participation, and suggestions for guiding and encouraging the young beginner. Matters pertaining to the development of regular time and place practice habits should be discussed and information about the eventual procurement of a specific band instrument and other subsequent steps should be aired. Time should also be allotted for a period of questions and answers from the floor to serve as a device for the further enlightenment of those in the audience.

If there appears to be a need to justify the use of pre-band instruments as opposed to beginning immediately on a legitimate band instrument—and this question might come up where a program of instrumental music is being offered for the first time—the music educator in charge can offer some of the following reasons for instituting the "exploratory" program:

1. Since it is an exploratory program, the music teacher is in a good position to assess the real interests of the individual.
2. The teacher will also be able to make some judgment of the individual's chance for success on a legitimate band instrument.
3. Through a period of observation the teacher can further evaluate the abilities of the individual and suggest consideration of certain instruments in keeping with the pupil's physical and mental capacities—not to mention his musical potential.
4. Through the use of a training device, the teacher is better able to note any particular deficiencies which might work against the pupil's being able to meet the greater demands of a legitimate instrument.
5. The use of a pre-band instrument can save the expense incurred in the rental or purchase of a band instrument.
6. The pre-band instrument offers no special embouchure problems, therefore pupils can concentrate on fingering and reading skills.
7. The pre-band instrument serves as a readiness device and can contribute to keeping pupil interest alive until such time as they are physically, mentally, and emotionally prepared to

tackle the problems associated with learning to play a regular band instrument.

If there is a felt need for demonstrating the pre-band instrument to the parents, the music teacher may readily display some of the techniques involved in blowing, tonguing, and fingering the instrument. He may also wish to use this kind of orientation meeting to demonstrate briefly a few of the band instruments upon which the majority of pupils will soon be involved in taking lessons.

The music specialist in charge of such a meeting may wish to inform parents about the preferred, accepted, or authorized methods of procuring an instrument of the band following the initial training period. Depending upon whether the program is about to be introduced in the schools, or is one of long and reputable standing, methods for procuring an instrument would include the following:

1. The use of a school-owned instrument on a free loan basis without any time period stipulation or restriction.
2. The use of a school-owned instrument on a loan basis but with a restriction placed on the number of months (or years) this may be used.
3. The use of a school-owned instrument on the basis of a "use" fee or tuition.
4. The rental of an instrument for a trial period from a music dealer in the area.
5. The purchase of an instrument involving a parent-dealer contract arrangement to permit either a time payment plan or other method for procuring an instrument.
6. The use of an instrument belonging to another member of the family.

While these six methods of procuring an instrument are most common, other variations or combinations of these plans are also in use.

In schools having a well established program including an abundance of equipment, instruments are loaned to pupils without charge. Others well equipped require a use fee based upon a semester or a full school year, with funds thus gathered channeled to the maintenance of equipment. Still other schools place a limit on the length of time an individual may use a school-owned instrument. This is sometimes done to promote a wider sharing of school-owned equipment, as well as to foster a sense of pride and responsibility among those students who must eventually procure their own instruments, particularly upon reaching the secondary level. While it is expected that most will want to possess an instrument of their own in time, it is the general practice of schools to supply, without restrictions, instruments that are considered to be large, costly, or unusual. Among these we would include: bass horn (sousaphone), bassoon, oboe, bass clarinet, alto clarinet, baritone saxophone, and large percussion equipment such as bass drum, tympani, field drums for marching band, etc. Many schools also supply baritone horns and French horns, and some even include cornets to be issued to individuals who desire to play in the band but own a trumpet instead of a cornet. The strict band director will require that cornet parts should be played on cornets, rather than substituting a trumpet for the specific role normally assigned to the cornet. While trumpets are used in the band, their particular role is somewhat different from that of the cornet which is regarded as the leading instrument of the brass section. Some directors use either, regardless of their intended role.

THE TRAINING PERIOD

Once it is determined whether the pre-band activity will be carried on as a classroom activity or on the basis of selectivity, those charged with the responsibility of the program will need to develop a schedule suited to the school offerings at large. Under most ideal conditions, this activity would be established on a daily basis for a period of from 20 to 30 minutes each, depending upon the grade level, whether organized as a class shared activity or selective groupings, and the size of the group or groups involved.

In some schools this activity is carried on in the regular period set aside for music and integrated in the music curriculum for the entire school year. Others have preferred to place a time limitation varying from six weeks to one semester, while still others have organized classes on a more selective basis and scheduled them once or twice each week during a portion of the lunch hour. Here again, the factors bearing on the number and length of these meetings will be determined largely by the intent or purpose of the program within a particular school system, the importance attached to this work by school authorities, the number of teachers in the system, and the nature of the school facilities related to this kind of activity.

OPPORTUNITIES FOR OBSERVATION, MOTIVATION, AND GUIDANCE

These classes, whether organized on a selective basis or as a class-shared activity, provide the teacher with an "arena" in which to observe the personal characteristics of the individual as well as his musical aptitudes. Such elements as are required for success in coping with the demands of specialized music study will become evident to the instructor as he works with those who participate in this activity. He will note quickly those who follow directions carefully and who respond without undue fanfare. He will observe those having difficulty with fingerings, those who encounter problems in tonguing, and still others who are unable to sustain tones for a required length of time. Some will exhibit a ready skill in reading basic rhythm patterns together with a mature sense of duration, while others will be found to have little conception of how to manage these elements. The eventual result of all of this exploratory experience will provide the teacher with a reservoir of information from which to draw for guidance purposes in subsequent stages of music activity.

During this pre-band instrument training period, the teacher may find it advisable to change or adjust the makeup of classes to improve the level of progress and achievement. Whether or not this can be done depends upon the nature of the program; that is, whether it is a classroom activity or a selected group, and whether it is scheduled during school or on an off-school time basis. Such a procedure, if possible to arrange, would permit certain pupils to move ahead faster while affording the teacher opportunities to devote more attention to those whose pace is slower.

The skill and patience of the teacher will be tested during the course of this period, and he may need to use certain motivative devices to maintain a reasonable rate of progress with each class. The use of weekly report cards has proven to be an effective aid in stimulating progress and in attracting parental interest and attention. Other techniques may be employed to foster individual and group advancement, such as exploration to learn new fingerings, learning to play certain intervals faster, and working for improved breath control through timed sustained-note contests. Beyond this, the use of flash cards on which are displayed various rhythm patterns and other items requiring a general knowledge of music can prove to be helpful in promoting progress.

Upon the successful completion of the pre-band training course, individuals deemed ready to learn to play on an instrument of the band may be awarded certificates of promotion. These may be used to signal a certain degree of attainment and as recognition of the pupil's preparation for instrumental training of the next higher order.

In schools where the pre-band instrument work is carried on as a part of the regular classroom music curriculum and implemented by the classroom teacher, it is both wise and necessary for the music specialist or band director to consult periodically with these teachers to ascertain progress and to offer assistance if desired or needed. In situations requiring the elementary vocal music specialist, who teaches and supervises the classroom music program, to be responsible for pre-band instrument activity, close coordination among staff members is vital. These specialists, as well as the classroom teacher, can exert great influence upon the pupils engaged in this activity which will ultimately affect the degree of success attained.

During the later stages of the pre-band instrument training period, a performance involving participants should be scheduled on an informal basis, with invitations issued to the parents, to serve as a "progress report." This kind of presentation is effective not only in motivating practice, but also in displaying what can be accomplished by children of this age and grade level in a relatively short period of time. It also provides the music educators with a springboard for disseminating information on subsequent steps in the program and for amplifying further the aims of this phase of the child's educational experiences. It is a good opportunity to include a display of instruments which these pupils will soon be playing and to describe the procedures involved in selecting an instrument suited to the child's interests and aptitudes. In addition to providing an initial performing experience, this presentation may also serve to underscore the role of the parent in encouraging the child in the development of constructive practice habits.

SELECTING AN INSTRUMENT

The process of selecting the right instrument for an individual is perhaps one of the most significant steps in the entire operation. As mentioned earlier, it is necessary for the instructor to be familiar with both the personal characteristics and the musical aptitudes of each enrollee if a high degree of success in the program is to be reached. It should also be understood that while the physical, mental, and emotional qualities of an individual may equip him to play more than one instrument, the chances are that his potential achievement level will be greater on one type of instrument than on another. Some of the influences brought to bear in the process of selecting an instrument are dealt with in this chapter.

Suitability

As people have personalities, it may be said that instruments also possess a kind of personality. While the role of some might be of a slow and plodding nature, others are required to play a more moving and active part. A thorough knowledge of the playing requirements of all instruments accompanied by a broad understanding of personality traits is needed to bring about positive results. The individual possessed of keen musical sensitivity, able to read rapidly and having a high degree of finger skill, would soon become bored in playing an instrument which serves in other than a leading role, while the individual whose musical sensitivities are less keen and who reacts slowly would find the demands of performing on a leading woodwind or upper brass instrument more than he can meet. It can be stated safely, however, that the majority will fall somewhere between these two extremes.

Some students select an instrument because of the appeal of a particular kind of tone quality, while others seem to be more captivated by its appearance. (I can remember as a youngster being intrigued by the action of the trombone slide and wondering where it went when drawn toward the player.) There are times too when a parent's life-long ambition to play a certain instrument precludes the child's choice of another instrument. This kind of situation may lead to an early termination of music lessons by the son or daughter who is thus persuaded. In any event, it is well worth the teacher's time to ascertain the real reason behind the selection of an instrument, particularly if he has taken the trouble to diagnose each separate case and prescribes the instrument which he feels is most suited to the individual. To be sure, there are many physical factors that influence the choice of one instrument instead of another, and a brief consideration of the more common of these is relevant at this point.

Dental factors

One of the most obvious of these factors is found in the individual who wears braces on his teeth and requires a continuing program of adjustment by an orthodontist. In cases of this type, the instructor should communicate by phone or in person, with the parent or orthodontist, if not both, to determine whether the particular instrument desired by the individual will impede or negate the effect of the corrective process. Depending upon the nature of the treatment and the effect a particular instrument may have, the pupil's interests and desires may have to be redirected toward percussion, string, or keyboard instruments.

Another condition which will have a marked influence in this matter of instrument selection is the degree of the overbite (major occlusion) or underbite (minor occlusion). Where the overbite is considerable, it might be advisable to avoid instruments such as clarinet or saxophone where pressures exerted on the mouthpiece need to be applied in an upward and outward direction, which would contribute to aggravating an already undesirable condition. Individuals in this catagory should consider an instrument in the brass family, where the pressure is inward and primarily concentrated on the upper teeth. If the overbite is rather exaggerated, however, problems related to "seating" the mouthpiece on the upper lip may be encountered. This situation would suggest trying one of the large mouthpiece brasses such as baritone or bass, or moving over to percussion, string, or keyboard instruments. In the case of an extreme underbite, here again a large cup mouthpiece instrument may be tried; however, it is likely that the person involved may need to make a selection from among the non-blowing types of instruments mentioned above. While these cases are rare, I knew an individual whose lower teeth extended well beyond the upper teeth and who played trumpet successfully in the professional ranks for years. The mouthpiece shank had to be bent downward and the rim of the mouthpiece was uniquely contoured to fit his unusual embouchure.

Embouchure pressure

Perhaps it should be made clear at this point that the pressures mentioned in relation to the lips and teeth, while not extreme, are nevertheless steady and can have an effect over the long term. It should also be recognized that the typical beginner, who has not yet learned to fully use the capacity of his lungs and the strength of his diaphragm, is inclined to concentrate disproportionate amounts of pressure against the lips. It may be some time before the young wind instrument player learns to equalize the breath pressure with the muscle pressure to attain the kind of balance required for sustained periods of playing. If the instructor is not a qualified brass major, it might be wise to arrange a clinic program where this can be demonstrated to young performers before they develop undesirable habits. The matter of pressure and balance also applies to woodwind instrument playing, although in a somewhat different manner.

While lateral or horizontal evenness of the teeth is desirable for the playing of all wind instruments, it is especially relevant in the playing of a brass instrument, since it underlies the very embouchure that is being developed and the pressure applied is directly felt. Pressure exerted against the lips and teeth varies according to the size of the mouthpiece. For example, compare the circumference of a dime, a quarter, and a half dollar and you will have a good idea of the amount of lip area involved in the playing of a cornet, trumpet, or French horn in the first instance, the trombone or baritone horn in the second case, and the bass horn in the third. The knowledgeable music educator should have sufficient playing experience on these instruments to be aware of the kind and amounts of pressure involved in each instance.

Lip types

With regard to fullness of the lips, a rule of thumb might be to look for a full upper lip which can provide an adequate cushion for a brass embouchure since the upper lip, being relatively stationary, affords the primary foundation of the embouchure; and to look for the full lower lip to provide an adequate cushion for the woodwind embouchure, since the greater amount of pressure will be borne by this lip. A good many years ago the thinking regarding the selection of candidates for cornet or trumpet was directed to finding individuals having thin lips. I believe this is a fallacy since the pressure applied against the lips, especially the upper lip, is concentrated within a small area, and the roles played by these instruments are quite demanding, particularly with respect to range and stamina. It would seem to follow that a fairly substantial cushion is preferred.

The length of the upper lip—that is, the distance from the red portion to the septum of the nose—is also a determinant in considering certain instruments. Think, for example, of the individual with a very short upper lip attempting to play a bass horn. The size of the mouthpiece could present quite a problem, since the rim would probably be pressing up against the player's nose!

In connection with lip contour, some authorities on flute playing suggest looking for an individual whose lips form a diamond shaped aperture at the center as the lips are parted slightly. They feel that it is easier for a person with lips like this to direct and control the stream of air introduced into the mouthpipe. Lip contour must also be considered by those wishing to play on a brass instrument with a small mouthpiece, such as cornet, trumpet, or French horn. Since the lip aperture for playing these instruments must be very small, individuals whose upper lip bows downward to a marked degree at the center may encounter problems relating to both articulation and range.

Other physical considerations

Finger length is of greater importance in the playing of the clarinet or bassoon, for example, than for brasses employing valves. Some fingerings encountered in playing the clarinet would prove to be very awkward, if not impossible, for a short-fingered child—particularly when one considers the use of the small fingers in reaching keys at the extremeties of the instrument. As for bassoon, unless the child of this grade level has unusually long fingers and is fairly tall for his age, the problems of holding and fingering this instrument may be insurmountable. It is a more common practice to introduce the use of this instrument at the junior high school level.

Another physical trait related to the hand and fingers is the width of the fingers. Young children whose fingers are very narrow might find it difficult to adequately cover the holes and rings of the clarinet, bassoon, or oboe, resulting in a great deal of squeaking and other non-musical sounds that could prove most frustrating for the individual. This problem could be handled through the use of a clarinet whose key design is like that of a flute employing pads.

Arm length is generally not of serious consequence except in the case of an individual wishing to play the slide trombone. The slide mechanism used in this instrument requires a reach of approximately 24 inches, from the shoulder to the knuckles, to manage the seven basic positions of the slide. For the beginner who will not be persuaded to consider the valve trombone or baritone horn as a temporary expedient, a handle may be attached to the slide to facilitate reaching the furthest positions.

In general, physical size as well as strength should be considered in pairing the child with an instrument, since some like the baritone saxophone, baritone horn, Sousaphone, and even tenor saxophone or French horn might be more than can be handled. While there are special chairs and stands to accommodate some of these instruments, there could still be the question of breath supply. It should also be pointed out that while the wise band director will carefully weigh the many physical and psychological aspects of selecting an instrument, he will also give due consideration to the interests and desires of the individual pupil. All other things being equal, the pupil who is paired with his first choice in selecting an instrument is likely to be more highly motivated than one who settles for less than his top choice.

ARRANGING FOR DEMONSTRATION PROGRAMS

During the course of the pre-band training period it is advisable to conduct a series of demonstrations to acquaint pupils with the playing characteristics of all band instruments to further aid them in making the proper choice. These demonstrations could be scheduled on the basis of displaying each "family" of instruments en masse, depending upon the time available and the number of staff members free to cooperate in this part of the program. They could be concentrated within a specific week or organized on a more integrated basis with the regular classroom music program and scheduled from time to time throughout the school year. In view of the nature of this activity, I would recommend a concerted effort within a limited span of time as being the more effective of the two general plans. Regardless of the time element, it should be obvious that a demonstration of instruments of a given family can provide a more detailed consideration of each, while one involving all the instruments at once may prove to be a somewhat confusing experience for pupils of this age group.

Depending upon the number of schools, the number of music teachers, the proximity to a city where professional musicians might be available, and the general philosophy of education that prevails, this demonstration activity may take one of several forms:

1. Demonstrations may be conducted in a concentrated manner by the individual music teacher initiating the program.
2. Demonstrations may be shared by "helping" teachers who have some knowledge and skill in instrumental music.
3. Larger systems with several instrumental music teachers might have each family of instruments covered by a staff member considered to be especially competent in either brass, woodwind, or percussion.
4. These sessions may also be organized to involve participation by professional musicians in the area during an assembly period, or at other times according to their availability.
5. Demonstrations may be conducted with the cooperation of "first-chair" players in an established senior high school band, or music students in a nearby college.
6. Demonstrations may involve performances by young pupils whose ages are not far removed from those about to start instrumental lessons. (This can be one of the most effective ways to generate interest among lower grade pupils.)
7. Demonstrations may be carried on throughout the pre-instrument training grade levels on a long term basis so that the youngest members of the school will come to recognize the various instruments by sight and sound.

8. Demonstrations may be conducted through the use of audio-visual aids such as films, charts, and recordings; however, it should be evident that live performances are more impressive in attracting and holding the interest of the prospective young instrumentalist.

TRYOUTS

Another step which can contribute to the success of this endeavor is the provision for opportunities for each candidate to "try out" on regular band instruments. While the majority are likely to become associated with the instrument of their choice, there are always a number of pupils who are either undecided or whose physical makeup mediates against that choice. It is in instances such as these where the knowledge, skill, patience, and diplomacy of the teacher come to bear most critically. Here too lies the opportunity for the band director to give special consideration to the need for developing a somewhat balanced instrumentation among the beginners. Pupils who are undecided may be led to select one of the less common variety, and those who encounter problems of a physical nature may also be persuaded to try one of the "needed" instruments. This is not to imply that these instruments require a lesser degree of musical aptitude or are less demanding; some of them actually require greater sensitivity and alertness. The important thing is to make every effort to retain these pupils in the ongoing program so that they too may enjoy the satisfaction that comes from being a part of a band!

For this tryout process, the instructor should be equipped with a few basic mouthpieces together with those used in playing the clarinet, saxophone, and flute, and one or more pairs of medium weight drum sticks and a practice pad. A set of mouthpiece visualizers or "rings," which come in different sizes, can serve to determine the kind of brass instrument most suited to an individual—at least where the lips and teeth are concerned (Illustration 1-3). Some teachers prefer to work directly with cup mouthpieces of various sizes for this procedure. They should have on hand a sanitizing solution for sterilizing mouthpieces and water for rinsing purposes, together with disposable tissues or paper towels for removing excess liquid from the items used in this operation.

The teacher should explain and demonstrate the position required and the method used to produce a tone on each instrument. Here again, the ingenuity of the teacher will be tested in managing this process without undue waste of time or loss of pupil attention. This

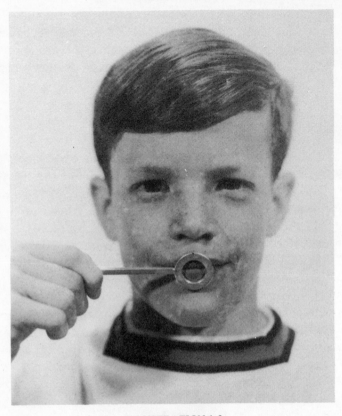

ILLUSTRATION 1-3

can be done by working with small groups of pupils interested in a particular instrument and giving some individual attention to each candidate. Pupils who can produce a clear "buzzing" sound on a brass mouthpiece, and whose other physical attributes measure up, can be encouraged to select an instrument of the brass family. The use of a flute mouthpipe section, without involving the body of the instrument, provides a means of determining those who can readily produce a good sound on this instrument. It may be of some help to the child to explain that this procedure is similar to blowing over the top of a soft drink bottle. Having a pupil blow into the mouthpipe, with the end of it first open and then covered with his hand, will produce a pitch change of an octave. This little device may reveal to the observant teacher other traits such as flexibility, breath control, and the like. The use of a clarinet mouthpiece is helpful in determining those pupils who can adapt most readily to the embouchure "posture" required to play this instrument. During this process pupils may need to be cautioned against "overblowing" and changing the position of the mouthpiece, since both lead to undue amounts of squeaking. The breath flow should be maintained at an even rate to induce a continuing sound. Music educators who prefer to involve the body of the clarinet along with the mouthpiece in order to obtain a more suitable tone, may assist the pupil in holding the instrument to assure obtaining the desired results.

During this process, the teacher should make notations concerning the adaptability of each individual to a certain instrument or family of instruments. Notation procedures could involve the use of pupil registration forms and the use of a tape recorder as well. The latter device might prove to be helpful for later reference. While the whole process of conducting tryouts on various mouthpieces and instruments is somewhat time-consuming, results achieved will more than compensate for the time and patience required. The percentage of dropouts will be found to be small, and the need to shift from one instrument to another will also diminish. While the compatibility of pupil and instrument is essential to the success of the program, it is even more vital as it concerns the needs, interests, and capabilities of the individual.

TESTING

The use of a music aptitude test as an aid in determining pupil readiness for participation in special phases of music is yet another step to improve the margin for success. There are a number of well known tests that are used in this connection, such as the Seashore Measures of Musical Talents, the Kwalwasser-Dykema Tests, the Drake Tests, the Lundin Tests, and others, including some distributed by leading instrument manufacturers. The use of some form of testing in arming the music educator with a more complete profile of each candidate will be of considerable value in this phase of the band building program. Information gained through this procedure will reveal pupil strengths and weaknesses and enable the teacher to guide the individual accordingly.

In order to avoid consuming a great deal of the instrumental teacher's time, the test could well be administered by the classroom teacher with the assistance or guidance of the elementary vocal teacher during a time of year that will best fit the needs of the planned program. Test scores of all pupils should be recorded on the registration forms and on pupils' permanent record cards in the main office for future reference. This kind of testing is frequently carried on at the fourth grade level, where most schools initiate the pre-band instrument training program. In situations where the instrumental teacher must carry on this work by himself, he may, with the cooperation of the principal, develop a schedule which will permit limited numbers of pupils to come to the music room to take this test. In systems staffed by an adequate number of music educators, this testing may be integrated with the regular music offerings of the selected grade and carried on as a musical experience for all to share, particularly since it has recognized values that reach beyond the immediate needs of the instrumental program.

PUPIL REGISTRATION

A well organized program of instrumental music should incorporate the use of pupil registration forms to enroll pupils in the specific phase of the music program. If the pre-band activity is carried on as a regular integrated part of the classroom music program, pupils would already be enrolled in individual classes. Specific registration forms for the instrumental program would then not need to be distributed generally until just prior to the beginning of the regular band instruction program. If, however, the pre-band training activity is carried on separately from the regular class routine, pupil registration forms would be required from the first meeting.

Registration forms should include the pupil's name, address, telephone number, names of parents or guardian, the classroom teacher's name, the grade level and classroom number, the date, and the pupil's age. In addition, there should be space provided to allow pupils to list their first, second, and third choice of instrument. Space should also be allocated for teacher use in connection with the instrument tryout process, for recording the music aptitude test score, and for recording any other data pertaining to the individual's progress. These forms can be forwarded with the pupil, for the use of music personnel, through the various grade levels and on up into the junior and senior high school. With the ever increasing use of IBM cards, computors, and data banks, especially in large systems, the whole process of pupil records will become more streamlined, more inclusive, and available to all departments of the school.

chapter 2

Setting Up the Instrumental
Instruction Program

Although numerous patterns are used to organize the program of instrumental instruction, some promise greater success than others. While many factors influence the choice of one plan in preference to another, the following are found to be the most fundamental and pressing:

1. The philosophy of education existing within the school system.
2. The socio-economic makeup of the community.
3. The ethnological character of the community.
4. The geographical location of the community.
5. The nature and size of the facilities provided for music education.
6. The number of music teachers in relation to pupil population.
7. Budget allotment for this segment of the program.

A broad philosophy of education will include provisions for a program of instrumental instruction in the school as a regular offering of the total curriculum. The basic provisions need to include:

1. Time during the school day.
2. Appropriate facilities in which to conduct these classes.
3. An adequate and properly trained staff to implement the program.

4. The furnishing of certain items of equipment such as instruments, music stands, and the like.

5. Methods books, instrument literature, and other materials.

An understanding by the administration of the values inherent in instrumental music will be of inestimable help, particularly in the early stages of establishing such a program.

TYPES OF CLASS ORGANIZATION

The structuring of the instrumental program may follow one of several courses. The most common of these will be listed here:

1. A heterogeneous grouping wherein all types of instruments are taught in the same class.
2. A limited homogeneous grouping wherein instruments of the same family are taught in the same class.
3. A strict homogeneous grouping wherein like instruments only are taught together.
4. Individual lessons scheduled during the school day and taught by members of the school music faculty.
5. Class lessons on like instruments given during the school day by "imported" professional musicians.
6. Private lessons given by professional musicians on school time.
7. Private lessons given by professional musicians after school or on Saturdays.

While these are among the plans most commonly used in organizing the instrumental program, there are apt to be variations in the administrative policies which govern them. These would include questions of whether lessons given by non-staff members are to be paid on a student fee basis or by funds allotted for this purpose from the overall school budget, and what charges, if any, may be levied against these professional musicians for studio privileges in the school. These and other questions of a similar nature must be determined by school authorities, since policies relating to these issues will vary from place to place.

A brief consideration of the advantages and disadvantages of the various plans suggested will help to determine the one best suited to a particular school in accordance with the six fundamental factors presented at the beginning of this chapter.

The heterogeneous grouping

The principal advantage of the heterogeneous class is that many pupils may be taught at once by a single instructor. Undoubtedly the prime motivating force for the adoption of this kind of grouping is that of economics rather than educational philosophy. While it might be claimed that this grouping would induce healthy competition among members of the class, this could also be said of other, more efficient, types of class organization.

The problems of scheduling this type of class would be relatively simple since such an arrangement gives little attention to selectivity. Classes of this description are frequently scheduled as a total band class with but slight regard for individual differences or for those existing between the many types of instruments represented. Another advantage of the heterogeneous grouping may emanate from its social climate; however, this would contribute little to the basic music goals of the program as a whole.

The obvious disadvantages of this multiple grouping include the inability of the teacher to give sufficient attention to players to help them overcome the problems that normally confront the beginner, such as the posture of the individual, the position of the instrument, the position of the hands and fingers, the placement of the mouthpiece, and other factors of a technical nature associated with each kind of instrument.

The problems of handling this type of class are further magnified by the great diversity of sounds being produced and the concomitant degree of confusion that can be brought about by such a conglomerate arrangement. Furthermore, this grouping requires greater patience, skill, and versatility on the part of the instructor who must be prepared to deal with the many and diverse problems that will arise during a typical class meeting. Classes organized according to this plan are all too frequently larger than is practical, resulting in a higher percent of dropouts than would be experienced in a more favorable grouping.

Since the making of music is based on the producing of sounds, it is vital that the teacher exert firm and consistent discipline in all classes. While some latitude may be permitted on occasion, since music is to be enjoyed, pupils must be made aware of the kind of behavior that is required to promote steady progress and to make this learning experience worthwhile.

The limited homogeneous grouping

Another type of class plan used in organizing the program of instrumental instruction is the limited homogenous grouping. This type of class, organized on the basis of instruments of the same family grouped together, is by its very nature more manageable and productive insofar as the level of musical achievement is concerned. Since instruments within the same family are alike in many ways, the number and variety of problems that are likely to arise during a lesson period are greatly condensed, especially when compared to the heterogeneous arrangement.

In a class of brass instruments, for example, the matter of tone production can readily be demonstrated to the class as a whole since all brass instruments employ cup mouthpieces and the tone of each is fundamentally produced in the same manner. Problems relating to tonguing may also be discussed in clear and precise terms, and shown easily through the use of mouthpiece visualizers or individual mouthpieces, before demonstrating on the instrument itself. The process of attaining embouchure flexibility can also be demonstrated more readily in classes organized according to this plan. Although there are greater differences existing among instruments within the woodwind family, it is still more efficient to organize classes in this manner than to have a mixture of all types.

Grouping instruments of a given family together is also more effective in broadening and developing the pitch range of the individual. In this respect the brasses again are more alike than the woodwinds, although they too have certain differences with which the knowledgeable music educator must deal. The process of dealing with the range development among instruments of the woodwind family is more complicated not only because of the multiplicity of fingerings involved, but also because of the differences in techniques applied in making register changes from one instrument to another. For example, while such a change may be accomplished on the flute simply by "overblowing," this process in the clarinet would require the use of a register key together with a different set of fingerings.

One of the most important reasons for advocating the organizing of classes by family groups in preference to the heterogeneous plan is the realization that each individual instrument embodies certain "favorite" tones from which to start beginners. The types of methods books which are required for the heterogeneous class frequently ignore these particular tones in the process of getting the mass of instruments started. Also, since the matter of economy must be considered, the item of class size among the two plans presented thus far need not vary to any great degree. I believe the average instrumental teacher would rather teach a class of eight or a dozen brasses or woodwinds than one composed of a similar number in a conglomerate type, and I would venture to suggest that the musical results would be considerably more gratifying for both teacher and pupil.

Grouping like instruments together

The third plan of class organization suggested is a further refinement of the second plan since it would limit classes to those which are alike. In classes of this type, the young cornetist would be playing with others learning to play the same instrument. This would eliminate the confusion of hearing instruments of differing tone qualities playing in different registers, as would be the case even in the family grouping. This strict homogeneous arrangement would provide for separate classes for all, or most, of the instruments. Exceptions might be found in a small school program where one of certain kinds of instruments such as oboe or bassoon are found. These would have to be provided for on an individual basis.

The many advantages of organizing classes on the basis of like instruments are obvious when compared to either the mass production mixed grouping or the limited homogeneous type involving instruments of the same family. The most obvious advantages are in terms of musical achievement and productivity. Teaching a class of six, eight, ten, or more clarinets at the same time enables the teacher to devote undivided attention to the specific problems associated with that instrument. Effort can be concentrated on embouchure development: the amount of mouthpiece taken into the mouth; the amount of lower lip to be rolled over the lower teeth to form a substantial cushion without smothering the reed; the amount of breath support needed and how to manage the air required to produce a resonant tone; the position of the chin to afford a firm foundation for the embouchure; the angle at which the instrument should be held; the position of the hands and fingers in relation to the holes, rings, and keys involved; and other technical considerations. Furthermore, this type of class organization would reduce the need for repeating directions, be less demanding on the teacher's patience and energies, and contribute to the maintenance of a faster rate of progress for the class.

Certain aspects of competition may be employed judiciously in classes of this makeup to motivate and stimulate individual progress, resulting in a higher level of proficiency in a shorter period of time. Having a group of pupils on the same instrument in a given period affords the teacher with a certain amount of flexibility in scheduling. For example, a period of 50 minutes may be divided in two, pacing faster members of the class according to their ability and at the same time allotting for the needs of those in the class requiring special help. This type of class organization is helpful in having pupils learn from each other. While this may be said of other types of class plans, the effect of having all instruments of the same kind in the same class emphasizes this element since playing problems encountered will be found to have much in common.

Other advantages prevalent in the use of this plan include the fact that methods books employed in classes of like instruments would provide for an in-depth consideration of all or most of the fundamental technical and musical problems associated with a particular instrument. Methods books designed for mixed instrument classes are generally more superficial and need to be structured musically on a course of continuing compromise. Furthermore, in the process of demonstrating proper playing techniques, the teacher is now in a position to perform on one kind of instrument during a given period and make this more meaningful and effective. At the same time the physical demands of shifting from one instrument to another quickly, as in classes of mixed instruments, are greatly diminished.

Individual lessons

A fourth plan which accommodates pupils on an individual basis is used by some schools where both an adequate staff and facilities exist. In these situations the lesson period is generally no more than 15 to 25 minutes in length so that a fairly sizable number of pupils can be met during each school day. While this plan is most costly, results are usually highly satisfactory since each individual receives separate and immediate attention. Methods books and supplementary teaching materials used under this plan are directly pointed to individual pupil needs and permit the teacher to focus upon special problems confronting the individual. Here too, the teacher is in a position to play with the student and demonstrate specific techniques which apply to the particular instrument being taught. Using this type of instructional plan, the teacher would be wise to schedule a series of lessons involving the same instrument in successive periods to further enhance his teaching effectiveness. Many music educators are trained and equipped to perform on various instruments; however, it should be understood that shifting from one to another throughout the day is very taxing, particularly when it involves demonstrating on a woodwind instrument immediately following a session on a brass instrument.

While this type of instructional plan is efficient, it lacks some of the advantages supplied by the larger class groupings since the element of competition is missing and the process of learning from other members of the class is also absent. The learning of the fundamentals of ensemble playing is also very limited since this plan stresses the person-to-person relationship of teacher and pupil, and the only kind of teamwork available is in the playing of duets, at least until the individual is ready for band membership.

The "imported" professional musician

Still another practice employed by schools in providing for instrumental instruction involves the hiring of professional musicians in the area to give class lessons during regular school hours. Although this practice is not a common one, where it does exist, classes are established on the basis of grouping the same instruments together. This is generally necessary since the professional musician is highly specialized in the playing of one instrument and is not usually equipped or interested in teaching others—especially in view of the risk of disturbing the sensitiveness of his embouchure.

The advantages of this kind of arrangement, beyond those already listed for the grouping of like instruments together, is that members of these classes would receive detailed instruction by highly qualified specialists and would therefore acquire knowledge that can only come through many years of broad professional experience. This plan would be of greater relative value for the advanced player since the finer points of playing that could be demonstrated by the professional might be lost to the young beginner.

There are certain disadvantages in this approach. While the professional musician may be a good performer, it does not necessarily follow that he will also be a good teacher. An individual brought into the school on a part-time basis often fails to develop any real affinity for the pupil or the school as a whole, but looks upon this kind of activity as merely a means of augmenting his income.

In some communities this plan is financed through funds allotted for the school system as a whole, while in others it is established on the basis of a fee charged each enrollee. If a fee is involved, it would most likely be the responsibility of school-connected personnel to manage the collection and record-keeping aspect of the program. It should also be understood that professionals contracted for this kind of service would require a guaranteed amount of money per hour or per day, depending upon how this arrangement is established at the outset.

Private lessons on school time

Another plan in use by a small number of communities involves the highly skilled specialist giving private lessons to individual pupils in the school during the day. This kind of plan is more likely to exist in communities which support a symphony orchestra of major or secondary proportions or in a college town with a substantial number of professionals. Arrangements are generally made by school authorities, including the music director, and schedules are set up with some degree of flexibility to accommodate both teachers and pupils. The main benefits derived from this kind of arrangement would be for the more advanced student and for those whose special interests in music may lead them to pursue this field as their chosen profession.

In some instances fees for this service are paid by the individual pupil, although more schools are tending to finance this kind of activity on the educational premise that it is their responsibility to provide for the gifted. At the present time a number of programs which recognize the need to provide for limited segments of the school population are functioning at the federal level. One of these encompasses opportunities for specialized music study for the gifted individual who otherwise could not afford it.

Private lessons after school

Some school systems solve the problems of providing for instrumental instruction by scheduling this activity after school and on Saturdays. While in the minority, the schools using this plan generally involve professional musicians in the area and schedule lessons privately for a stipulated fee. This kind of arrangement usually schedules lessons on a half-hour basis so that as many pupils as are interested may be accommodated. Here again, while there are benefits in this program for the beginner, the greater advantages are enjoyed by the more advanced player since he can more readily absorb the specialized instruction that is normally afforded by the professional musician. Also, as in other situations, members of the school music staff or clerical personnel in the institution are likely to be involved in certain record-keeping processes. Generally it is within the province of the band director to establish contacts with the professionals in the area and establish a workable schedule of lessons to be given after school or on Saturdays.

Policies regarding the use of school facilities for this or any similar type of activity would necessarily have to be established by the local

Board of Education. As originally stated in this chapter, the plan of organization adopted for providing instrumental instruction in the schools will be influenced by the reigning philosophy of education, by the socio-economic makeup of the community, by the ethnic character of the area, by its geographical location, by the nature and size of the music facilities, and by the number of music teachers in relation to the pupil population.

METHODS BOOKS RECOMMENDED
FOR VARIOUS TYPES OF CLASSES

The following list of methods books, while not a compendium of this type of material, is offered as a guide in the selection of books suited to various types of instrumental instruction prevalent in schools throughout the country.

For the heterogeneous class

Title	Author	Publisher
Belwin Band Builder Book I,II,III	Weber and Douglas	Belwin Inc.
Easy Steps to the Band	Taylor	Mills Music Inc.
Intermediate Steps to the Band	Taylor	Mills Music Inc.
First Division Band Method - Part I, II, III	Weber	Belwin Inc.
Hal Leonard Elementary Method - Book I		Hal Leonard Music
Master Method for Band - Book I, II	Peters and Yoder	Kjos Music Company
MPH Band Method- Book I,II,III	Kinyon	Music Publishers Holding Corp.
Tune a Day - Book I	Herfurth and Stuart	Boston Music Company

For the "limited" homogeneous class

All of the foregoing books may be used.

For the "strict" homogeneous class

FLUTE:

Breeze Easy Method for Flute - Book I,II	Anzalone	Witmark Pub. Co.
Method for Flute	Eck	Belwin Inc.

Rubank Elementary Method	Peterson	Rubank Inc.
Rubank Intermediate Method	Peterson	Rubank Inc.
Tune a Day - Book I	Herfurth and Stuart	Boston Music Company
The Beginner Flutist	Moyse	Leduc Music Co.

CLARINET:

Belwin Clarinet Method - Vol.I, II	Gekler	Belwin Inc.
Breeze Easy Method for Clarinet - Book I	Anzalone	Witmark Pub. Co.
Hendrickson Method Book I	Hendrickson	Belwin Inc.
Rubank Elementary Method	Hovey	Rubank Inc.
Rubank Intermediate Method	Skornika and Miller	Rubank Inc.
Tune A Day - Book I	Herfurth and Stuart	Boston Music Company

OBOE:

Oboe Method -Book I, II	Gekler and Hovey	Belwin Inc.
Rubank Elementary Method	Hovey	Rubank Inc.
Rubank Intermediate	Hovey	Rubank Inc.
Tune A Day - Book I	Herfurth and Stuart	Boston Music Company

BASSOON:

Breeze Easy Method -Book I, II	Anzalone	Witmark Pub. Co.
Rubank Elementary Method	Skornika	Rubank Inc.
Rubank Intermediate Method	Voxman	Rubank Inc.

SAXOPHONE:

Breeze Easy Method -Book I, II	Anzalone	Witmark Pub. Co.
Calliet Method -Book I, II	Calliet	Belwin Inc.
Rubank Elementary Method	Hovey	Rubank Inc.
Rubank Intermediate Method	Skornika	Rubank Inc.
Tune A Day -Book I, II	Herfurth and Stuart	Boston Music Company

Universal Fundamental Method	Melnik	Universal Music Publishers

CORNET OR TRUMPET

Beginning Trumpeter, The - Book I	Hering	Carl Fischer Inc.
Method for Cornet Vol. I	Beeler	Remick Music Corp.
Rubank Elementary Method	Robinson	Rubank Inc.
Tune A Day - Book I	Herfurth	Boston Music Company
Universal Fundamental Method	Pease	Universal Music Publishers

FRENCH HORN:

Breeze Easy Method -Book I, II	Kinyon	Witmark Pub. Co.
Method for French Horn - Book I, II	Pottag and Hovey	Belwin Inc.
Rubank Elementary Method	Skornika	Rubank Inc.
Universal Fundamental Method	Pease	Universal Music Publishers

TROMBONE

Breeze Easy Method -Book I	Kinyon	Witmark Pub. Co.
Beeler Method for Trombone - Book I, II	Beeler	Remick Music Corp.
Rubank Elementary Method	Long	Rubank Inc.
Tune A Day - Book I	Herfurth	Boston Music Company
Universal Fundamental Method	Pease	Universal Music Publishers

BARITONE (EUPHONIUM):

Breeze Easy Method for Baritone	Kinyon	Witmark Pub. Co.
Method for Baritone - Vol. I,II	Beeler	Remick Music Corp.
Rubank Elementary Method for Baritone	Long	Rubank Inc.
Rubank Intermediate Method for Baritone	Bolz and Skornika	Rubank Inc.

TUBA:

Method for Tuba - Vol. I, II	Beeler	Remick Music Corp.

Rubank Elementary Method	Hovey	Rubank Inc.
Universal Fundamental Method for Tuba	Hovey	Universal Music Publishers

PERCUSSION:

Art of Playing the Cymbals, The	Denov	(Adler) Belwin Inc.
Bell Lyra and Orchestra Bell Method - Book I	Pease	Pro Art Pub. Inc.
Breeze Easy Method for Drum - Book I, II	Kinyon	Witmark Pub. Co.
Method for Snare Drum - Book I, II	Buggert	Belwin Inc.
Haskell Harr Drum Method - Book I, II	Harr	M.M. Cole Pub. Co.
Rubank Elementary Method	Yoder	Rubank Inc.
Rubank Intermediate Method	Buggert	Rubank Inc.
The Three "R"s for the Snare Drum - Book I, II	Ostling	Belwin Inc.
Universal's Fundamental Method for Percussion	Melnik	Universal Music Pub.

For use in individual lessons and more advanced students

FLUTE:

Complete Method for Flute	Popp, Soussman	Carl Fischer Inc.
Foundation to Flute Playing	Wagner	Carl Fischer Inc.
Melodious and Progressive Studies	Cavally	Southern Music Company
24 Instructive Studies, Op. 30	Anderson, Cavally	Southern Music Company
26 Selected Studies	Altes	G. Schirmer Inc.

CLARINET:

Celebrated Method for Clarinet, Complete	Klose-Bellison	Carl Fischer Inc.
Complete Method for Clarinet	Lazarus	Cundy Bettony Co. Inc.
Hendrickson Method Book II	Hendrickson	Belwin Inc.

Method for Clarinet Book I, II, III	Langenus	Carl Fischer Inc.
32 Etudes	Rose	Carl Fischer Inc.
40 Studies - Book I, II	Rose	Carl Fischer Inc.

OBOE:

Barrett Oboe Method	Barrett	Boosey and Hawkes
Method for Oboe	Nieman-Labate	Carl Fischer Inc.
48 Famous Studies	Ferling	Southern Music Company

BASSOON:

Practical Method	Weissenborn	Carl Fischer Inc.
Studies for the Bassoon	Weissenborn	Carl Fischer Inc.
Solos for the Bassoon Player	Schoenbach	G. Schirmer Inc.

SAXOPHONE:

Foundation to Saxophone Playing	Vereecken	Carl Fischer Inc.
Selected Studies for Saxophone	Voxman	Rubank Inc.
25 Daily Studies	Klose	Carl Fischer Inc.
24 Studies in Duet Form	Luft	Carl Fischer Inc.

CORNET OR TRUMPET:

Complete Conservatory Method	Arban	Carl Fischer Inc.
40 Progressive Etudes	Hering	Carl Fischer Inc.
40 Progressive Studies	Tyrrell	Boosey and Hawkes
Method for Cornet Vol I, II	Beeler	Remick Music Corp.
Selected Studies for Trumpet	Voxman	Rubank Inc.
32 Etudes	Hering	Carl Fischer Inc.
24 Melodious and Technical Studies	Hering	Carl Fischer Inc.

FRENCH HORN:

Complete Method	Franz	Carl Fischer Inc.
French Horn Passages	Pottag	Belwin Inc.
50 Etudes for French Horn	Kopprasch-Franz	Carl Fischer Inc.
Method for French Horn - Book II	Pottag-Hovey	Carl Fischer Inc.

Art of Brass Playing, The	Farkas	Wind Music

TROMBONE:

Arban Method, Complete	Arban-Mantia	Carl Fischer Inc.
Cornette's Method for Trombone	Cornette	Cundy Bettoney Company
Melodious Etudes Book I, II, III	Rochut	Carl Fischer Inc.
Beeler Method for Trombone - Book II	Beeler	Remick Music Corp.
40 Progressive Studies for Trombone	Tyrrell	Boosey and Hawkes
The Simons School	Simons	Elkan Vogel Company
Trombone Virtuoso	Mantia	Carl Fischer Inc.

BARITONE (EUPHONIUM):

Cornette Method	Cornette	Cundy Bettony Co. Inc.
Complete Method	Arban	Carl Fischer Inc.
Selected Studies for Baritone	Voxman	Rubank Inc.

TUBA:

Eby's Scientific Method for Sousaphone	Eby	Big Three Music Corp.
Foundation to Tuba Playing	Bell	Carl Fischer Inc.
Method for Tuba - Book II	Beeler	Remick Music Corp.

PERCUSSION:

Intermediate Drum Method	Schinstine-Hoey	Southern Music Co.
Modern School for Snare Drum	Goldenberg	Chappell & Co. Inc.
Standard Method	Podemski	Mills Music Inc.
Modern Method for Bell, Xylophone, Marimba, and Chimes Book II	Gardner	Carl Fischer Inc.
Modern Method for Tympani	Goodman	Mills Music Inc.

THE FUNCTION OF THE SMALL ENSEMBLE

The complete instrumental program will include provision for the establishment of a number of small ensembles which can offer a kind of performance experience not otherwise available in the full band. Here the role of the individual assumes greater relative importance since he is likely to be the only one playing a particular part. The individual in the small ensemble tends to pay closer attention to the various elements of performance since mistakes are not covered by others, as would be the case in a band of fairly large proportion. The individual player will also develop greater independence in reading, since each part in a quartet will undergo a certain amount of rhythmic movement at a time when other parts are relatively inactive or sustained. Ensemble playing for most students provides new incentives to practice, since each member of the group soon comes to recognize the transparent nature of the music and is therefore inclined to put forth greater effort to match the competency of the others. It frequently kindles new interest in playing, particularly among advanced players who may tend to become bored with the music of the large band, which usually requires a certain amount of repetitious drill work before it is ready for a public performance.

Furthermore, where an active ensemble program exists as an integral part of the instructional program, this kind of practice and experience contributes to the musical refinement of the band as a whole. Elements of performance such as intonation, blend, balance, attack, release, dynamics, phrasing, rhythm, and interpretation are handled with new insight by the performer. This leads to the development of a more mature sense of musicianship which in turn is reflected in the playing of the large instrumental units.

SCHEDULING ENSEMBLE REHEARSALS

The scheduling of ensemble rehearsals may present a problem to the director who already has a full schedule of band rehearsals and performances, the teaching of instrumental classes, teaching one or more of the formal music subject courses, and directing the many music activities of the school in general. Although it will be the responsibility of the band director to organize these ensembles, select the music, and get the program started, he can make effective use of section leaders of the band or available members of the faculty to provide leadership for these groups. This kind of experience is of infinite value to students who are planning to go into the field of music where they will be involved in leadership roles.

In some schools, ensemble playing is closely integrated with the program of instrumental instruction, especially where like instruments or those of the same family are grouped together in small classes. Here the playing of trios, quartets, and other small ensemble forms may be introduced as part of the weekly lesson assignment.

Some ensemble activity, directed by capable students, can also be provided for during the regularly scheduled band rehearsal periods from time to time. Where student leadership functions in connection with the ensemble program, the director should oversee the selection of music and spend some time with these individuals to promote an understanding of the correct tempos, the style of the music, and the basic interpretive aspects. Other provisions for scheduling ensemble activity may be made during study periods, before or after school, or on week ends.

ENSEMBLE PERFORMANCES

Because of the size of these ensembles and the intimacy afforded by them, a high level of "espirit de corps" is often attained, resulting in a greater enjoyment of music in general. The activities of ensembles may include performances in school assemblies or in formal concerts, with time allotted to one or more of the better qualified and experienced groups. Recitals involving a number of small ensembles may be scheduled from time to time throughout the year on an informal basis to promote opportunities for the less experienced player as well. These recitals may serve as a "proving ground" for units preparing for an appearance at a state or regional festival, and also afford a method for selecting groups which are felt to be prepared for this kind of activity. Beyond these kinds of activity are opportunities to perform at meetings of community organizations such as service clubs, patriotic groups, church clubs, and civic bodies. These "arenas" afford the individual member a variety of experiences and tend to motivate his continued enjoyment and interest in the small ensemble.

For pupils possessing creative tendencies, the small ensemble offers a natural vehicle for learning to arrange and compose music, helping him to become familiar with certain writing techniques which will be of benefit later when he attempts to write for the larger and more complete units, such as the band or orchestra. Additional benefits may be derived from participation in the ensemble program since the literature of many kinds of ensemble combinations would be found to be unlike that written expressly for the completely instrumentated groups. A band building program operating on the premise that all members should be involved in at least one small ensemble during the course of the school year gives promise of achieving goals heretofore unattained.

In addition to performing in bands and small ensembles, the

student has countless opportunities for developing individual skills through the use of solo literature which affords new experience and enjoyment for the budding young instrumentalist. This facet of performance has been made even more interesting and challenging through the use of recorded materials such as are available in the "Music Minus One" series and "Accompaniments Unlimited," which offer an ever expanding library of recorded material on disc and tape respectively.

chapter 3

Scheduling the Instructional Program, Band Rehearsals, and Other Performing Groups

At the elementary level, scheduling is relatively uncomplicated since a common nucleus of subject matter forms the base of the offerings from grade to grade, and pupils within a grade level share the same subjects. At the junior high school where electives are introduced and the curriculum is somewhat broadened, the matter of scheduling becomes more complex. Scheduling for the senior high school with its vast array of subjects and their subdivisions has become a highly demanding process that is further complicated by having to provide for co-curricular and extra-curricular activities as well.

The responsibility of establishing a general time schedule on which the school will operate usually lies with the building principal. In addition to determining the type of schedule, the number and length of periods per day, he must be concerned with the school facilities and faculty.

The music educator must be familiar with various scheduling techniques so that he can understand and interpret the aims and purposes of the total school program and at the same time act in the best interests of those engaged in the music offerings of the curriculum. On occasion he needs to communicate closely with the principal in working out certain schedule items which are associated with music instruction and performance activity. He needs to be well versed in the advantages of the various types of schedules so that he can act in an advisory capacity when called upon by general administrators.

Fortunately, the importance of music as a force in education is becoming recognized by educators in general, and the need to justify its place in the overall curriculum has greatly diminished. For the most part, music classes, instrumental instruction, voice training, and choral and instrumental performance groups are scheduled within the framework of the regular school day. In many schools, the major performance groups rehearse each day and students receive credit commensurate with other subjects of the general curriculum. The more formal aspects of music such as those studied in courses like Music Appreciation, Music Theory, and Harmony have enjoyed this status for some time.

Scheduling provisions for music will vary considerably from school to school in accordance with the predominating philosophy of education, the understanding and tolerance of music by administrators and teachers in general, the size of the student body, the number of music teachers serving the school, and the facilities available for music study, rehearsal, and performance. The type of schedule employed will also have a direct bearing upon the results attained, since some afford greater latitude and flexibility than others. The ensuing sections of this chapter will deal with some of these matters.

SCHEDULING INSTRUMENTAL INSTRUCTION

The success of the instrumental instruction program hinges to a great extent upon proper scheduling. If instruction on instruments of the band (or orchestra) is to be a meaningful and truly educational experience, it must be accorded status equal to other areas of learning. The administrator with breadth of vision and understanding recognizes the values inherent in this kind of learning experience and provides accordingly. Although certain aspects of the program may be scheduled during part of the lunch hour or after school on a limited basis, particularly at the elementary level, the basic program of instrumental instruction needs to be structured within the framework of the school day. In this way it will be accorded a "posture" commensurate with its physical, mental, and emotional demands and will result in a higher level of achievement and satisfaction for those who participate. Activities scheduled after school, especially those involving young children, should be limited to programs whose requirements are of a less stringent nature.

While schedule patterns or techniques will vary somewhat from one school level to another, several methods have proven to be both practical and workable.

MUSIC INSTRUCTION AT THE ELEMENTARY LEVEL

One of the most common practices used in providing for instrumental instruction during the school day at the elementary level is the establishment of a series of separate classes of limited size on a fixed time basis each week for a period of from 30 to 40 minutes. A limited number of pupils would be drawn from several classes of the same grade level to form a class for instructional purposes. In this way, no one class would be depleted to any extent and therefore could carry on as usual. The few from each class who are scheduled for a music lesson would be required to get the day's assignment from the classroom teacher or from others in the class. In some instances make-up periods are arranged for this purpose during the regular school hours, at lunch time, or after school. Since most instrumental instruction is scheduled on a weekly basis, pupils would miss only a total of 30 or 40 minutes a week from other subject areas.

A similar plan would avoid having pupils miss the same class each week by requiring the classroom teacher to stagger or rotate periods within the day so that a given subject would be missed only once every seventh, eighth, or ninth week depending upon the number of periods in the daily schedule. The alternate plan to this would be a reversal of the rotation process, with instrumental classes meeting during a different time period each week while the regular classroom activity remains fixed. It should be realized that while these plans are workable, young people, who are sometimes forgetful, would need to be reminded on the day before their lesson to bring their instruments and instruction books.

Still another possibility is to schedule pupils for instrumental classes at the time of the day when the classroom teacher would normally be conducting a regular music period. While this method merits consideration, it is generally more complicated to schedule, particularly if the instrumental class is organized according to the like instrument plan. This practice would of course be frowned upon by the elementary vocal supervisor who would justifiably suggest that individuals of this age level should be concerned with developing their voices and learning reading skills and other musical insights. This plan could prove unwieldy from the point of view of the instrumental instructor whose teaching load is quite heavy and whose services are divided among two or more schools.

Depending upon the type of class organization used and the size of each instrumental class, some schools allot two shorter periods per week for instructional purposes. This plan has certain advantages which it might be well to consider. Pupils having two lessons per week for 20 minutes each would miss less class time on any given day and are likely to attain a higher level of musical achievement due to the greater frequency of teacher directed sessions. Some authorities hold that the difficulty of the instrument should be a determinant in deciding the number of weekly lessons to be given. It should also be pointed out here that in some parts of the country, the values of this phase of education are so highly esteemed that instrumental lessons are conducted on a daily basis.

It is suggested that the type of class organization adopted in connection with the instrumental instructional program should be the result of deliberate and cooperative efforts by the school administrator, the music instructor, and the classroom teachers.

MUSIC INSTRUCTION IN THE JUNIOR HIGH SCHOOL

At the junior high school level, the manner in which instrumental lessons are scheduled would deviate to some extent from methods applied at the elementary level. The curriculum of the junior high school is generally constructed with greater latitude than that of the elementary school since electives are offered at this level and study periods are incorporated in the overall school schedule.

Among the most common plans used for scheduling instrumental instruction at the junior high school level are those described here. Where the basic school subject curriculum is scheduled on a rotating plan, music lessons may be scheduled on a fixed time plan. In this way a class of clarinets, for example, scheduled for a lesson at 8:15 on Monday morning would meet at that same time each week, while subjects in general would rotate and fall at different times on succeeding Mondays. Assuming the school operates on a seven period cycle, pupils would then miss one subject class only every eighth week. It should be pointed out here that a rotation or staggered period plan could be established on either a daily or weekly basis. Where some form of rotation is used, it is found to be very effective in equalizing the various advantages of certain clock periods of the day when pupil efficiency is at its highest or lowest.

Where the school subjects are scheduled on a fixed plan, the music lesson period would function on a rotating basis. The clarinet class which was scheduled for 8:15 on Monday, for example, would then meet at approximately 9:00 on the following Monday.

In a situation where study periods are interspersed in each pupil's weekly schedule, music lessons could be planned for during one of these periods. The biggest problem in using this plan is that pupils having the same study periods may not necessarily play the same instruments, which could result in a series of short individual lessons with relatively few pupils available each period. Beyond this, if a number of pupils playing the same instrument were available during the same period, care would need to be taken to group those at a similar stage of advancement together.

In some junior high schools where music is required of all pupils for two or three periods per week, those engaged in instrumental study may be scheduled for the weekly lesson during one of these regular music periods. This plan assumes the presence of two or more music teachers in the building at the same time, and also requires adequate facilities. Some of the larger and more progressive junior high schools are staffed by three music specialists. In these instances one would be assigned to teaching choral music, directing choral groups, and teaching General Music classes. Another, well versed in the playing of wind and percussion instruments, would teach these instruments and direct the band or bands and carry on an ensemble program. A third staff member, presumably a string major, would provide instruction on string instruments, direct the orchestra, and assist in other areas such as General Music and ensemble activity. It should be pointed out that the scheduling of one instrumental class lesson per week would be the very minimum recommended and that some school systems provide for this activity two or more times per week.

While the four plans for scheduling instrumental lessons presented here are among those most frequently used, variations and combinations of their basic elements are employed with some success in junior high schools throughout the country. One that comes to mind involves the rotating of instrumental music classes around the fixed subject schedule; however, instead of the rotation being confined to a fixed day from week to week, the classes are rotated throughout the entire week. This would mean that lessons occurring on Monday of the first week would fall on Tuesday the second week, on Wednesday the third week, and so on. Although this method may permit greater efficiency in grouping larger numbers of like instruments together while avoiding conflicts with other subjects, it can be rather confusing to the pupil who might be inclined to forget when his lesson occurred on the preceding week. This problem would be most prevalent during the first several weeks of school and would affect seventh grade pupils more than those in the eighth or ninth grade who would be more accustomed to this kind of schedule.

As in the elementary school, the scheduling of music lessons for the young instrumentalist would require close cooperation between administrators, music staff members, and the faculty at large. Furthermore, the type of class organization adopted for a given junior high school should be determined on the basis of the six factors listed at the beginning of the previous chapter.

MUSIC INSTRUCTION IN THE SENIOR HIGH SCHOOL

The methods employed in the scheduling of instrumental lessons at the senior high school level are essentially the same as those applied at the junior high school level, with perhaps further refinement. Where the importance of music is understood and the need for continuing study is recognized, administrators charged with the responsibility of scheduling make every effort to see that these needs are met. These efforts include: (1) the scheduling of students during at least one of their study periods; (2) the scheduling of instruction on a fixed time basis where other subjects rotate; (3) the use of a rotating plan for instrumental lessons where other subjects are scheduled on a fixed pattern; (4) the use of a rotating plan which provides for this activity on a different day each week in succession; and (5) the scheduling of class or private lessons within the school day, after school hours, or on Saturdays. On the other hand, where the needs in music are not understood or felt to be important, little provision is made for continuing instrumental instruction on the premise that this kind of activity need not be provided for beyond the junior high school, or if desired, should be arranged and paid for by the individual. This assumption presupposes that there is a sufficient number of qualified instructors on the many different types of instruments readily available, and that all individuals desiring to continue this learning experience at a higher level can afford it. What a sad day for education if this were the kind of thinking that prevailed with respect to all areas of the senior high school curriculum!

Schools having a vital and forward looking program of music education make every effort to provide for individual differences among students of this age level. These differences, in fact, become more pronounced as young people approach adulthood. In music, this becomes very evident when we consider the great strides in technical proficiency and musical understanding achieved by so many. Some of the performance levels reached, especially by juniors and seniors, are quite remarkable and in some cases border on the professional. In view of the increasing numbers of students going into the teaching and performance of music and the many who engage in it as a leisure time activity, it would appear obvious that a varied and challenging program of music should be made available throughout the senior high school years.

SCHEDULING BAND REHEARSALS

The provision of adequate amounts of time during the school day for music performance units is essential if the program is to be worthwhile and productive for all concerned. While the number and length of rehearsals will vary somewhat from the elementary to the high school level, this function of the educational program should be incorporated within the framework of the school day. Elements affecting the number of rehearsals scheduled on a weekly basis for school bands of whatever level will include: (1) the length of the school day; (2) the number and length of the periods; (3) the number of music staff members available to conduct the program; (4) the nature and size of the facilities provided for music; and (5) the performance demands made upon the group as it relates to both school and community.

Elementary band rehearsals

At the elementary level, band rehearsals are generally provided for during the school day two to five times per week. In consideration of the physical, mental, and musical requirements of this activity, rehearsals at this level are usually from 30 to 40 minutes long. While some schools resort to scheduling some of this activity during part of the lunch hour, many establish it as a regular class period during the school day either on a fixed time basis or on a staggered time or rotation plan. Obviously, in schools where a large majority of pupils are transported by bus, rehearsals must be provided for within the limits of the school day.

Factors that will help to determine the number and length of band rehearsals at this level will include: (1) the general breadth of the educational "climate"; (2) the availability of the instrumental specialist in charge of this activity (since some are required to service several schools); (3) the number and kind of other activities competing for time in the schedule; (4) the time of year as related to extra rehearsal time required to prepare for a concert or other special event; and (5) the desire and enthusiasm evinced in connection with band activity in general.

Junior high band rehearsals

Rehearsal activity for bands of the junior high school is likely to be scheduled more frequently and for longer periods than its counterpart at the elementary level. By this time, the young performer has developed increased stamina and has also learned to concentrate for longer periods of time. In addition, he has generally matured to the point where he begins to understand the language of the conductor and to know what is expected of him in rehearsal. Also, since he has gained in knowledge and proficiency on his chosen instrument, he gets greater enjoyment from these experiences.

Band rehearsals at this level are generally provided for during the school day in periods of 40 to 50 minutes. While most junior high bands rehearse two or three times per week, some share in this activity on a daily basis. Many junior high schools also employ the practice of alternating band rehearsals with those of the orchestra on the basis of a two-week rotation ("A" week and "B" week), which allows for three band and two orchestra rehearsals on "A" week, and two band and three orchestra rehearsals during "B" week. In this way, each group enjoys the same number of meetings during the course of the school year.

Since the offerings of the junior high school curriculum are somewhat more like those of the senior high school than those of the elementary school, and scheduling patterns, with the introduction of electives and study periods, are fashioned after those in vogue at the senior high school, the frequency, length, and character of band rehearsals are often similar. Furthermore, the facilities for music at the junior high school are generally more sophisticated than those found at the elementary school.

The two types of scheduling most commonly used at the junior high school are the fixed time schedule and the rotating schedule. The former type, which is more traditional, requires each class to meet at the same time of the day throughout the week, while the rotating type permits the scheduling of each class at a different time of the day from day to day. While the traditional type of schedule may be simpler for the administrator to arrange, it lacks the flexibility of the rotating schedule, which may be altered according to circumstances. Furthermore, the rotating type of schedule is more equitable since no one class is required to meet the last period of each day when pupils' energies and attention spans are at their lowest, or just before lunch when pupils tend to become rather restless, or immediately following this period when they become sluggish and dilatory.

Another factor to be considered in scheduling weekly band rehearsals at this level is the number of assemblies, concerts, and special events in the school and community which may require the services of the band. The subject of performances by school bands, which is of concern to band directors and administrators, will be discussed in a later chapter. Also, as in the case of the elementary school, the number and length of rehearsals scheduled at this level will be determined to some extent by the number of qualified music staff members available in proportion to the size of the school population and the number of schools each would be required to serve.

Senior high band rehearsals

Band rehearsals in most senior high schools run from 45 minutes to one hour and are generally scheduled from three to five times per week. In addition to regular rehearsals, provision is made in some schools for sectional rehearsals as well. These would normally be provided for either after school or during an activity period, especially where the facilities and staff are limited. In some instances, sectional rehearsals may be scheduled during the regular band periods, assuming that the facilities will permit dividing the band by sections and assigning each to a separate room in the music wing. This arrangement would require the assistance of additional staff members or competent section leaders on whom the director can rely. Beyond the regular rehearsals scheduled during the school day, it is often necessary to call extra rehearsals after school or on Saturday mornings, especially during football season or when preparing for some event of special significance.

Since the rotating type of schedule mentioned earlier is more equitable and has more flexibility than the fixed time type, it merits very serious consideration for adoption at the senior high school level. It should also be understood that one of several types of rotating schedules may be chosen, according to the advantages afforded to the school at large in the judgment of those charged with this responsibility. One example of this kind of schedule provides for rotation from day to day with each "numbered" period occurring at a different clock time each day. A six period day might be planned as follows:

Clock Period	Mon.	Tues.	Wed.	Thurs.	Fri.
1	[1]	2	3	4	5
2	2	3	4	5	6
Recess	–	–	–	–	–
3	3	4	5	6	[1]
4 (Lunch)	4	5	6	[1]	2
5	5	6	[1]	2	3
6	6	[1]	2	3	4

Since the actual number of minutes allotted to each class period will vary from school to school, the above example does not include specific time indications. It will be noted, however, that with this plan the number sequence of periods is in order whether it is examined horizontally or vertically. Assuming band meets Period 1, it will be noted that it meets five times per week and at a different clock time each day. In some schools this period is assigned to the band and orchestra on alternate days. To insure rotation, each day must begin and end with a different "numbered" period. Furthermore, the ensuing week may either follow the same pattern as the first week, or begin with Period 2 and follow the same sequence that occurred on Tuesday of the first week and so forth. This plan may, of course, be applied to a seven period day as well. It should also be understood that the period indicated for lunch would be made up of the number of minutes required for class plus time allotted for eating.

Another type of rotating schedule which works effectively at the senior high school level is that which involves a seven period sequence in a six period day. Each period would be 50 minutes long, and classes would be scheduled on an average of four times each week. Also, on weeks where there are no assemblies or other special meetings which might affect the continuity of the regular sequence, two classes would meet five times per week. Again, the period prescribed as the lunch period would involve class time plus the number of minutes set aside for eating. In the example of the schedule illustrated here, let us assume that band rehearsals occur during Periods 1, 8, 15, and 22 (shown in squares) while an individual's instrumental lesson could be scheduled during one of his study periods (shown in circles). The latter is frequently scheduled back to back with Physical Education. As before, specific clock times are omitted since these will vary from school to school insofar as class periods, recess, home room periods, and lunch periods are concerned.

Upon examination of these two schedules, it will be noted that band meets five times the first week and four times the second week. Also, an assembly (labeled "X") is scheduled during the second clock period on Friday of the second week. A special event period such as this can be inserted readily and will merely delay the progress of the number sequence for the length of one period. Generally these kinds of programs are planned for well in advance so that the members of the faculty are informed and may make lesson plans accordingly. Copies of the weekly schedule are usually placed in the teachers' mail boxes two or three days before the beginning of the new weekly cycle. As mentioned earlier, music lessons could fall during one of the student's study periods, and this information would be contained on a separate schedule placed in the hands of all teachers on a quarterly or semester basis.

Under this schedule system, students enrolled in a four subject program and physical education, meeting twice a week, will have ample time in which to schedule music subjects and performing units such as band, orchestra, and choir. Those carrying five subjects could still schedule band since it will be recalled that each subject meets four times per week on the average; thus the seven period cycle would provide for a total of 28 periods per week plus two more in an uninterrupted cycle. Period 1 following Period 28 begins another new cycle.

This type of schedule has flexibility and equality since all classes share in the "preferred" times of the day for holding class, and each has a certain number of less desirable times of the day to contend with. Its flexibility permits changing periods out of sequence if necessary, as when a speaker scheduled for an assembly appearance is delayed for some reason, or special activities of a given class require a temporary adjustment in meeting time. While it may take time at the beginning of the year for pupils to become oriented to this schedule, the advantages of operating under it far outweigh the disadvantages.

A Rotating Schedule
(Based upon a seven period rotation in a six period day)

The First Week

Clock Period	Mon.	Tues.	Wed.	Thurs.	Fri.
1	[1]	7	13	19	25
2	2	[8]	14	20	26
Recess	–	–	–	–	–
3	3	9	[15]	21	27
4 (Lunch)	4	(10)	16	[22]	28
5	5	11	17	23	[1]
6	6	12	18	(24)	2

The Second Week

Clock Period	Mon.	Tues.	Wed.	Thurs.	Fri.
1	3	9	[15]	21	27
2	4	(10)	16	[22]	X
Recess	–	–	–	–	–
3	5	11	17	23	28
4 (Lunch)	6	12	18	(24)	[1]
5	7	13	19	25	2
6	[8]	14	20	26	3

□ band
○ private lesson

X assembly

MODULAR SCHEDULING

A relatively new form of scheduling that has come into wider use in recent years is the modular schedule. In keeping with the meaning of the word module, which means "a small measure," each hour of the day is divided into segments. These may vary from 15 to 30 minutes or more in length in accordance with the best judgment of administrators in charge of making the school schedule. Assuming, for example, that a 20 minute module was adopted, a six hour school day would contain 18 modules; therefore a full five day school week would encompass 90 modules.

Major subjects would be assigned a minimum of two modules per day for five days which would then conform to the 200 minutes per week of class time required by many Boards of Education. The number of modules allotted to individual subjects could vary with needs. For example, in chemistry lab or in music group rehearsals, two 20-minute modules may be considered to be insufficient; therefore three modules may be assigned. The number of times classes would be required to meet would also vary since three 20-minute modules allotted to a given subject would permit scheduling such classes for fewer than five times per week, thus providing room on the schedule for other pursuits. These pursuits could include taking an instrumental lesson, doing library research, consulting with a teacher on a specific problem, or engaging in activities of the student council or school publication during these so-called "free" periods. To meet the needs of the instrumental instruction program, a series of modules can be established during the day. Classes in this activity could be scheduled for one or two modules, depending upon the size of the classes and the type of class organization adopted for this purpose. Also under this system, individuals wishing to devote one or more modules on certain days to practicing in a studio may be permitted to do so.

Assuming major subjects under this plan occupied ten modules (200 minutes) each week, a student taking five subjects would still have time to be in band, while one pursuing four major subjects would have even greater latitude regarding electives. In general, administrators doing the scheduling would be wise to place large single class groups in the framework of the master schedule early in the process of schedule construction to avoid conflicts.

The modular schedule has great flexibility in meeting the needs of the individual since the administrator skilled in its use can tailor schedules to accommodate both the required and elective choices of each student. It should be pointed out that this feature, while making scheduling more complicated, nevertheless offers benefits which justify its adoption, at least on a trial basis.

Factors bearing on the construction of a modular schedule include: (1) class size; (2) the number of minutes required per week; (3) the number of times a class will meet in relation to the length of the module; (4) the provision of an adequate staff to meet student needs; and (5) an adequate number of rooms of various types in which to conduct individual and class activity.

chapter 4

Planning New Band Facilities and Renovating Existing Structures

In communities where a new school is to be built, music personnel should be involved in planning the music facilities from the earliest stages. Periodic consultations with the administration, the building committee, and the architect should be held to exchange ideas relating to both the general and specific needs of the school music program. Among the elements that need to be considered in the planning of music facilities are location, size, function, traffic circulation, ventilation, heating, lighting, and acoustics.

The members of the music faculty should meet together to plan for the many special needs of educating through music. Sketches or layouts of music areas should be submitted to those in charge of the building program, bearing in mind the type of community for which it is planned—that is, whether urban or rural, industrial or residential, the size and makeup of the student body, and the scope of the proposed program. These plans should be developed in view of population growth trends of the community or area being served by the school. In all too many instances, the time that elapses between the early planning stages and the final acceptance of the building has resulted in situations where the adequacy of the facilities may be the subject of some doubt. In recognition of the important contributions of music to the educational, social, and cultural development of the individual and to the community at large, facilities for music in the senior high school should be developed in accordance with the best practices in music education throughout the country.

LOCATION

Obviously, since music is a performing art, rehearsal facilities should be located near the auditorium stage and on the same floor level to expedite the movement of personnel and equipment. These facilities should also be near the area to be used for drilling the marching band, so that rehearsal time is not wasted in getting to and from the field. Furthermore, an outdoor stage adjoining the instrumental rehearsal room for summer band concerts and other special school and community activities should be considered. Adequate provision would need to be made for the parking of cars and the seating of audiences. For the latter purpose, the contour of the land and the direction of the setting sun would be of prime importance.

In view of the nature and size of most music performance groups and the activities engaged in by these groups, the music area should have direct access from the outside of the building. This will avoid the necessity of opening the building at large and at the same time will contribute to the ease of supervision by staff members when conducting special rehearsals after school or in the evening. It can also facilitate matters relating to concerts, festivals, parades, and other activities in which music groups are involved.

Special attention needs to be given to the location of the music area so that disturbance caused by sound will be kept to an absolute minimum. Also, while the music area should be close to the stage and auditorium, the acoustic treatment of the area should be such as would permit the use of the auditorium while rehearsal activity is in progress in both the large instrumental and choral rehearsal rooms.

The location of music rooms within the music wing is important, especially with regard to the matter of supervision. Large rehearsal rooms and practice studios should be located in close proximity to the director's office to facilitate observation of activity taking place in those areas. Storage rooms for instruments, uniforms, choir robes, and other special equipment should be planned to promote ready access and easy distribution. A design with rehearsal rooms, studios, offices, and storage areas all on the same floor should promote the smooth flow of traffic and at the same time will be safer than those involving two or more different floor levels.

A floor plan such as the one shown in Illustration 4-1[1] which was originally designed by the author, is arranged on the basis of single floor level. Close examination of this plan will reveal ready access to all major practice areas from a main corridor in the music wing. Furthermore, a smaller corridor permits direct access to both of music directors' offices and practice studios without having to pass

---

[1]Used by permission: Milton E. Nelson, A.I.A. - Architect. Charles A. Maguire & Associates, Consulting Engineers–Wethersfield, Connecticut; Providence, R.I.; Boston, Massachusetts.

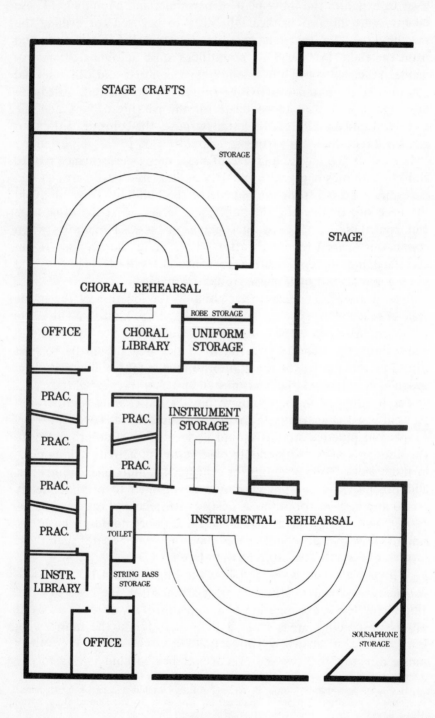

STAGE CRAFTS

STORAGE

STAGE

CHORAL REHEARSAL

ROBE STORAGE

OFFICE

CHORAL
LIBRARY

UNIFORM
STORAGE

PRAC.

PRAC.

PRAC.

INSTRUMENT
STORAGE

PRAC.

PRAC.

PRAC.

INSTRUMENTAL REHEARSAL

PRAC.

TOILET

INSTR.
LIBRARY

STRING BASS
STORAGE

SOUSAPHONE
STORAGE

OFFICE

ILLUSTRATION 4-1

through either of the large rehearsal rooms. This corridor also serves as an acoustic buffer between the choral and instrumental rehearsal areas. Storage of large instruments is provided for apart from the main instrument storage room yet within the the rehearsal area itself. Additional instrument storage facilities are available through lockers installed in the studio corridor. Separate music library facilities for instrumental and choral music are provided, with each being situated near the respective director's office. Ready access from the outside is possible by way of a double-door main entry to the music wing and through doors leading directly into the two large rehearsal rooms. Studio activity can be supervised readily since these are in close proximity to both the instrumental and choral directors' offices. Upon closer examination, other design features such as the relationship of the music area to the auditorium stage and an outdoor stage may be noted.

If for some reason two levels are dictated because of a peculiarity of design or layout of the building such as might be encountered in connection with the contour of the land, areas other than rehearsal rooms and directors' offices could be located on the second level. These could include storage areas, practice studios (provided means for supervising these are planned), an instrument repair room and perhaps a recording control room with a large double window through which one may look down upon the large rehearsal room or rooms.

In some instances, although rare at the high school level, a separate building is provided for all music classroom and rehearsal activity. There are some advantages to this arrangement since disturbance of other subject areas is kept to a minimum. Sound emanating from music rooms is thus more isolated from the main school complex. Furthermore, this eliminates certain inhibiting influences which are sometimes brought to bear upon music rehearsal activity and generally affords greater freedom in the performance of music. Special rehearsals held after school and in the evening can also be conducted with greater latitude since students may come and go without having to enter the main building. While there are many advantages to having such a building, the most notable disadvantage would be the need to transport music stands, percussion equipment, and many other items to the auditorium stage or pit area for performances and concerts. Also, depending upon the geographical location of the community, it may be necessary to have the music building connected to the main building by means of an enclosed corridor of underground tunnel. For most communities the cost and maintenance of of a separate building for music would negate the feasibility of such a plan.

THE SIZE OF MUSIC ROOMS

The size of music rooms will vary according to their specific function. The largest of these would be the rehearsal rooms for both instrumental and choral groups which may need to accommodate as many as 125 or more individuals at a given time. The smallest would most likely be the practice studios which would be required to accommodate but a few at a time.

The instrumental rehearsal room

Authorities in the field of school design recommend allowing from 20 to 25 square feet per pupil in planning the room which will be used by instrumental groups. On this basis, a band of 60 members would require a room of from 1,200 to 1,500 square feet of floor space to accommodate the needed chairs and music stands in addition to the large pieces of equipment such as bass horns, bass drums, snare drums, and timpani. With respect to dimensions, the discerning planner will make allowances for the future growth of performing units in this room. If a permanent riser installation is planned for this room, riser widths should be at least 54" and preferably 60" to insure having adequate space for the chair, the performer, and a music stand. The topmost riser, which is usually occupied by the percussion and bass sections, should be at least 72" in depth. The step from one riser level to another should be no more than 8" to afford easy movement from level to level. A semicircular design is generally preferred over an angular riser arrangement from the standpoint of appearance and visual communication. (See rehearsal room shown in Illustration 4-2.)

For the sake of economy, flexibility, and for other reasons, the instrumental rehearsal room may be designed with a single floor level rather than with risers. The conductor would then require the use of a podium to afford ample visual contact with all members of the group. In such schools, if desired, portable risers which would normally be assembled on the stage for concerts could be used in the rehearsal room throughout the year. While this plan is economical, it may work a hardship on members of the custodial staff responsible for moving the risers from place to place. This question may need to be given special consideration, especially in schools which sponsor an

ILLUSTRATION 4-2

active program of music. Beyond its economical benefits, this plan has certain other advantages which will be touched upon later.

Obviously, the main question of a permanent riser installation versus a single floor level in the rehearsal room is one that will need to be determined early in planning the music area of a new building or in altering an existing structure. Factors which will influence the decision regarding the design of the room will include the kinds of use for which the room will serve, the cost of one type of plan compared with another, the need for flexibility, especially if the room is to be shared by others, and the personal preference of the band director occupying the position during the planning stages. It should be understood that directors will vary in their preferences on this matter. Furthermore, since band directors are known to move from one community to another during the course of their careers, it goes without saying that they will need to adjust to the physical plant regardless of their personal preferences. Those that remain in the same position for an extended period of time are more likely to realize their own goals in this regard, since these individuals can generally exert greater influence when it comes to designing the music area of a newly proposed high school or in renovating an existing structure.

Since certain advantages and disadvantages will be found to exist in relation to both the single level floor plan and the multi-level design, it will require studied evaluation of each to determine which arrangement will be most compatible with individual school needs. While the permanent riser installation is sturdy, durable, and easier to maintain, it will prove to be most costly, at least initially. It should be recognized that separate portable risers would have to be provided for in connection with performances given in the school auditorium and that storage space would be required for these units when they are not in use. Beyond this, it should be realized that the uses for which a room with risers can serve will be somewhat more restricted.

The primary advantages of a single level floor plan lie in the direction of economy and flexibility. Since but a single level is involved, original costs will be less than the multi-level type, and there will be few restrictions on the use of such a room. Other important considerations which may be overlooked in planning music facilities are those relating to traffic and safety. Obviously, the movement of personnel and equipment will be safer and more efficient when only one floor level is involved.

If desired, portable risers could be assembled in the rehearsal room and used throughout the year in this location except when needed for concerts on the stage or elsewhere in the school or community. With this arrangement players could rehearse according to a prescribed seating plan which would not need to be altered when these risers are assembled in other areas. However, excessive movement of these units from the rehearsal room to the auditorium and other locations will contribute to a certain amount of deterioration since they may not always be handled with the greatest of care. Also, as indicated earlier, the number of times custodians will be required to assemble and reassemble these may place some limitations on their use. It should be further noted that when portable risers are pressed into service in the rehearsal room, they will add to the problems of room maintenance since dust, dirt, papers, and miscellaneous debris will tend to collect underneath them.

Where extended music facilities are planned for in a proposed new high school, it might be wise to consider an arrangement whereby one of the large rehearsal rooms would be constructed to include permanent risers while another would be designed on the basis of a single floor plan. In this way, the music area could secure the benefits of both kinds of rehearsal facilities. Generally speaking, risers, of whatever type, in a rehearsal room will assure a certain symmetrical arrangement of chairs, stands, and other physical equipment which can contribute to an air of orderliness. This condition in turn can influence the general atmosphere of the rehearsal area.

The height recommended for rehearsal rooms for large groups will vary somewhat in accordance with the width and depth of the room and whether or not the room is equipped with risers. Because of the volume potential of a 100 piece band, one would expect to plan for a higher ceiling in this room than in a choral room with a capacity of 100 singers. It should be pointed out, however, that the factor of height would not be the overriding consideration, since the shape of the room and the type of acoustic material used in its construction would affect its acoustic character. In general, ceiling heights of from 12 to 16 feet are recommended as being adequate for the average high school instrumental rehearsal room.

The choral rehearsal room

Choral music rehearsal rooms require somewhat less space than that recommended for instrumental purposes. This is primarily due to the fact that music stands are not needed and there are no bulky instruments to provide for. It is recommended that a minimum of 10 square feet per pupil be allotted, although 12 to 15 square feet would be more suitable, particularly for larger groups, considering the traffic problems involved. One needs also to take into consideration the space requirements of furnishings and equipment necessities such as a grand piano, a record player, a tape recorder, and certain storage areas associated with choral music activity.

Most choral rehearsal rooms are equipped with risers to provide singers with ready visual association with the conductor and to promote a more balanced listening condition for singers and conductor alike. These risers are generally 36" in width with steps of approximately 8" from level to level and are arranged in a semi-circular fashion to foster listening across the entire group. (See Illustration 4-3.)

It might be well to point out that the doors of all large rehearsal rooms should be wide enough to permit easy movement of large items of equipment, including grand pianos which are periodically pressed into service on the stage. Also, it is a general practice to design large rehearsal rooms with emergency exits strategically located and leading directly out of the building.

Another important detail in planning the large music rehearsal rooms is providing sufficient depth in the room so that the conductor does not have the impression that he is "on top" of the group, and also to promote an easy visual sweep of the entire group. As mentioned in connection with the instrumental rehearsal room, ceiling heights for large rehearsal rooms generally vary from 12 to 16 feet, depending upon whether or not the room is equipped with risers, the general shape of the room, and its acoustic treatment.

ILLUSTRATION 4-3

The music classroom

In some of the largest and most active programs of music education at the high school level, provision is also made to include a music classroom in addition to those areas designed to accommodate instrumental and choral group rehearsals. These classrooms are designed to house groups of students whose interest in music is deeper than that of the average student and who wish to learn about subjects such as the fundamentals of music, music history, appreciation, harmony, arranging, and composing. In size, this room may approximate other typical classrooms; however, space considerations should include provision for at least one piano (several more if piano instruction is offered), a small electronic organ, a record player, tape recorder, and certain storage areas for records, general supplies, and textbooks used in these courses.

Because of the nature of the activity that will take place in this room, it would be preferable to design it without risers. Furthermore, it should be planned acoustically to accommodate sectional rehearsal activity of various instrumental and choral groups within the school and located in between large rehearsal areas to serve as a further acoustic buffer. In most high schools, the choral rehearsal room serves as a general music classroom and the size, shape, and facilities needed are planned for at the outset.

Practice studios

The smallest rooms of the music area are likely to be those designed for individual practice purposes, with special consideration for pupils who play the largest instruments which cannot easily be transported to and from school. It is suggested that these rooms be not less than 70 or 80 square feet and preferably larger to accommodate more than one person, as would be the case if used for instructional purposes. Where several of these rooms are planned for, some should be larger than others to include space for a studio piano and for small ensemble activity. It is vital that special attention be directed to the acoustic treatment of these rooms since they are frequently located adjoining each other. The problem of sound transmission from room to room can be a disturbing element, and the degree of reverberation in the room itself can be bothersome to individuals practicing.

In addition to the normal furnishings in these rooms, such as chairs and music stands, a corner shelf should be installed for the instrument case or books normally carried by each student. A 16" by 20" mirror should be placed on a side wall to reflect posture, position, and embouchure peculiarities during instructional or practice periods. An electric outlet of the double plug variety should also be supplied in each studio for tuning devices, record player, tape recorder, and other electronic equipment. Bumper strips to prevent excessive marking of the walls by chairs should be installed either on the walls approximately 30" from the floor, or on the floor approximately 6" from the wall. For an example of a practice studio, see Illustration 4-4.

It should be noted here that one of the most prominent manufacturers of school music furnishings and equipment recently introduced a series of acoustically treated practice studios to its ever expanding line of products. These carrels, which are available in several sizes, can be readily installed individually or collectively in areas of schools where such facilities are lacking. In addition to serving as practice areas for both vocal and instrumental music, they may be pressed into service as an office, a listening lab, a recording studio, for speech correctives, for office machinery, and for many other kinds of activity. Sturdily constructed of steel with floor level adjusting screws, each is supplied with acoustical glass for easy supervision, an air blower for ventilation, and a means of supplying light and power for electronic devices.

ILLUSTRATION 4-4

The director's office

The office of the director should be located immediately adjoining the large rehearsal area for ready access and to facilitate supervision. Some also prefer the installation of a large double glass window in this room to permit ready surveillance of the adjacent rehearsal room. The dimensions of this room would be determined by its intended function. Since it should contain a desk, chairs, storage cabinets, records, and personal effects of the director, it should not be less than 100 square feet at an absolute minimum. If it is intended to serve as a teaching post where instrumental lessons are given to small numbers of pupils, it should be at least 150 square feet or 10' x 15'. If this office is also to be used for storage of certain items such as a tape recorder, record player, Stroboconn, or trophies, it should be somewhat larger than the aforementioned rooms.

The office of the director usually contains a set of legal files in which to keep recordings or various instrumental methods books and other teaching materials. A telephone is essential, as is a communication system connected to all practice areas and to the main office. Since this office is also used frequently for conferences with students, parents, staff members, and sales personnel, provision should be made for extra chairs and perhaps a closet for hanging coats and other apparel.

If the band director and the Supervisor of Music are one and the same person, this office should be somewhat larger since it is likely that single copies of all music texts used in the system would be kept on file for reference purposes, as well as other teaching materials and records. Furthermore, if this office is large enough, music faculty meetings could be held here with the desired degree of privacy. Executive board meetings of student and parent music groups could also be carried on here.

The music library

If sufficient space is allotted to music needs in a new building, it is recommended that separate library rooms for instrumental and choral groups be planned for with each immediately adjacent to the room to be served. These rooms should not be less than 10' x 12' (preferably larger to allow for growth), and should contain a sorting rack on one wall. It is suggested that wall cabinets for storing music classroom materials and counter space for stamping, sorting, and filing music be provided. It is further recommended that a small sink be installed in at least one of the library areas to afford a water supply for the many purposes this room will eventually serve (Illustration 4-5).

For storing music, some directors prefer open shelving combined with the use of music storage boxes which are especially designed for this purpose. Others lean toward the use of file cabinets, both legal size and letter size. Since most concert band music is printed on large

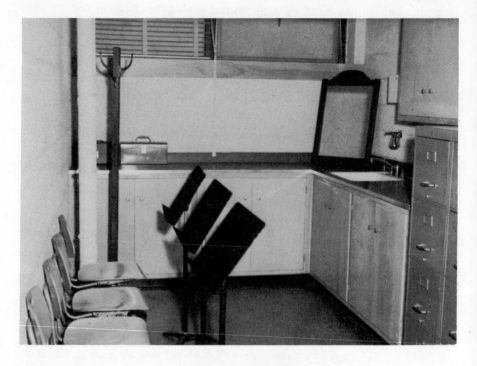

ILLUSTRATION 4-5

paper, the legal-size cabinets would be required for filing and storage of the majority of selections. The octavo-size band numbers could be accommodated in the letter-size cabinets, while the march-size music would require small multi-drawer cabinets. In general, the storage of music in music filing boxes on open shelves is a somewhat more efficient use of space. This method is also more economical since metal filing cabinets are fairly expensive.

In smaller schools, where one library room must serve the needs of instrumental and choral groups, it would be wise to store music against opposite walls to provide some kind of separation. A common sorting rack could serve both segments of the department. It is recommended that a card file system be developed to identify all music by title and composer, and under various catagories, to expedite the handling of music.

The instrument storage room

There are various techniques used for the storage of instruments. Among them are the use of a single room designed with open shelving, a room with lockers of various dimensions, open shelving within the rehearsal room itself, lockers along the band room walls, shelving underneath the ends of the highest risers with sliding doors, lockers along the corridors leading to the rehearsal room, and specially designed units such as are now available from prominent manufacturers of school music equipment. If the band director is involved in the first stages of planning the music area, he can select the type of storage plan he feels will be most effective for his purposes and proceed accordingly.

If a single storage room is involved, it should have two separate doors with adequate space between these doors to promote ready entrance and exiting of traffic. The shelving should be spaced along the three walls of the room with dimensions varying somewhat to allow for cases of different sizes. The shelving would need to be 40" deep for storage of instruments like trombones, baritone horns, tenor saxes, bass clarinets and the like. While sousaphones could be stored on upper shelves, it would be better to arrange for separate storage for them, located in close proximity to where they will be positioned in the band. In some instances they are allowed to remain on chairs of special design (Illustration 4-6[2]). If this practice is followed, their mouthpieces, bits, and perhaps even neck sections should be removed to discourage others from tampering with them. Another effective method for storing these instruments includes the use of a rack which can be mounted on the wall of the band room or a nearby storage area. Such a rack should be constructed of sturdy material and include padding to prevent marring the finish. This type of rack was recently introduced on the market and is shown here (Illustration 4-7[3]).

With reference to the storage of percussion equipment, it is common to leave large items such as bass drum and timpani in place in the band room while all accessory items including snare drums, cymbals, bells, and other traps are stored in a specially designed cabinet (Illustration 4-8). Through the use of such a cabinet these items can be cared for properly and are readily available in rehearsal. The top surface can accommodate bells and other accessories and the entire cabinet can be moved about in the rehearsal room or on stage. Field drums used for marching band activity could be stored on the top shelves of the instrument storage room or in cabinets in or near the band room. A mobile rack such as is pictured here could serve

---

[2]Sousaphone Chair and Percussion Cabinet:
Manufactured and sold by Wenger Corporation, Owatonna, Minnesota 55060

[3]Sousaphone/Tuba Wall Hanger:
With the permission of the Western Music Specialty Co., Grand Junction, Colo. 81501

effectively for the various types of drums used in association with the marching band (Illustration 4-9[4]).

The size of the instrument storage room would be determined by the size of the band and in consideration of protracted statistics for

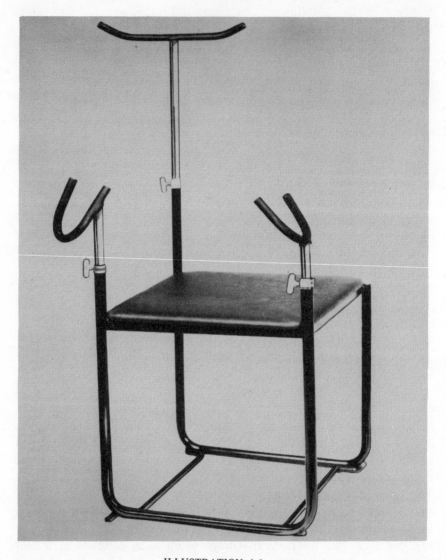

ILLUSTRATION 4-6

growth in the immediate future. If the architectural pattern of the music wing seems to call for a long narrow room between the choral and instrumental room, which could also serve as a sound barrier, I

[4]Schreiber's Drum STOrack DSR 41
Made and distributed by Schreiber's Inc., 31 Schreiber Building, Airport Road North, Bloomington, Illinois 61701

ILLUSTRATION 4-7

would suggest a room of not less than 14 to 16 feet in width and from 24 to 28 feet in depth. Shelving or lockers on either side could be of varying dimensions in a mixed or alternating pattern, so that all players of similar instruments do not flock to the same area when band rehearsals are convened or dismissed. In larger schools, the single storage room for instruments should be 500 or more square feet regardless of its shape.

It should be noted here that while the open shelf type of storage would be the most economical, it affords little security for the protection of the instruments. The amount of money allotted to the design and building of facilities for music will have a direct bearing upon the type of instrument storage plan adopted.

Individual lockers of various sizes with combination locks is perhaps the best method to use in providing maximum security. Lockers of wood or metal are available through several manufacturers of school furniture or may be custom built according to

ILLUSTRATION 4-8

specifications supplied by the music director. The publication of the Music Educators National Conference dealing with this subject supplies the following dimensions for instrument lockers:[5]

6" x 6" x 36"   Drum Pad, Flute, Piccolo
12" x 6" x 36"   Clarinet, Oboe
12" x 12" x 36" Bass Clarinet, Bell Front Alto, Cornet, Trumpet
12" x 15" x 36" Alto Saxophone, Bassoon, Tenor Saxophone
12" x 46" x 36" Baritone Saxophone, Bass Trombone
15" x 8" x 36"   Violin, Viola
15" x 34" x 36" Cello
36" x 36" x 36" Basses (Brass)
18" x 18" x 36" Alto Clarinet, Baritone, Field Drum, French Horn

---

[5]Reproduced with permission from page 101 of "Music Buildings, Rooms, and Equipment," 1966 edition, publication of the Music Educators National Conference, Washington, D.C.

ILLUSTRATION 4-9

While it is obvious that some instruments do not require the depth suggested above, the dimensions are given with a certain amount of uniformity for reasons of appearance and ease of construction. Upon close examination, one might conclude that the dimension suggested for brass basses would not accommodate a sousaphone unless the bell were readjusted if not detached at the time of storing.

Some schools with limited facilities for music and little space for storage require band members to leave small instruments in their regular lockers while providing for large instruments by means of open shelf storage in the band room. This would be the least desirable method for storing instruments since it would afford little protection for larger instruments owned by individuals or by the school itself. It would be preferable to install a number of lockers along one or two sides of the rehearsal room, or build shelving under the highest risers with lockable sliding doors.

To expedite traffic in the large rehearsal room, it would be wise to have several different storage areas to provide for dispersion of traffic rather than condensing it. This can be done by installing lockers for small instruments in corridors of the music area or in practice studios if necessary. Some could be stored under risers as suggested,

ILLUSTRATION 4-10

and, where feasible, wall racks could be located in various places throughout the rehearsal area.

In recent years, leading manufacturers of school music furniture and equipment have devoted countless hours and large sums of money to research special needs of the school music program. As a result, a number of new products have been introduced on the market. Among these are units which are designed for the storage of instruments. To add to their adaptability, some are equipped with casters to permit their being moved from a central storage room to the rehearsal room itself. Some have even greater latitude in design by providing storage space for music folders on the reverse side, as shown in Illustration 4-10.[6] Players can thus obtain instruments and music at the same time as they enter the rehearsal room, reversing the procedure when they leave. This arrangement not only contributes to a smoother flow of traffic but also can be a rehearsal time saver.

Companies such as this also offer consultative services to band directors planning new facilities or engaged in renovating existing areas.

[6]Schreiber's Wind STOrite S:L 16W25.
Made and distributed by Schreiber's Inc., 31 Schreiber Building, Airport Road North, Bloomington, Illinois 61701

Storage rooms for uniforms, robes, and jackets

In planning the music area, space should be allotted for storing the various types of uniforms worn by music performance groups. To facilitate the distribution of these when needed, it is advisable to design the room so that it borders a wide corridor. Furthermore, to expedite this process, the room should be oblong with the longer dimension of the room parallel to the adjacent corridor. This will bring the uniforms within easier reach of those in charge of distributing them to band members lined up in the corridor. A Dutch door with a small counter attached is suggested, and if two or more students will be involved in giving out uniforms, two such doors would serve more effectively than one. These could be either directly bordering each other, or spaced several feet apart with wall space in between. The latter technique could accommodate two separate lines of students and speed the distribution process.

The dimensions of this room would depend upon the number of uniforms to be stored; however, here again anticipated growth should be planned for. A room 8' x 14' should be adequate for the storage of approximately 50 uniforms. Larger bands would require rooms of 10' x 16' or 12' x 20'. It is suggested that the rods on which the uniforms are hung be of 1½" or 2" steel pipe with bracing provided every four to five feet along the length of the pipe to insure proper support. Uniforms could be hung in two tiers with some space allowed between tiers, and with the lower tier sufficiently high so that uniform coats will hang several inches off the floor. Hats could be stored on shelves on the side walls and above the uniform racks or on a separate roll-out rack which could be moved into the corridor or band room. If a single pipe rack is used around the borders of the room, hats could be stored in cubicles directly above the uniforms. Number tags should be placed on the pipe rack to correspond with the uniform number, and the pipe should be notched to keep hangers in position. It is also recommended that wooden hangers rather than steel wire hangers be used for all types of uniform storage.

Provision should also be made for one or more wall cabinets in this room for the storage of plumes and various uniform accessories.

In some instances, uniforms are stored in lockers or sections of the wall along corridors leading to the band room. This arrangement could eliminate the need for having students wait in line on occasions when uniforms are required.

Facilities for storing choir robes may be planned on a somewhat similar basis, although they are more often found to be stored in elongated closets along the walls of the choral room or an adjacent corridor. It should be pointed out that many choral directors prefer to uniform their choirs with jackets or blazers with uniformly colored skirts or trousers either of a similar or a contrasting color. In cases such as these, the handling of this apparel would be similar to the procedures used in connection with band uniforms.

Recording or control room

This room should be located in immediate view of the large rehearsal room or rooms being served. Specially designed windows would be required for this room, with particular emphasis given to the acoustic factors involved. If the building plan employs an "island" design where a series of offices and storage rooms separate the main rehearsal rooms, the recording room could be included in this so-called island and serve both the choral and instrumental rehearsal rooms. Furthermore, if this room were next to the office of a music director it could be entered through that office, thus eliminating the need for doors leading directly into either of the large rehearsal areas. This could further reduce the noise factor involved in recording sessions. Verbal communication needed between the control room and either large rehearsal room could be managed through the use of wall phones or a microphone and speaker. Beyond this, for recording purposes it may be considered necessary to have a flashing light to signal the beginning of a recording session.

This room should contain a master control panel to monitor the process of recording. Equipment should be of the highest quality available within reasonable budget limitations to insure obtaining reproductions of good quality. Also included should be a desk, chairs, a table or work counter with cabinets above for storing and filing tapes, and a splicing machine and winding device such as is used in editing tapes. In view of the special purpose for which this room is intended, it is important to consider the acoustic qualities desired in it and in the rooms immediately adjoining.

Some schools engage in a considerable amount of recording of concerts and other performances in the auditorium and prefer to have a room of this description located in the auditorium itself.

Instrument repair room

Although general repairs on instruments are usually handled by specialists in the field who are employed by instrument dealers in the area, occasions arise when minor repairs or adjustments need to be made during the school day. A small room, or section of a room, of approximately 100 square feet could be planned for this purpose. A countertop or workbench would be required as would some cabinet and drawer space for basic tools and supplies. Among items needed for quick repairs are an assortment of pads and springs for woodwind instruments, stick or tube glue, various thicknesses of cork for woodwind needs, corks for brass instrument water keys, various springs for these water keys, and different types of lubricants for both brass and woodwind instruments. Some of the leading manufacturers of instruments have made repair kits available to band directors for use in connection with minor repairs. In addition to containing basic supplies, they are equipped with certain tools which come into frequent use in these minor repair operations. (See Illustration 4-11 for one of the more complete types of kits available.[7])

Since it is expected that the band director's time should be devoted to teaching, he should not feel impelled to take care of other than emergency needs. Serious malfunction of instruments should be dealt with by those who are trained and experienced in the field. It is understandable that this burden might be proportionately greater for the band director situated far from a city where these services would normally be available. We might add, however, that courses in instrument repair are being offered in many schools throughout the country engaged in preparing people for the field of school music.

If space permits the inclusion of a room or area for instrument repair, it should be equipped with electrical outlets, a gas supply or Bunsen burner, a sink and water supply, and a number of the basic tools needed to make minor repairs.

Dressing rooms

The practice of keeping uniforms in the school to insure proper care and storage is followed by many band directors throughout the country. It cases such as these, it becomes necessary to distribute uniforms each time the band is to make a formal appearance in the school or community. Provision therefore needs to be made for changing attire before and after such occasions. It is recommended that several small dressing rooms be planned in the music area and near the stage so that these facilities may be shared by other departments of the school. These rooms should vary somewhat in

[7]With permission of Erick Brand Repair Supplies and Musical Specialties, 1117 West Beardsley Avenue, Elkhart, Indiana 46514

ILLUSTRATION 4-11

size and should contain chairs, mirrors, electric outlets, hangers, and shelving. In addition, it would be well to have a small sink in each dressing room, particularly in view of dramatic production needs. In some of the larger rooms, closets should be built in to provide for the storage of costumes and makeup materials used in dramatic productions. These closets should have folding louvered doors to provide ventilation and take up less room space when open. Ironing boards that are recessed in the wall when not in use should also be planned for, as well as cabinets for storage of specialized types of equipment and materials associated with staged activities.

Other facilities

Lavatory facilities for student use should be planned for in close association with the dressing rooms and music area in general. Provision should be made for separate facilities for faculty members. Where space and budget permit, it is recommended that shower facilities be included for band directors whose services in connection with concerts, parades, and other events are required frequently and at all seasons of the year.

THE SHAPE OF MUSIC ROOMS

In general, rooms used for rehearsing large instrumental and choral groups should be rectangular in shape with the larger dimension being the width of the room as viewed from the director's podium, and the smaller dimension being the depth. For example, a band room designed to accommodate 100 players would be 50' wide and 40' deep. A room of this shape would facilitate visual communication between performer and conductor. The depth of rehearsal rooms should be adequate in relation to the width to give the conductor an easy visual sweep of the room without having the feeling that he is "on top" of the group.

In choral rooms, or in rooms which serve for both instrumental and choral groups, sufficient floor space should be allowed on the main floor level in front of the risers to accommodate a grand piano, a record player, and other equipment such as is required in music rehearsal activity.

Music classrooms, while not as large as rehearsal rooms, could also be planned on a rectangular basis so that pupils seated in the rear are not too far away from the teacher, the piano, and any other equipment that will be pressed into service in various kinds of music classes. Although risers in such a room promote improved visual communication, they are not considered essential.

The director's office and practice studios could be of either square or rectangular design depending upon the general layout of the entire music area. Dimensions for these have been suggested earlier. It might be mentioned that walls in practice studios are often non-parallel for acoustic reasons.

To promote ready handling of uniforms and choir robes, it was suggested that the long dimension of these rooms should parallel the adjoining corridors. This design not only affords faster handling of apparel and equipment, but also expedites the traffic situation associated with this process.

Storage rooms for instruments and other equipment could also be either square or rectangular, depending again upon the general plan adopted for the music area at large. However, in some cases, these rooms are designed as long and rather narrow areas to serve as acoustic buffer zones between large rehearsal areas.

Finally, it is important to note that rooms used for rehearsing large groups, for ensembles, for sectional rehearsals, and for individual practice purposes are designed with non-parallel walls to promote a more even diffusion of sound within the area as well as to avoid echo, dead spots, and other acoustic peculiarities.

VENTILATION

In recent years there has been a trend toward providing air conditioning in areas of the building, such as the music wing, that are used during the day, after school, and in the evening, and during the summer months for the summer music programs of the school and community. Systems such as these are installed with temperature and humidity controls accessible to faculty members and custodians. Separate controls are needed to regulate levels in various areas of the music wing since areas used for storage would require a constant level for both temperature and humidity. Rehearsal rooms which accommodate large groups during regular rehearsal periods and relatively small groups during other periods may need to be adjusted from time to time. It should be understood that the increased breath-taking activity of wind instrument playing requires a greater volume of air in a given time span, and the heat generated by large numbers of people within a room further complicates the matter of ventilation.

When air conditioning is not available, ventilation of the music area is provided either through windows, hopefully including some cross ventilation, or by a motor driven system involving exhaust fans and air ducts. If a mechanical system is used, the location of the motor responsible for circulating the air must be chosen very carefully since the noise caused by this unit can prove to be very distracting to either individual or group practicing. This type of unit should be installed either above the ceiling of a storage area, or better still, above the ceiling in a corridor leading to the music area.

When ventilation is completely by natural means, the number and accessibility of windows that can be opened and their location in relation to side and rear walls must be considered. Attempts should be made to avoid glare for players and conductor. In some instances tinted or colored glass may serve effectively to reduce glare. Large rehearsal rooms should be designed with double doors leading to adjacent corridors, and with an additional door located on another wall for emergency use. This kind of door arrangement will be found helpful in providing ventilation when the weather is particularly warm, as is often the case during certain months of the school year. Some authorities advise using as little glass as possible in music areas for acoustic reasons; this can also serve to maintain cooler temperatures since a large amount of brick wall area will tend to provide lower temperatures than will large areas of glass. It should of course be recognized that provision for ventilation through natural means could cause a certain amount of disturbance to nearby areas of the school since some sound will escape from the band room, especially at certain seasons of the year.

In areas where ventilation is supplied by mechanical means and through the use of air ducts, these ducts need to be treated with sound-absorbing materials; otherwise sounds emanating from one area of the music wing may be transmitted to another area.

Another area not necessarily in the music wing, though generally nearby, and frequented by music groups, is the auditorium stage which in too many instances is sorely lacking in provisions for ventilation. This area can become almost unbearable for members of performing groups and the conductor, particularly at certain seasons of the year. When one considers the increased activity with respect to the inhalation and exhalation of air required in the playing of wind instruments and the size of some of the groups on the stage at a given time, it is not difficult to appreciate the degree of discomfort to the performers. Exclusive of the kind and amount of energy expended by each member of the band, the mere fact of massing bodies in a limited area is enough to raise the temperature from five to ten degrees during the course of a concert. This problem is further magnified by the fact that the uniforms worn by school bands are designed to serve outdoors as well as indoors. Add to this the lighting of the stage, which is generally supplied by several long banks of overhead lights also generating a certain amount of heat, and the need for special attention to stage ventilation becomes even more apparent.

In the newest buildings, provision for control of temperature and humidity is afforded through the installation of air conditioning units in this and other areas where the physical energy requirements are considerable. In some instances, depending upon geographical location, entire buildings are air conditioned. The added costs are further justified where the building is used throughout the summer months. However, it might be of interest to note that the difference in the cost of installing air conditioning for certain areas of the building and that of installing a mechanical air system with its many air ducts is not great.

If the ventilation of the stage and auditorium is supplied through a mechanical air system with exhaust fans and ducts, the location of these is very critical in view of their noise potential. When the exhaust fans are turned on to cool the auditorium before and during a concert, the motion of these fans causes a humming sound which at times becomes quite audible. This sound is particularly noticeable during the playing of soft and transparent passages of both instrumental and choral music. The problem is more serious in schools where a great deal of recording of concerts is engaged in as a regular practice.

In designing the stage, every attempt should be made to afford adequate ventilation, including the locating of double doors in the three wall areas surrounding the stage to allow for possible cross ventilation directly from the outside or by way of adjacent corridors. At the present time, however, factors relating to noise disturbance emanating from off the stage need to be considered. This latter item might also be felt to be a two-way street, depending upon the amount of usage the stage may be put to during regular school hours. Doorways leading to and from the auditorium should be planned so as to provide maximum ventilation for this area where air conditioning is not made available.

LIGHTING

Lighting of music rooms is generally provided by banks of fluorescent lights running across the room and spaced four to six feet apart from each other from front to rear. Through the use of the very newest of these units, the temperature change caused will be kept to a minimum, since they are engineered to generate very little heat.

Some music areas are dependent to a great extent on natural lighting from the outside. While this may be necessary in certain cases, it should be remembered that large areas of glass in music rooms can be responsible for peculiar acoustic conditions. The use of glass bricks for portions of the walls of music rehearsal areas is a fairly common practice in an effort to introduce natural light into these rooms. Here again, however, the problems relating to absorption and reflection of sound must be weighed carefully, especially in rooms where rehearsals of large and fully instrumentated bands will take place.

Because of the demands of reading music and in consideration of the many sizes and types of manuscripts encountered in this process, the lighting of music rooms should be somewhat above the level of the average classroom. The distance from the eyes of the player to the printed page on a music stand is greater than that from a reader's eye to a book held at arm's length. This situation is more pronounced in relation to certain instruments such as the trumpet and trombone, since the music stand cannot be brought too close to the individual without affecting his posture or tone production. Furthermore, where the light is adequate and evenly distributed throughout the room, the posture of players in general is enhanced.

Other factors that need to be considered in lighting as it relates to music rooms is the manner in which players in a band are distributed throughout the room and at different riser levels. Attempts should be made to equalize the lighting for those on the floor level and those situated on the topmost riser. This may be done by installing banks of lights at varying heights from the floor in relation to the height of the riser or by using somewhat larger and brighter units over floor level areas. Furthermore, depending upon whether the lighting is direct or indirect, the element of ceiling height, the degree of reflection, and the texture and color of the walls and ceiling will contribute in different ways to the lighting in these rooms.

With reference to color, authorities suggest soft shades of medium and light colors such as cream, beige, tan, peach, green, blue, and aqua. Colors are generally selected with the room exposure in mind, using warm colors for those on the north side of the building and cool colors for those with a southern exposure. Painted surfaces and wood paneling should have flat or non-reflective finishes and should be devoid of any unusual patterns or designs that may be distracting. I can recall visiting one school where the wall behind the conductor contained sections of perforated acoustic tiling which, when viewed from the players' positions, created an illusory effect that gave one the feeling that the wall was moving!

The average band rehearsal room is supplied by both natural and artificial light. Where natural light is afforded through windows, it is important to plan the room so that neither the conductor nor the players are facing directly toward them since the amount of glare that might result from this arrangement could be very troublesome. For example, in a room having a bank of windows along the wall in back of the highest riser level, individuals seated there are hard to distinguish due to the silhouette effect produced on extremely bright days. This can result in eye strain for the conductor looking directly at these windows. In reverse, this situation would work a hardship on band members. Although window shades could be drawn, the benefits of natural lighting would be lost and the ventilation of the room would also be affected.

In connection with lighting, we must consider the provisions made for electric outlets in music rooms and music rehearsal areas. In view of the increasing number of electronic devices for instrumental and choral music in use by music classes and performance groups, it is essential to plan for enough outlets for such items as electric tuners, metronomes, the Stroboconn, a record player, tape recorder, an electronic organ, the vibraphone, and so on. It may be of passing interest to note that some band rooms are equipped with enough outlets to accommodate music stand lights for rather sizable groups, although I dare say these would have limited use in this area and would be more useful in the auditorium pit.

ACOUSTICS

We might begin our consideration of acoustics by saying that music is an art that deals with the science of sound. Since the message of music is conveyed through the medium of sound, it is of prime importance that all areas in which music is produced be treated in special ways insofar as acoustics is concerned. As we become more aware of the effects of sound on both the producer and the consumer we need to exert greater effort toward its direction and control. This then becomes a matter of consideration of the shape of music rooms and the reflective and absorptive qualities of materials used in their construction.

The matter of acoustics in the music area is concerned with factors of both the production and consumption of sound—that is, the various media employed in the making of sound and the reception and absorption of these sounds. Rehearsal rooms need to be designed and constructed so that they will have a certain degree of "liveness" or reverberation without distortion or echo, and so that the performers will be able to hear each other readily in the process of achieving correct intonation and proper balance. On this general basis, it would be expected that the large instrumental rehearsal room would require more "deadening" of sound than the large choral rehearsal room.

Attempts should also be made to separate large rehearsal areas so that there is no sound transmission between them. This can be done, as mentioned earlier in this chapter, by interspersing storage areas or offices between the rehearsal rooms. Generally these rooms are planned with non-parallel walls to promote the diffusion of sound and provided with wall panels of thin plywood, usually perforated, and with fiber glass backing to absorb sound. Where several rooms are directly adjoining each other, as is often the case with practice studios, it may also be necessary to allow for air spaces on either side of these rooms. This would require a double wall construction pattern for this part of the building. Some builders prefer to take up this space with mortar and use more absorptive materials within the studios. Also, if music offices in this area are to be used for instructional purposes at times, it will be necessary to use similar application in their planning and construction.

The subject of acoustics as related to school construction is generally complicated by the fact that provisions for the distribution and control of sound are not only concerned with the immediate music area, but relate to other areas adjoining the music wing where subjects of an entirely different nature are being taught. This problem may be further magnified during certain months of the school year when doors leading to corridors are open to promote better ventilation. If possible, music rooms should be set somewhat apart from the library and academic areas to reduce to a minimum any distraction that might result from the transmission of sound. By the same token, shop areas should not be located near the music wing since noises from these areas could make it difficult for both the conductor and the performers to concentrate on the score. Apropos to this is a definition of music attributed to the well known orchestra conductor, Leopold Stokowski: "Music is the art of painting with sound upon a canvas of silence." This further underscores my earlier reference to the fact that in planning for acoustics in music areas, one must not only be concerned with the factors of sound production but must also bear in mind those related to hearing.

While outside noises need to be considered in planning music areas, the acoustic qualities within the rooms themselves are of prime concern. In view of the broad range of dynamics involved in the performance of music, it must be possible to hear sounds at the level of a whisper and yet not have the distortion that can arise when large instrumental groups, especially, are performing at high volume levels.

The best time to be concerned with the acoustical characteristics of the music area is when planning a new building. During this time, periodic conferences involving the architect, music personnel, and administrators should be held to develop the desired acoustical atmosphere in the music and adjoining areas. However, this is not always possible since some situations revolve about the making of alterations in an old building where a portion of the building is to be allotted to music needs. In cases such as these, steps can be taken to modify the acoustical character of rooms through the application of acoustic tiling on the ceilings, by changing the angle of wall surfaces through the use of thin plywood paneling backed by air space, fiber glass fill, or other absorptive material, and through the use of drapes and carpeting.

Other factors relating to the kind and amount of acoustic treatment required in music rooms are the size of the room and the purpose for which it was intended. While it is obvious that storage rooms for instruments and uniforms do not require special acoustic conditioning, as mentioned earlier, they can serve as buffers for areas where sounds are produced. Also, problems which might be encountered in connection with the auditorium and large rehearsal rooms would be virtually non-existent in the average music classroom or practice studios, thus different treatment would have to be accorded the various types of rooms in the music area. For example, the auditorium or large rehearsal room might have echo problems, which would probably not arise in connection with practice studios or other small rooms.

Beyond this, if the music area encompasses a control room or recording studio, special care must be applied in its construction. In addition to acoustic provisions for the room itself, some must be made for the walls and ceilings of bordering rooms. Furthermore, there should be a specially designed control window, and doors of heavy construction with rubber insulation around the frame. Doors in the music wing in general should be of heavier construction and more soundproof than those serving the average classroom needs. And, speaking of doors, in certain areas of the music wing it is necessary to plan for double doors to allow for the movement of pianos and other large pieces of equipment needed on stage from time to time.

An excellent and detailed coverage of the subject of acoustics is contained in the M. E. N. C. publication on Music Building, Rooms, and Equipment, 1966 edition, contributed by Richard Bolt of the Acoustic Laboratory of the Massachusetts Institute of Technology. This author recommends that music educators involved in planning new music facilities should have a copy of this publication for reference purposes.

chapter 5

Dealing with Equipment for the
Band Building Program

In view of the ever increasing interest in and demand for music and the changes occurring in this field, authorities charged with the responsibility of educating the young have attempted to meet their obligations by providing for the special needs of the music department. As they supply shop areas with many special pieces of machinery; commercial departments with typewriters, adding machines, and mimeograph machines; mathematics departments with calculating devices and computors; science departments with microscopes and mockups of parts of the human body; it would naturally follow that the music department should be provided for in similar manner.

FURNISHINGS NEEDED IN THE MUSIC DEPARTMENT

The equipment needed to carry on the activities of the music department of the high school includes the basic furnishings ordinarily associated with music rooms such as chairs, music stands, pianos, storage cabinets, chalk and bulletin boards, record players, and the like. In addition, one would also expect to find certain more highly specialized pieces of equipment including a percussion cabinet, music sorting racks, electric tuning devices, a tape recorder, and other items generally associated with the performance of music.

Chairs

For many years the chairs found in music areas were made of wood, metal (folding types), or both wood and metal. In recent years, the trend has been more in the direction of using contoured plywood and molded fiber glass in the manufacturing of school furniture. These chairs are generally the non-folding type which can be stacked for easy movement from the rehearsal rooms to the stage or pit area of the auditorium. The seats and backs of these chairs are generally fastened to tubular steel which provides the legs and framework. In consideration of the height of the average high school student, it is suggested that while the majority of chairs should be 18" in height, some which are 17" should also be available. Some thought should also be given to procuring chairs with a shelf or book rack, depending upon whether the room involved will be used exclusively as a rehearsal area or will also serve as a music classroom or study hall. If a folding-arm chair is used in a room which must serve as an all-purpose music room, the tablet arm surface should be made of hard synthetic material to discourage marking upon it.

Music stands

While the collapsible or folding music stand is light and easy to carry, it is not recommended for the kinds of use music stands are subjected to in schools today. The type most commonly used is the telescopic variety made of steel and other metals with a heavy base, sometimes of cast iron, to provide stability. These are adjustable for height and the angle of the desk, and will last for a good many years under normal conditions. In addition to being more durable, they are more reliable than the folding type since the latter have a tendency to collapse at most inopportune times. Actually, these heavier metal stands will also prove to be more economical since they will take more abuse for a longer period of time. They are generally finished with a non-reflective surface to eliminate glare and usually come in black, although gray is also available. For band rehearsal purposes, some authorities suggest that one stand for every two players be provided, while others recommend a more suitable ratio of one stand to every one and one half players. I would personally recommend the latter figure, assuming that the budget will allow it. Obviously, additional stands can be purchased from time to time to achieve the preferred ratio.

The conductor's podium

In rehearsal rooms equipped with risers it is not necessary for the conductor to use a podium to afford visual communication with all members of the performing group, unless the individual is uncommonly short. Regardless of the height factor, however, some directors prefer to mount a podium as a signal for players to prepare to begin the rehearsal. For concert purposes on stage, the podium not only serves to elevate the conductor, whether or not risers are used, but also serves to indicate to the audience that the performance of a given number is about to begin or has finished.

The average podium height is eight inches while the platform section usually measures about three square feet. Personally, I would suggest having one of greater depth since there are times when the conductor wishes to have a more direct view of performers sitting on the outside of the topmost risers. Occasionally the conductor may wish to back away from his music stand in order to focus specific visual attention upon certain individuals or sections. It is advisable to equip the top surface of the podium with a measured piece of corrugated rubber matting to insure good footing.

Bulletin and chalkboards

Bulletin boards of different sizes should be available both in and directly outside the rehearsal room. The one located in the rehearsal room would serve for the posting of notices concerning specific activities of the group and for displaying fire drill and civil defense instructions, music lesson schedules, and similar material. The board immediately outside the room would be used to post notices of a more general nature including guidance posters on music as a career, scholarships available to music students, and publicity releases on band concerts and other appearances. If it is located near the uniform room it could provide a place on which to post a list of band members together with the numbers of their uniforms, hats, and other such items. The board located in the room should not be less than four square feet while the one located in the adjoining corridor should be considerably larger.

Chalkboards are usually mounted on the front wall of the rehearsal room within easy reach of the conductor. They are usually of green non-reflective surfaces, and for purposes of writing music may be lined with one or more music staffs. In some instances, provision is made for a double chalkboard with one mounted on the wall while the other operates on wheels or rollers, allowing it to be raised or lowered in front of the one on the wall. In this case, one board may be completely lined for music writing purposes while the other is blank. For rehearsal room needs, the chalkboard should be a minimum of six feet in length and four feet in height, while for music classes the board space should be considerably more generous.

Display cases

Display cases, lighted by fluorescent units and lockable, are desirable for displaying trophies, plaques, and other citations awarded to the band and other performing groups. Cases such as these are generally built into the wall immediately outside the rehearsal room. While some may be reached from within the room, most often they are accessible from the outside via sliding glass panels. They may also be used to display the most recent pictures of the school's performing units, and from time to time should undergo changes to afford new interest for the viewer. Cases of this sort mounted on the wall are generally about five feet long and four feet high, and six to ten inches deep. Usually two or more adjustable shelves are provided in each case.

STORAGE AREAS IN THE MUSIC DEPARTMENT

In the music department, there is the need for storage of many types of equipment. To have a well organized department, areas and methods must be designated for the storage of music, instruments, recordings, and uniforms.

Music storage areas

While the matter of storing music was dealt with in some detail in the previous chapter, some further consideration of this subject may be in order especially as it relates to the handling of music folders.

In general, the music library of the band and other music groups is stored in a separate room either on shelves or in filing cabinets. In some cases, however, such accommodations have not been provided for, especially in older buildings, and makeshift arrangements have to be made. Some provide for this need through the use of wall cabinets in the rehearsal room, while others purchase ready made units which rest on the floor and are placed against the wall. Units of this kind are available in various dimensions from manufacturers of school furniture or may be custom made by members of the school maintenance staff or by a local carpenter with special skill in cabinet making.

Some band directors use a conductor's console containing two rows of shelving to accommodate music folders following rehearsals. While this might appear to be a good way to store folders on a day to day basis, I have noticed that a traffic bottleneck results around this unit as each player attempts to place his music folder on a specific shelf. It might be better to arrange for music folder storage in some other manner which would tend to disperse the traffic rather than channel it. This could be done by having shelves in different parts of the room, or by having members keep folders in their regular school lockers between rehearsals. However, this technique may be troublesome if members share folders as is often the case.

Other directors prefer to have folders kept in a cabinet in their offices or in the rehearsal room (or library, if one exists), and have them distributed and collected by band librarians before and after rehearsal periods. Others delegate this responsibility to section leaders or different individuals within each section on a rotating basis. In this way each member of the band learns, at least in some measure, to appreciate the amount of work entailed in the handling of music by regular librarians.

An effective device in handling music folders from day to day is a cart mounted on wheels or casters, designed with vertical slots with pressed wood separators every 1½" to 2" apart, and built in at least two tiers. Each slot would be identified by a number assigned to each folder. This kind of unit can be custom made by members of the school maintenance department, a class in woodworking if the instructor of such classes sees merit in the project, or by a local carpenter. It can be rolled out of the library or store room prior to each rehearsal and wheeled back immediately thereafter. (See Illustration 5-1.) The pressed wood separators used either in vertical slot arrangement or as shelving should be fashioned with a semicircular cut-out to facilitate grasping the folder. Another point to consider in designing roll-out cabinets for music storage or other uses is that the material used for the base should be sufficiently broad and heavy to prevent their being tipped over.

A unique design for the handling and storage of music folders consists of a series of vertical slots approximately 1½" or 2" apart, set in two or three tiers along one wall of the rehearsal room and leading directly into the music library room. This unit can be equipped with lockable sliding doors. In this arrangement, librarians can place band folders in numbered slots from within the library and make them accessible to band members on the other side of the wall. To avoid a traffic jam in this area, folders could be picked up after rehearsals by section leaders or by a number of individuals within large sections and returned in a similar manner. The sliding doors could be locked at the close of school or at any time during the school day when it is deemed advisable or necessary by the director.

ILLUSTRATION 5-1

It was suggested earlier that a music sorting rack be made available to band librarians and to other music groups in order to expedite the handling and sorting of music. If a separate music library does not exist within the facilities provided for music, one could be installed on a section of wall in the rehearsal room or an adjacent corridor. It should also be mentioned that units for the storage and care of music and equipment used in the music wing are available from a number of leading manufacturers of school furniture.

Storage of recordings

Special provision needs to be made for the storing of recordings used in connection with music classes, such as Music Appreciation, or to illustrate certain performance styles and techniques during band rehearsals. These recordings should be stored in an upright position in file cabinets (legal-size) or on shelves. Vertical separators should be installed every three or four inches to keep records in position and to offset the possibility of warping. As suggested in the handling of music folders, these partitions could be designed with semicircular cut-outs to facilitate grasping the records. Care should be taken to plan record storage areas away from any sources of heat that may be in the room. To further expedite the handling and use of recordings in the music area, a library system should be developed, including sign-out cards for each record which might be borrowed for listening assignments given in music courses.

Storage of instruments

While the matter of storing instruments was dealt with in the previous chapter, particularly in relation to the planning of new buildings, further attention should be given to this and to the storage of equipment items in new or existing buildings.

If the space allotted to the music department does not contain a separate storage room for instruments, provision for this needs to be made in the main rehearsal room. This may be done by installing lockers, cabinets, or shelving along the available wall space in the room. Lockers which provide the best protection for individual instruments may be purchased from manufacturers of school furniture or can be custom built. These should be designed in various dimensions to accommodate instruments of different sizes. The larger and more cumbersome instruments should be stored in the lower lockers while those of medium and small size could be kept in the middle and upper units. Some consideration should be given to having students share lockers, especially those playing flute or clarinet which are generally in abundance in school bands. In fact, this procedure may be necessary where storage facilities are limited or where the student population growth has exceeded existing provisions. Specific locker dimensions are listed earlier; however, if these are installed on a custom basis they can be apportioned according to individual school needs. If lockers are used, each one should be identified by number and supplied with a combination lock. Because of the noise factor in the opening and closing of metal doors, some directors prefer to have these units constructed of wood.

The installation of open shelving in existing buildings, adapted to accommodate the storage of instruments and other equipment, is the most economical method to use for this purpose; however, it should be understood that this system applied to a larger rehearsal area provides little, if any, protection for equipment except when this room is locked. Somewhat better provision could be made through the installation of lockable sliding doors of various dimensions to accommodate groups of instruments.

For large instruments such as sousaphones, string basses, and cellos, roll-away racks are available through a leading manufacturer of school music equipment. Also, as mentioned earlier, a strong metal rack that can be mounted on the wall for the storage of sousaphones is now available. Some directors prefer to use sousaphone chairs and to leave instruments in place following rehearsals. While this may be necessary due to a lack of storage space, it tends to invite a certain amount of experimental playing by others during the course of the day. Sousaphone shelf racks may be made of wood and mounted on the wall with heavy brackets of wood or metal to support the weight of the instrument. These should be contoured to the shape and size of the tubing of the instrument, and cushioned with strips of felt or soft rubber. Whichever type of rack is used, it should be located close to where the bass section is seated during rehearsals to expedite handling.

For storage of percussion equipment, including snare drums, cymbals, mallets, and other small drum accessories, most schools use specific cabinets designed for this purpose. These are generally equipped with fairly heavy casters to promote mobility, and the top surface is usually fitted with a piece of carpeting or other sound-absorbing material. While these are available in the general music merchandising market, some directors prefer to design such a cabinet with their specific needs in mind, and, perhaps motivated by economy, have it built by the school maintenance or industrial arts department. These cabinets are built with the surface table approximately 36" from the floor (including the height of the casters), 48" or more in overall length, and 24" or more in width to accommodate large cymbals within and for holding a set of orchestra bells on top. This type of cabinet may be designed to include one or more drop-leaf extensions for additional surface space. In the event that a cabinet such as this is built, it would be well to consider the installation of sliding doors with facilities for locking. Drawers for the storage of small accessory items should be included.

Uniform storage

Uniform storage in most new buildings is provided by a room designed for this express purpose. If space is at a premium, whether in a new building or an existing structure undergoing alteration, uniform storage may have to be provided along the wall in the rehearsal room itself, or along the corridors leading to this room. Doors should be louvered to afford some measure of ventilation. It is also recommended that serious consideration be given to the use of sliding doors of standard size, particularly if corridors where uniform closets are situated are less than ten feet across. Furthermore, if at all possible, wall uniform storage sections should be spaced somewhat apart from each other to avoid congestion.

Uniforms may be hung in wall cabinets on the basis of a double tier arrangement, or on a single tier plan with shelving or compartments directly above for hats. The bar used to hold the uniforms should be placed not less than 38" above the floor of the cabinet with a second tier placed a similar distance above the first. Since the standard width of most cabinet doors used in this kind of construction runs from 30" to 34", a cabinet section employing sliding doors would need to be 64" to 72" overall. Assuming that uniforms are hung with 3" spacing from hanger to hanger, a cabinet of this size should hold from 18 to 20 uniforms per tier. In consideration of the weight of this number of uniforms, it is suggested that the cross bars bearing this weight be made of 2" piping with adequate end supports.

Some directors prefer a wall cabinet arrangement in which uniforms alternate with hats, so that band members may get both at the same time. Another arrangement that would permit this procedure is one employing a single tier with hats placed on shelves or compartments immediately above the uniforms. With the latter arrangement, additional shelving could be provided above the hat storage area for storing certain items of equipment which come into use at limited times throughout the year. These would include field drums, music carrying cases, color guard equipment, flags, and uniform accessories.

In general, to facilitate the cleaning and maintenance of music areas where cabinets play an important part in the storage of instrument, uniforms, and equipment, these cabinets should be faced off up to the ceiling wherever this is feasible. Special attention should also be. given to the treatment and materials used in connection with the mop boards to expedite easy maintenance by the custodial staff.

RISERS

Since the question of risers in relation to the large rehearsal rooms was considered at some length in the previous chapter, comments here will be pointed to the portable types which are generally pressed into service at various times during the school year.

There are presently on the market a number of well constructed portable risers, of both instrumental and choral types, which have come into wide use throughout the country. These may be purchased in sections and readily assembled on the stage, in the pit, or on the floor of a school room or community hall, and may also be used in connection with outdoor performances.

Risers of this type designed to serve instrumental needs are generally made of heavy plywood with legs of tubular steel capped with heavy rubber or synthetic material. Platform sections of these risers are usually 8 feet long by four feet deep, and have legs of 8, 16, 24, and 32 inches to afford consistent graduation from the floor level upward. While these are most commonly assembled in a U-shaped pattern, they are available with pie-shaped segments to permit a semicircular design. Some manufacturers also construct risers in 8 foot sections at varying heights but with depths of 33 inches, to which may be attached sections 15 inches deep, affording the necessary 48 inch depth required for seated instrumental groups. The advantage of this type of riser design, as purported by the manufacturer, is that of flexibility. The 33 inch deep sections may be used for seated choral units, while the 15 inch sections could serve standing groups when assembled as directed. The selection of risers is generally left to the discretion of the music director whose choice will be determined by the frequency and kinds of use these units will receive.

The advantages of using risers in connection with either instrumental or choral performance activity are obvious with respect to both visual and aural aspects, since performers and conductor will have improved sight communication and, equally important, performers will be able to hear each other better. Beyond these reasons for using risers in performance are those related to appearance and discipline, neither of which require further amplification for the trained music educator.

If for economic or other reasons it is necessary to have riser sections constructed by the maintenance staff or woodworking department, care should be taken to keep the weight and size specifications to a feasible minimum to facilitate easy handling of riser sections.

AUDIO-VISUAL EQUIPMENT

The music department of the high school should also be equipped with certain special items of the audio-visual category. Among these should be record players of good quality, one or more tape recorders, electric metronomes, tuning devices, a slide projector, perhaps a movie camera, and other electronic and mechanical devices which may be effective in the promotion of learning in the field of music.

It will probably be agreed that one of the best ways to develop conceptions of musicianship among young players of high school age is to invite outstanding college groups or professional musicians to perform in the school or to arrange field trips to concert halls in nearby cities. Through these means, the individual band member is given the opportunity to experience a live performance by highly skilled musicians. In addition to observing certain visual details of performing such as the position of instruments, the posture of the players, and the general discipline of the group, he can broaden and enrich his conception of fundamentals such as tone quality, sonority, phrasing, intonation, articulation, dynamics, and precision. If these opportunities are limited because of geographical location, the director could then turn to the use of high quality recordings by professionals or outstanding school and college units. Color slides and sound films can also be used to advantage to promote interest and progress.

Record players and recordings

If recordings are used to foster a better understanding of "bandsmanship" among members of the group, it is essential that both the recordings and the record player be of a high quality. Leading manufacturers of record players have become increasingly aware of the need for good equipment for the school field and have turned to designing units with diverse capabilities. These must be more durable and versatile than those found in the home since they are exposed to a variety of uses by different individuals. Once such unit is shown here, and according to the manufacturer: "It gives the instructor the capability to provide the full impact of high quality sound from records and tapes to classes of any size. It also enables him to conveniently make tape recordings from records with his own comments superimposed. The public address channel enables the instructor to comment on music being played or to lecture to a large audience. Live performance and rehearsals can conveniently be recorded in stereophonic sound and played back at full volume immediately after the performance. Headphone monitoring facilities permit monitoring of the program as it comes through the microphones or from immediate playback of the tape after it has been recorded."[1] (See Illustration 5-2.) A unit containing features such as these will prove to be a valuable asset to the band director and to music educators in general. For band directors who occasionally resort to the practice of playing recordings in rehearsals and who wish to enlarge their band record libraries, the following partial list can be of value:

---

[1] By permission: Radio Matic of America, Inc., 760 Ramsey Ave., Hillside, New Jersey 07205.

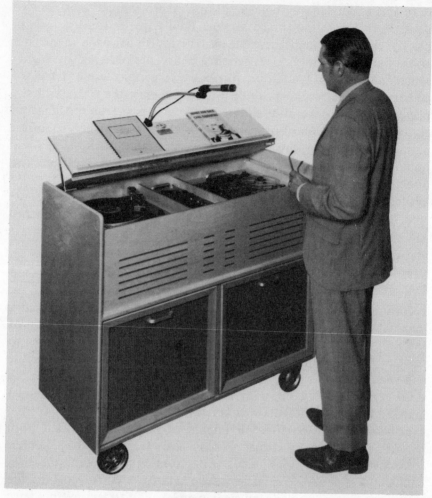

ILLUSTRATION 5-2

Companies Carrying Recordings of Works for Band
(Note: In some cases these include recordings of their own publications.)

Bandland, Inc., 407 Fox Building, Detroit, Michigan 48201

Belwin-Mills Inc., 250 Maple Ave., Rockville Centre, New York 11570

Bourne, Inc., 136 West 52nd Street, New York, N.Y. 10019

Crest Records, 220 Broadway, Huntington Station, New York 11746

Educational Record Reference Library,, 16 West 61st Street, New York, N.Y. 10023

Instrumental Music Inc., 1416 Lake Street, Evanston, Illinois 60204

Kenyon Publications, 17 West 60th Street, New York, N.Y. 10023

Hal Leonard Music, Inc., 64 East 2nd Street, Winona, Minnesota 55987

Lyons Band Instrument Co., 688 Industrial Drive, Elmhurst, Illinois 60127

Mercury Record Corp., 35 East Wacker Drive, Chicago, Illinois 60601

Music Minus One, 43 West 61st Street, New York, N.Y. 10023

On the Spot Recording Co., 11359 Lothair, Chicago, Illinois 60643

Regal Records, 7816 North Interstate, Portland, Oregon 97217

Salvation Army Music Co., 120 West 14th Street, New York, N.Y. 10011

Shawnee Press Inc., Delaware Water Gap, Pennsylvania 18327

Summy-Birchard Co., 1834 Ridge Ave., Evanston, Illinois 60204

Vanguard Recording Society, Inc., 154 West 14th Street, New York, N.Y. 10011

It should be noted that band recordings may be had by writing directly to large colleges and universities which sponsor active band programs that include the making of records on a fairly regular basis. Perhaps one of the most complete listings of recordings of band literature is that published by the Instrumentalist Company, 1418 Lake Street, Evanston, Illinois 60204.

The tape recorder

The tape recorder has become an increasingly important aid to the high school band director. Its use by individuals in the practice studio and by the band in rehearsal and concert has proven to be invaluable in analyzing results and determining progress. When used by individual players, it affords an effective means of evaluating performance, whether sight reading, playing a segment of a prepared lesson, or performing a solo work. Since it only records what it "hears," the results are starkly objective.

Through the use of this device, elements of performance such as tone, articulation, intonation, tempo, phrasing, dynamics, attacks, and releases can be appraised with a view to improving these areas of performance. In connection with group activity, elements such as sonority, blend, balance, precision, and unity can also be appraised.

Selecting the tape recorder

In selecting the tape recorder to serve the requirements of the instrumental program, the band director should investigate the makes and types considered to be practical for school uses. While it is recognized that the best recording results are likely to be obtained under studio conditions, most recording of school bands will necessarily take place in the rehearsal room or school auditorium. Furthermore, in selecting equipment such as a tape recorder, microphones, and microphone stands, it should be apparent that the portion of the budget available for the purchase of these items will have a direct bearing upon the quality and amount of equipment that can be procurred. To insure the acquisition of good equipment, it may be necessary to establish priorities in the process of obtaining the desired items.

The tape recorder that is to serve the many needs of the senior high school music department should be of top quality. While the average home recorder might prove adequate for individual use, it will be rather ineffective when it comes to recording large groups, especially bands. Because of their size and makeup and in consideration of their volume potential, high school bands require a professional grade of equipment if satisfactory results are to be achieved.

The recorder chosen should include a selector to permit recording at speeds of either 7½ or 15 inches per second. The higher speed provides the greatest frequency response and superior fidelity since the amount of hiss (signal to noise ratio) will be minimized. Speed accuracy is also important since any appreciable amount of variance will have an adverse effect on the recording. The recorder should also be equipped with some type of "V U" meter to afford visual control of the recording level. Without this feature, one may be confronted with problems of distortion created by recording at too high a level, or under-recording (hissing) by using a level that is too low. It should also be possible to monitor the incoming signal through the use of a set of earphones of good quality. The recorder should further be equipped with a digital counter which measures the number of revolutions made by the supply reel. This is a time saver in locating specific places on the tape when playback is desired and is also functional when it comes to splicing or editing. Most machines are supplied with a safety lock switch which guards against the accidental erasing of portions of the tape already recorded upon.

A tone control adjuster should be included to permit the balancing of high and low frequencies. The recorder should be adaptable to the use of output jacks for connecting to external amplifiers and input jacks for recording directly from a tuner, record player, or another tape machine. It is recommended that when the recorder has been selected, ordered, and subsequently delivered, the band director and others who may be involved in its operation carefully study the owner's operating manual which accompanies the machine. A thorough knowledge of its proper care and use will not only afford the most satisfying results, but also insure its length of service.

Choice of microphones

Beyond the nature and quality of the components contained in the tape recorder itself lies the critical choice of microphones. These must be compatible (having the same impedance) with the recorder and be adapted to their intended needs. For maximum fidelity, low impedance microphones are preferred to the high impedance types. Microphone cables used in conjunction with low impedance "mikes" can be from 20 to 200 feet without loss of signal. In general, since microphones may be said to be the "ears" of the recorder, it is essential that they possess a high degree of sensitivity.

In selecting microphones, the band director needs to keep in mind the kinds of use these will serve and the acoustic qualities of the areas where most of the recording will be done. Many school band rehearsal facilities are found to be too small and bright with many sound reflecting surfaces to provide a good "copy" of that which is being played. In most cases, better results would be obtained by recording in the auditorium. This large area can offer greater latitude with respect to the placement of microphones, and the chances are that the acoustic character of the hall will be more favorable.

Microphone types include crystal, ribbon, dynamic, and condenser mikes. Those most commonly in use today include the dynamic and condenser types. Crystal microphones which were in popular use in the early days of broadcasting and recording were found to be too sensitive to changing weather conditions and were limited in frequency range. The ribbon type requires greater care with periodic readjusting of the ribbon necessitated by abrupt movement or jarring. It is also felt to be somewhat limited, especially in its response to upper frequencies.

The dynamic microphone has proven to be sturdy, dependable, and quite accurate in terms of flat frequency response. It can serve effectively for recording at close range and at some distance, provided neither dimension is extreme. The condenser microphone, which requires its own power supply, is the most expensive of the types mentioned. Through the use of a pattern switch, certain makes and models possess great adaptability in accommodating different recording conditons. These patterns include the cardioid or heart shape design, the figure "8", and the omni-directional pattern.

Since stereo recording calls for a certain amount of separation, it is suggested that a cardioid (uni-directional) microphone pattern be used. In view of the directional character of the cardioid microphone or microphone pattern, some of the audience noises encountered when recording in the school auditorium can be eliminated. In situations such as this, one would not use an omni-directional microphone since sounds emanating anywhere in the hall would be picked up. The latter type of microphone would be effective if a round table discussion were to be recorded. Under this kind of condition, one such microphone placed in the center of the table equi-distant from each speaker would meet the needs.

Microphone placement

For recording large groups a minimum of two microphones should be used. Microphones should be positioned from 6 to 12 feet above the heads of the players and for stereo recording purposes should be placed (or hung) from 8 to 10 feet apart. Furthermore, microphones should be located some 10 to 15 feet in front of the group; however, this may require some experimentation with respect to the acoustic character of the room or auditorium where the recording will be done. In some instances, and to avoid picking up background noises such as one experiences when recording with a live audience, it may be necessary to move the microphones closer to the performing group. Care should be taken to avoid placing these too close, however, because of the possibility of picking up certain individual instruments to the detriment of the total balanced effect. For recording soloists, it is suggested that a separate microphone be used and monitored through the tape recorder.

Directional microphones, such as the cardioid type, should be aimed at sections to be picked up; however, special care should be given to the placement of microphones with respect to certain sections. The percussion section, whose sounds are distinctly differ-ent from those produced by the wind instruments, is notorious for creating an overloading of microphones and contributing to a distorted or muffled effect. This can be especially true with respect to the timpani which may tend to "cover" the wind instrument sound. It is true also of the bassoons because of their distinct tone color and the manner in which it comes over the microphone. The director and the individuals operating the recording machine will probably need to experiment in microphone placement to bring about the desired balance. In the event that one section of the band is notably weak, placing one of the microphones somewhat closer may help to achieve an improved balance. It should be understood that the use of greater numbers of microphones can contribute immeasurably to the overall effect, assuming that they are judiciously placed and that the individual controlling the recording process is sensitive to all aspects of recording and has some knowledge of music.

As mentioned earlier, the finest recording results would probably be obtained by transporting the band to a professional recording studio. Here the acoustic conditions are scientifically established, a multiplicity of microphones of different types are available, trained engineers seated at the mixing console in the control room can monitor the session and supervise the details of the whole operation. It would be wise to plan for some consultation between the engineers and the band director before the recording session so that both will understand the problems which might arise. The feasibility of holding a recording session under professional conditions such as described here would have to be determined by the band director in cooperation with school administrators. Factors that would come to bear upon such a decision would include the amount of time needed to prepare for such a session, the amount of studio time required to record a sufficient number of selections to occupy a standard 12" disc, the cost of transporting the group to the studio, the provision of one or more meals in the event of a lengthy session, the hourly charge for the use of the studio and its staff, and the general demand for such a recording in the school, community, and area. These are but a few of the items which would need to be considered in assessing the practicality of such a venture.

Selecting tapes

For recording the high school band, it is suggested that a good quality acetate or polyester tape be used. While the quality of the former is good, the latter is more durable although somewhat more expensive. Furthermore, it can be stored for longer periods of time without fear of deterioration. Obviously, low noise tape is preferred over other types, and for best results, new unused tapes should be required for recording at formal concerts, particularly if disc records are to be made from the tapes. For casual rehearsal use or for studio practice purposes, used tapes will be adequate. Material on these tapes will be erased as the tape passes over the magnetic eraser head. Care should be taken to avoid the purchase of "off-brand" tapes since these might be those rejected by certain manufacturers because of imperfections. These imperfections could include variations in the dimensions of the tape due to faulty slitting or uneven coating. In either case, the fidelity of the tape will be affected and a certain amount of distortion will result.

Methods of recording

Since there are many ways in which the tape recorder can serve the needs of the music department, the director will be required to determine the feasibility of recording monaurally or stereophonically at various times throughout the year. Monaural recording involves a single channel while stereo recording requires two. While one microphone can be used to record monaurally, at least two are needed to record in stereo since two channels are involved in the latter process. These provide for the tonal separation which characterizes a stereophonic recording. For certain purposes, such as recording individual pupils for analysis or evaluation, the use of a single channel would be adequate. For recording small ensembles such as a trio or a quartet, this method is also acceptable. However, if the performance of a work by a small ensemble is to be included on a disc record and some separation of sound is sought, the taping should be done stereophonically through the use of two or more microphones. While it is possible to record large groups, such as the band, monaurally, much of the depth and sonority of the group will be lost. Recording stereophonically, however, will bring about much more satisfying results since this method takes advantage of the full sonority of the band together with its wide range and variety of tone color. Recording in stereo is further preferred since it permits greater latitude in the mixing of sounds and the controlling of dynamics for the purpose of equalizing or balancing various sections of the band when this is desired or becomes necessary. In addition, the individual tone controls on a stereo tape machine allow for the boosting of the highs and lows of certain instruments.

Depending upon the intended use of a particular tape, the band director will have to determine in advance the most suitable method of recording—that is, whether to record monophonically using the entire width of the tape (full track), or to record monophonically using two tracks (dual-track). The latter method involves taking the full reel which has been recorded in one direction, turning it over, and placing it on the feeder or supply spindle and rethreading it for recording in the opposite direction. While economical, this method will not permit editing without first redubbing (recopying). Another method of recording is in stereo through the use of a two-channel system and requiring two or more microphones. If the tape is used in one direction only, editing and splicing will be relatively easy. Here again, however, if the position of the reels is interchanged for the purpose of recording on the same tape in the opposite direction, it will not be possible to edit without first redubbing. The two-track and four-track (sometimes called half track and quarter track) methods of recording, particularly in stereo, have gained increasing popularity.

As the director and members of the band, having a special interest in tape recording, become more skilled in the use of the school equipment, they will apply certain refinements in its use. Among these refinements is starting the motor before the actual sound is picked up to insure having the motor warmed up and moving at a regulated and consistent speed. Also, in stopping the tape the recorder should be permitted to run for five seconds or more, gradually turning down the volume on the applause—assuming we are talking about recording at a concert. Another refinement would include taping wires and power cables to the floor with masking tape to guard against their being tripped over. It might also be helpful to place microphone stands on rubber mats or other sound absorbing material to avoid the transmission of stage or auditorium floor noises. Furthermore, if the playing area is acoustically dull, it may be necessary to place microphones further away from the performing group to pick up some of the liveness of the hall itself.

In general, it is recommended that the individual operating the recorder practice using it under conditions similar to those that will exist during the actual recording session, insofar as possible. This procedure will help to eliminate some of the problems encountered in recording, especially those relating to recording at too high a level (resulting in distortion), or too low a level (picking up too much tape hiss and motor noise). Recording at a point midway between these two extremes should produce satisfying results. It is assumed that the matter of microphone placement will have been determined in advance through some experimentation, and that the acoustical character of the hall (and the cooperation of the audience) will enhance the final product.

Making records from tapes

Since many band directors have disc records made from tape recordings made at concerts and other important events, the following list of companies which provide the many kinds of services relating to this practice is offered for reference purposes:

Angel Records, 1750 N. Vine Street, Hollywood, California 90028

The Audio Recording and Manufacturing Co. Inc., 4 New Hyde Park Road, Franklin Square, New York 11010

Century Custom Recording Service, P.O. Box 308, Saugus, California 91350

Continental Recording Co., P.O. Box 1026, Mobile, Alabama 36601

Crest Records, 220 Broadway, Huntington Station, New York 11746

Findlay Recording Co., P.O. Box 39127, Cincinnati, Ohio 45239

Fleetwood Custom Recording, 321 Revere Street, Revere, Massachusetts 02151

Full Fidelity Recordings, 9475 Lockland Road, Cincinnati, Ohio 45215

Ken-Del Productions, Inc., 515 Shipley Street, Wilmington, Delaware 19801

On the Spot Recording Co., 11359 Lothair, Chicago, Illinois 60643

R.C.A. Victor Custom Record Dept., Station B, Box 7031, Dayton, Ohio 45407

Recorded Publications Co., 1575 Pierce Ave., Camden, New Jersey 08105

Regal Records, 2302 North Going, Portland, Oregon 97217

Vogt Quality Recordings, P.O. Box 302, Needham, Massachusetts 02192

This is only a partial list, but some of these companies have franchised agents throughout the country who can supply the needed services.

OTHER ELECTRONIC AIDS

Other electronic aids known to assist the band director in achieving desired goals in both individual and group performance include the metronome. While spring wound metronomes are still available, the electronic models are more widely used today. Although its original and main purpose is to provide a means of measuring tempo, the metronome can also serve as an effective aid in learning to play difficult rhythm figures. For example, if a student is having difficulty performing a dotted quarter note followed by an eighth note, it can be taught by holding the first note for three

metronome beats and the second for one, thus: ♩· ♪ etc. When the
pupil grasps the relationship of the two notes, the metronome can be
speeded up. The teaching of a dotted eighth note followed by a
sixteenth, and other difficult patterns, can be approached in a similar
manner.

In selecting a metronome, care should be taken to check its
accuracy. (This can be accomplished through the use of a
chronometer, a quality time piece, or a stop watch.) It should be able
to maintain speed even though a change may occur in the line
voltage. Other features to consider concern the ease of reading the
dial, its ability to start instantaneously, its volume consistency as
tempos are changed, and the inclusion of a flash-beat device to
permit visual guidance. These features, and more, are contained in
the unit pictured in Illustration 5-3.[2]

ILLUSTRATION 5-3

Another device, powered by electricity, which is very effective in
matching certain tones by individuals in the process of tuning is the
Tempo Tuner. It can also serve as a metronome since it includes a
separate control dial for this purpose. As a tuning device, it can
supply four fixed pitches. For use with bands, the model which
sounds F A B♭ and C should be procured. (Two other models are
available which sound G D A and E, and B D G and E respectively.)
A fifth reference tone can also be supplied which can be made to
vary within a 2½ octave range.

---

[2]With permission of the Franz Manufacturing Co. Inc., New Haven, Connecticut 06519

This device is especially useful as an ear training aid since, through its use, pupils will become more conscious of the need to tune individual tones. Furthermore, while one of the selected tones is sounded, the individual can play an arpeggio or other interval exercises against it, thus improving his awareness of tone relationships. Among its other advantages, this device can sustain a given tone for as long as it is needed, thereby eliminating the need for using an individual player to supply a series of tones for tuning a group of players. (See illustration 5-4.[3])

Still another device that has served as an effective aid to the band

ILLUSTRATION 5-4

director is the Billotti TriNome, which can function as a metronome, a bell metronome, and a rhythm metronome capable of reproducing all sorts of rhythm patterns. Furthermore, these patterns can be demonstrated at almost any desired speed. While this device can be used to good advantage in band rehearsals, its application with individuals and small groups, such as would be scheduled for music lessons, will prove to be especially effective in contributing to the

[3]Photo courtesy of Selmer Division of Magnavox Co., Elkhart, Indiana 46514

understanding of the element of rhythm. Note the many possible settings on the model in Illustration 5-5.[4]

The Stroboconn, which permits quick and accurate measurement of the frequencies of all tones within the range of a piano, has been widely used by band directors throughout the country. The sound picked up by the microphone is visually "translated" by means of whirling discs which may be seen through the 12 scanning windows on the large model. The smaller Stroboconn contains only one window; however, through the use of a dial it can provide for the measurement of all 12 tones.

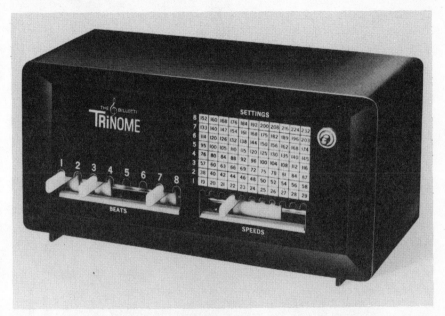

ILLUSTRATION 5-5

If the tone is below the desired pitch, based on A - 440, the visual pattern will move to the left. On the other hand, if the tone produced on the instrument being tuned is somewhat higher, the pattern will move to the right. If the tone is precisely in tune, the pattern will remain stationary. In addition to indicating the pitch tendency of the tone sounded, the Stroboconn can measure the amount of deviation to the 1/100th of a semitone. On the larger model, a pointer can be moved to the left or right to measure the degree (in cents) of the pitch variance. In effect, this device enables the player to "see what he hears" (as the manufacturer puts it)— in

---

[4]With permission of Targ & Dinner Inc., 2451 N. Sacramento Ave., Chicago, Illinois 60674

other words, sound can be measured by visual means. (See Model 6T-5 shown in Illustration 5-6.[5]) In addition to its popular application in tuning band instruments, the Stroboconn has often been pressed into service by piano tuners with good results.

While the Stroboconn can be used in connection with rehearsals of the full band, some of its finest applications are brought about with

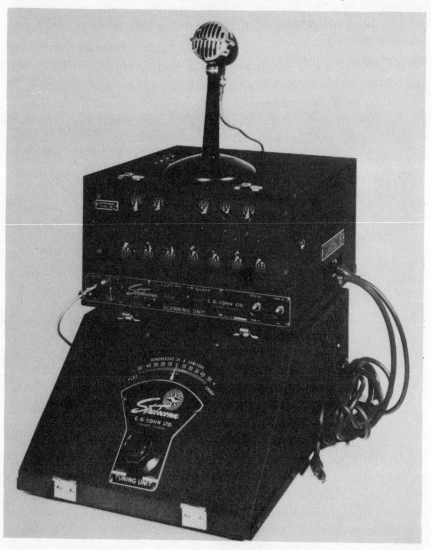

ILLUSTRATION 5-6

[5]Permission to reprint photo of Stroboconn, Courtesy Conn Corporation, Elkhart, Indiana 46514

individuals in the practice studio. Here the student can become thoroughly familiar with the peculiarities of his own instrument and thus learn to make the necessary adjustments that will bring about improved intonation.

MOTION PICTURE AND TELEVISION EQUIPMENT

The use of motion pictures and television in connection with certain kinds of music performance activity is becoming more widespread as this equipment comes closer to the reach of school budgets. While both motion pictures and closed circuit T.V. have certain applications in common, each can meet individual needs in ways that the other cannot.

One of the obvious advantages of closed circuit television is that it is possible to have the video tape played back through the monitor immediately following a performance. The use of a motion picture camera requires a period of time for the processing and developing of the film before it can be viewed. On the side of motion pictures, however, a 16 MM color sound (or silent) film, which is easily carried from place to place, and which can be shown on all standard 16 MM projectors, can be an effective aid in the promotional and public relations phase of the music program. A specially prepared color film, for example, showing the highlights of the year's activities can be a positive influence in recruiting and for "selling" the educational benefits of band membership. The use of good quality color film will insure the accenting of certain details which might not be as sharply defined except on the more expensive video "packages."

The initial costs of closed circuit T.V. for school use may appear high; however, the many uses that it can serve in the school at large will more than justify its procurement by the audio-visual department, if not by the music department itself. While the costs of motion picture film and television tape are not far apart, the latter will prove less expensive in the long run since it can be used over and over. Beyond this, since the video tape can be monitored as the action takes place, the feasibility of retaining all or a portion of the tape for future reference can be determined almost immediately.

USES OF CLOSED CIRCUIT T.V. IN THE BAND PROGRAM

Among the uses of closed circuit television in the band program are the analysis and evaluation of performing abilities. Through the use of the T.V. camera and monitor in a studio environment, it is possible to observe and identify certain idiosyncrasies of each player and to offer on-the-spot suggestions to rectify these. Peculiarities such as may relate to the embouchure, to tonguing, to the position of the fingers or hands, to the breathing process, and to other playing habits can be observed. Since direct viewing is possible and immediate playback of the tape is available, the advantages of video recording are obvious and countless.

Another application of closed circuit T.V. is that dealing with rehearsals and performances of the marching band. Here again, the band director is afforded a means by which he and the members of the band can assess results as they prepare a pre-game or half-time show. Since video tape playback is possible without special processing, the group can gather in the band room following the rehearsal and engage in an evaluation of its efforts. This procedure will give each member a clearer understanding of his particular role as it relates to the whole. Players will respond more quickly in subsequent rehearsals and results should be noticeably improved. Since the sound of the band is also involved, this aspect of the performance can be assessed as well. The achievement of consistent sound balance in connection with marching band maneuvers is extremely difficult, if not impossible, in view of the movement of the group and the changing locations of the various instruments and sections of the band. Some attempts are being made by manufacturers of electronic devices to solve some of these problems by equipping each member of the marching band with a power-pack to amplify the tone of the individual instrument.

For indoor use, which involves special lighting, a different kind of planning will be necessary. An indoor video taping session such as might take place in the band room or on stage in the auditorium can provide unique opportunities for the evaluation of both the visual and aural aspects of performance. Performing under conditions such as these will be considerably less demanding than those existing during a formal concert. The rehearsal set-up and atmosphere will provide opportunities to experiment with camera placement, the location of microphones, and other details of recording. In a concert situation, on the other hand, all visual and audio details as well as the continuity of the program must be carefully planned and rehearsed in advance. Once the concert begins, there will be few if any opportunities to readjust equipment. For an undertaking such as this, the band director and the technical staff responsible for the control of the lighting, the placement of microphones, the positioning of the camera (or cameras), and the production director will need to engage in one or more consultation sessions to coordinate all the details to assure satisfactory results.

SELECTION OF EQUIPMENT

The procurement of closed circuit television components including the camera, the recorder, the monitor, speical lights and other equipment will, in most cases, be the responsibility of the audio-visual director or a member of the faculty who has a special interest in and some knowledge of this kind of equipment. Otherwise, the band director will have to study up on the subject and depend upon the reliability of a particular dealer following some personal surveillance of the field.

In general, the five most critical considerations in the selection of a video unit for school use are: (1) durability, (2) reliability, (3) portability, (4) simplicity of operation, and (5) suitability for school purposes. In addition to these basic concerns, it will be necessary to determine in advance the tape width deemed most practical for school use. Popular dimensions include ½", 1", and 2" tapes. For most school uses, the 1" tape should prove adequate. With reference to the acquisition of the recorder itself and compatible microphones, the information supplied earlier in relation to the selection of a tape recorder should provide some guidelines.

Since most school equipment is used by a number of different individuals, it is essential that the unit purchased be of rugged construction. All those who will use the video equipment may not be technically oriented, therefore the unit must also be reliable and not require the services of special personnel for operating purposes. In this regard, however, most audio-visual departments train groups of students who exhibit special talent and interest in this field; therefore, they are in a position to supply student aid on a voluntary basis. Since the video equipment might be used outdoors as well as indoors, it should be portable. It may be noted that school cameras run from 10 lb. battery operated units to models of considerable weight (100 lbs. or more). While early models of video recording units called for the services of skilled technicians and controlled conditions under which to operate, many of those designed for school use today require little special knowledge or training. It should of course be understood that while the larger and heavier recorders provide a better picture, they are somewhat more complicated to operate. Also, since models vary in benefits and convenience offered, it will be necessary to determine their basic suitability for the majority of school uses.

Other considerations in the selection of a video unit for school use should include: (1) tape speeds, (2) writing speed, (3) head configuration, and (4) modulation systems. It should be noted that there are about 27 different formats for video taping at the present time, and others will probably be added in time.

CARE OF TAPES

Like tapes used for other recording purposes, the video tape requires some special care in its handling. Since temperature and humidity affect the quality and life of tapes, they should be stored in a controlled atmosphere. It is especially important to store tapes vertically in individual containers for protection against dust and to make them easy to locate. If dust particles are present on the tape as it passes over the playback head there will be a noticeable loss of picture. The white lines which will appear are referred to as "drop-out." To extend the life of a tape, a log of its use should be kept to indicate the amount of use in 100-foot sections. If the first one or two hundred feet of a tape are used repeatedly, it might be wise to wind the tape off the original reel and rewind it on another reel. Care should be taken not to rewind tapes either too tightly or too loosely since breakage or distortion may result in subsequent uses.

In conclusion, it should be noted that there are many other electronic and non-electronic aids available to band directors, with new devices in a state of research and development. Those mentioned here are felt to be among the most frequently used by the band director in his efforts to foster a stimulating and worthwhile program of band activity.

chapter 6

Developing the Proper
Instrumentation

For many years it has been the practice of schools throughout the country to provide, in various ways, for the procurement of the large and unusual instruments of the band. These are generally needed to cover certain basic parts of both a rhythmic and harmonic nature and to achieve a balanced instrumentation. Beyond this, they add to the tonal enrichment and sonority of the band and perform other functions that would otherwise be weak or entirely missing. For the most part, these instruments are of a less common variety and cost more than the average parent can afford. Expenditures of substantial sums of money on equipment such as this is justified on the same basis as supplying typewriters, microscopes, lathes, and other specialized items for all departments of the school. Generally a number of these instruments are purchased each year until an adequate inventory is achieved. While many schools lend instruments of this kind to students without charge, some with more limited budgets require an annual rental or use fee. Furthermore, where funds allotted for music are held to be inadequate, certain fund-raising activities are pursued in efforts to secure the needed instrumentation.

Since the needs relating to instrumentation very considerably from school to school, it would be difficult to recommend specifics with regard to this matter. The music educator in charge of the program of instrumental music should determine the needs and establish a list based upon priorities. While some music educators are fortunate enough to inherit a generous supply of instruments because of the efforts of those who preceeded them, most have to make a concerted drive to obtain the desired instrumentation.

At the outset the director should outline specific equipment needs to school officials responsible for developing the total school budget. The list of items should include descriptions, quantities, and costs, together with the names of authorized and reputable dealers in the area. It should be presented on the basis of priorities and revised annually in keeping with changing needs and growth trends. If the equipment items sought by the director are not supplied within a reasonable period of time, it may be necessary to engage in certain forms of fund-raising activity. Beyond this, and to speed up the procurement of needed instruments and equipment, the band director may organize a band parents association to assist in securing needed equipment and in other matters relating to the many activities of the band.

In view of the different types and sizes of bands together with the changing conceptions of bands and band music, the listing of different instrumentations for bands of varying sizes, while not the complete answer on the subject, will afford some guidelines that can be of help. For our purposes here, we shall consider the matter of school-owned instruments and instrumentation as one integrated subject.

PERCUSSION INSTRUMENTS

Assuming the high school band building process is in its early stages, the band director will first need to point his efforts to the procurement of large instruments of the percussion section. Instruments such as bass drum, timpani, chimes, and certain other percussion equipment not readily transportable should be considered in the same light as basic school furnishings and supplied by the school. While concert snare drums may be carried to and from school, they are more commonly held to be part of the school-owned percussion equipment. Field drums which are used for marching band functions are also supplied by the school in most cases. These are generally ordered in the official school colors or in those which complement the band uniforms. Small percussion accessories such as tambourine, castenets, wood blocks, and triangles are similarly treated as school-owned equipment.

Other instruments of this section which are normally regarded as part of the school instrument inventory include bells, xylophone, vibraphone, and gong. Since some of these items are quite expensive and of more limited use, they might be considered to be in the luxury catagory and relegated to a low priority rating. While timpani are quite expensive, their early purchase is justified on the basis of frequency of use and the role they play in supporting the basic harmonic structure of the music, not to mention their assistance to both the rhythmic and dynamic elements of band literature. In procuring a set of timpani for school use it is recommended that one should have a diameter of 26 inches, and the other 29 inches. A pair of this type would provide both an adequate range for the bulk of the music performed by school bands and an ample body of tone for all normal uses. As funds become available, it might be well to procure additional timpani of the 23 inch and 32 inch variety to accommodate the range and technical requirements of some of the contemporary band works.

Cymbals should also be placed high on the priority list of school-owned percussion equipment. In view of both the indoor and outdoor aspects of band performance, more than one pair of good quality cymbals should be planned for. While the initial pair could be 15 inch medium weight cymbals for all general purposes, a subsequent purchase should be a pair of 17 or 18 inch medium weight cymbals to serve in connection with concert band activity. Band directors should exert great care in selecting a pair of cymbals whose tonal characteristics will complement each other and whose responsiveness will meet the needs of the kind of music performed. Furthermore, they should take into account the size of the band and the types of performance activities planned for the group—not to mention the size and strength of the members of the percussion section who will be called upon to play them! For marching band purposes it is suggested that cymbals no larger than 14 or 15 inches be supplied for the average high school band. Additional percussion equipment generally provided by the school should include a set of bells, timbals, bongo drums, maracas, claves, and an assortment of mallets and small traps.

BRASSES IN THE BAND

Instruments of the brass family which should be acquired in the early stages of building the band instrument inventory include bass horns, baritones, and French horns. Instruments such as cornet, trumpet, and trombone are usually owned by individual members of the band. In some instances, however, where the cornet tone quality is felt by the director to be highly desirable, effort should be made to supply these to all members of that particular section in the interest of promoting a more uniform tone. It should be pointed out that composers and arrangers are coming more to the writing of separate parts for trumpet when the brilliance and color of that instrument is desired. Trends in instrumentation shift from time to time in accordance with the general evolution of the band and its literature. At present there seems to be a move in the direction of a wider use of the trumpet in conjunction with cornets in concert bands throughout the country. A number of contemporary works are arranged in such a manner as to have the cornets and trumpets complement each other while a few have called for the use of trumpets exclusively.

Instruments such as the fluegelhorn and the upright alto horn which contribute a somewhat different tone quality than either the cornet or trombone are not normally held to be essential and therefore are unlikely to be included in most school instrument inventories. Where budget amounts are especially generous and marching band activity engaged in on a large scale, upright alto horns may be procured and issued to horn players during certain times of the year.

Basses

For practical purposes, sousaphones are generally used in school bands rather than upright basses since they can serve for both the concert and the marching band. In view of their high cost, the director starting to build a band will be fortunate to be supplied with one or two of these at the outset. He will, of course, plan to acquire more of these as the band grows in size and as more individuals become interested in playing bass horn. With reference to the number of these that would be needed for balance purposes in bands of different sizes, I would recommend the following: For a band of 25 to 40 pieces, at least one bass would be needed and another should be sought when the band reaches a membership of 40. For bands of 40 to 60 pieces, at least two if not three basses should be planned for, while in groups as large as 80, four should be sought. Larger units of 100 to 120 should be supplied with five or six basses to provide an adequate foundation upon which to develop real sonority in the band.

While these are offered as general recommendations, it should be understood that bass parts would be supported by other low-voiced instruments and the director's judgment will influence the number desired in proportion to the other instruments available, assuming of course that there is an adequate supply of players of these instruments. If few other supporting instruments such as bass clarinet and baritone saxophone are available, the need for more basses will be greater.

Baritones (euphoniums)

Baritone horns, sometimes referred to as the 'cellos of the band, should be counted among the instruments supplied by the school. Their role in providing interesting countermelodies and adding to the over-all sonority of the band makes them indispensable. Since these too are expensive, they are likely to be acquired one by one as the band grows and the part they play in the band becomes more apparent to players of other instruments. In general, it should be safe to say that a rule of thumb for the number of these needed in bands of different sizes would be the same as applied in connection with bass horns. Again this may vary somewhat depending upon the available number of other instruments that play similar parts, such as tenor saxophone and trombone.

French horns

While French horns are usually thought of in terms of quartets, it is not likely that the band director starting a band program will be supplied with four of these from the beginning. He may also be confronted with the problem of finding candidates for them. This may be done either by seeking volunteers to switch from other instruments, or by starting new pupils. At the high school level, this process could be aided by finding pupils who have had prior training and experience on piano or in choral music, since they will have some knowledge of reading music.

For the most part, it is expected that these players would have been started prior to the high school level. For bands of 25 to 40 pieces, a minimum of two French horns should be planned for, while those having a membership of 40 to 60 should be equipped with four. Bands ranging in size from 60 to 80 pieces would be expected to have at least four and very likely six horns, and those of 100 to 120 pieces should include a double quartet of horns. In procuring French horns for use at the high school level, the director would be wise to consider the advantages of the double horn over the single horn and plan budget expenditures accordingly.

Trombones

Trombones are generally owned by individual members of the band and need not be supplied by the school under normal conditions. Of course, if a scarcity exists, it may be necessary for the school to provide some. As the instrument inventory of the school is enlarged, the band director should consider the acquisition of bass trombones which are not usually purchased by the average high school student and which will help to increase the sonority of the band. With respect to the number of trombones needed to promote a desirable balance in the band, the following is offered: For bands of 25 to 40 pieces, two to three trombones should be included while in groups of 40 to 60, three or four would be required. Bands of 60 to 80 pieces should be equipped with at least six trombones with perhaps two bass trombones among them. In bands of 80 to 100 members, I would expect to find eight or nine trombones, including not less than two bass trombones. In groups totaling 100 to 120, ten to 12 trombones including three bass trombones would be required to balance all the other instruments that go to make up large organizations such as these.

Cornets and trumpets

Instruments such as the cornet and trumpet are generally owned by individuals in the band and are not purchased by the school, particularly in the initial stages of equipping a group when funds are needed for the large, more unusual, and costly instruments. When an adequate number of these have been accumulated over a period of time, the director may find himself in a position to purchase cornets or trumpets in line with instrumentation needs and with some consideration of the kind of band sound he is trying to promote. Since we are concerned with the subject of building the school instrument inventory while engaged in the process of developing a balanced instrumentation in the band itself, I would offer the following recommendations concerning cornets and trumpets:

For bands of 25 to 40 pieces, four to six cornets should prove adequate, while bands ranging in size from 40 to 60 should be equipped with six cornets and two trumpets, unless the director prefers all cornets. For bands of 60 to 80 in number, eight cornets and two trumpets would be appropriate in promoting balance, and those having 80 to 100 pieces should include ten to 12 cornets plus a pair of trumpets. Bands in the 100 to 120 membership range should include a dozen cornets and one or two pairs of trumpets.

Before proceeding with a consideration of woodwind needs, the reader should be reminded that while the numbers of brass instruments suggested may afford the proper balance within the band, other influences will come to bear upon the degree of success achieved in this process. Numbers of instruments do not guarantee the attainment of balance, since within each section there will undoubtedly be strong, capable players amid those of lesser ability. Whether the band engages in a great deal of marching activity or is primarily a concert ensemble will also have some bearing upon the course of its development. The director's conception of a band sound will also have a marked influence. Furthermore, the whole process of accumulating an adequate supply of instruments and attaining the proper balance is one that demands a great deal of skill, patience, persistence, salesmanship, and musicianship on the part of the band director over an extended period of time. As the saying goes: "Rome wasn't built in a day."

WOODWINDS IN THE BAND

As in the case of brass instruments, the band director will need to focus his attention on the procurement of the large and expensive woodwind instruments which are not customarily owned by individuals. From the outset, he should attach a high priority to the acquisition of bass clarinets and tenor and baritone saxophones in an effort to promote richness and sonority in this section of the band. Once these instruments have been acquired, he should seek additional funds to purchase double reed instruments such as oboes and bassoons. As the band grows in size and maturity, he should plan to add alto clarinets and at least one contra-bass clarinet to the school inventory. Furthermore, in the event that none of the members of the flute section own a piccolo, it may be necessary to secure one or more of these in proportion to the size of the band and in consideration of the kinds of activities the band engages in most frequently.

Flutes

Flutes are among the instruments normally possessed by individual members of the band, and therefore are not usually supplied by the school or included in the school inventory. Piccolos may be included however, since their use is more limited, and the average student who owns a flute may not be able to afford a piccolo too. There might be an exception in the case of an individual who is planning to pursue a career in music and owns both a flute and piccolo, or one whose parents are financially able to provide both. With reference to the number of flutes needed for balance in the band, the following is recommended: In bands of 25 to 40 pieces, one or two flutes would be needed with one doubling on piccolo if possible. Bands of 40 to 60 members should be equipped with from four to six flutes with one doubling on piccolo. For bands of 60 to 80 in number, six to eight flutes should be sufficient, with one doubling on piccolo also. Larger bands of 80 to 100 members should have from eight to ten flutes with two doubling, and bands of 100 to 120 should include ten to 12 flutes with at least two doubling on piccolo. For marching band purposes, the tone of the flute is quickly dissipated; therefore several players might need to be assigned to piccolo. If the director feels so inclined, he may involve the entire flute section in the marching band regardless of the number of piccolos available, on the premise that all should share in the vicarious experiences afforded through membership in the band. In some instances, flute players are assigned to function as part of the color guard, as a member of a flag twirling group, or even as a helper in the percussion section. For general purposes, in relation to the number of flutes required for balance in the band, I would suggest that a figure of ten percent could be used as a guideline.

Clarinets

As in the case with flutes, B^b clarinets, with few exceptions, are owned by individuals in the band. School budget allotments for instruments do not usually include clarinets, especially in the first steps of building the band—particularly if the budget is limited. In rare cases they might be supplied by the school if a scarcity of players exists and there is an accompanying urgent need to develop them. Schools with an adequate budget and a fairly complete equipment inventory have been known to supply clarinets made of metal or ebonite during the fall football season and for other marching band events, since individuals owning costly instruments made of wood are justifiably reluctant to expose them to rough use and low temperatures.

With regard to the matter of instrumentation balance, I would recommend having from six to ten clarinets in small bands ranging in size from 25 to 40 members. Bands of 40 to 60 members should include ten to 15 clarinets, while larger units of 60 to 80 would be expected to have 15 to 20. Bands of 80 to 100 would need approximately 20 to 25 B^b clarinets, and those in the 100 to 120 membership range should include 25 to 30 clarinets. As another guideline to the number of B^b clarinets needed for balance in the band, a figure of 25 percent of the total band membership is suggested.

Oboes

In the process of building a band and developing the school instrument inventory, I would not be inclined to expend funds for the purchase of an oboe until I had procured certain other wood-winds which could contribute more significantly to the development of the band tone. Since these instruments are expensive and difficult to play together, and since few pupils are interested in playing them, I would not press to include one in the beginning. However, as the band progresses, I would plan to acquire one or more of these since their role, particularly in the concert band, is unique. They are rarely if ever played in a marching unit.

In regard to the table of instrumentation, I would not expect to include an oboe in a band of 25 pieces. Perhaps when the size of the group approaches 40, particularly if the main aim is to develop a wind ensemble, I would recommend the inclusion of one oboe. For bands of 40 to 60 members, I would still suggest only one oboe in consideration of other more urgent priorities. Bands numbering 60 to 80 pieces should afford a pair of oboes playing first and second parts respectively. Bands ranging in size from 80 to 100 up to 120 pieces would be expected to include either one or two pairs of oboes to cover both parts in a balanced manner. In some instances, one player may be assigned to the English horn or alto oboe, since it is capable of producing a distinctive tone quality that is frequently soloistic in character. These too are very expensive and would not normally be found in other than extremely well equipped bands.

Bassoons

Bassoons too are expensive instruments which seem to have limited appeal to students. In view of other pressing needs, I would delay buying a bassoon until the band program is fairly well developed, from the point of view of both quality and numbers. As in the case of some of the other less common instruments, it may be necessary to transfer a clarinet or saxophone player to bassoon unless the band building program of the lower school levels is well developed, in which case one might expect to find bassoon players starting at those levels.

Although I would not look for a bassoon in a band of 25 pieces, I would expect to find one in a band of 40 pieces, particularly if the group functions primarily as a concert organization. In cases where the band director has switched either a clarinet or saxophone player to the bassoon, these individuals could play their first instrument in the marching unit. Bands of 40 to 60 members should include at least one bassoon, while those of 60 to 80 could include a pair. As in the case of the oboe, bassoons function in pairs since two parts are generally supplied in most band arrangements. On that basis, and for balance purposes, bands of 80 to 120 should be equipped with at least one pair of bassoons. (Groups of 120 could easily accommodate four.) If the budget permits, one of these might well be a contra-bassoon, especially if a great deal of concert work is planned.

Bass clarinets

Bass clarinets are generally included in the school instrument inventory in the early stages of building a high school band, since they are among the most essential instruments in contributing to the sonority and the balance of the band. Because of their cost and size, they are rarely owned by an individual band member, but are usually provided by the school. In my opinion, the bass clarinet should be placed high on the agenda in the process of accumulating school-owned instruments.

In bands of 25 to 40 pieces, I would expect to find at least one bass clarinet, while in those numbering between 40 and 60 a pair of these should be included. Bands ranging in size from 60 to 80 should have three bass clarinets, one of which could very well be a contra-bass to afford even greater sonority. Bands with 80 to 100 members should include four bass clarinets, among which there should be one contra-bass. Group as large as 100 to 120 could well afford to include five bass clarinets. These would be most effective if distributed as follows: three regular bass clarinets, one E^b contra-bass clarinet, and one BB^b contra-bass. It is recognized that a contra-bass is a very expensive piece of equipment and would therefore not be sought until a rather complete instrumentation was developed.

Alto clarinets

While alto clarinets contribute to the tonal make-up of the band, they are not generally regarded as being highly essential. This is due in part to the fact that parts written for them are often covered by alto saxophones, bass clarinets, and in some instances by B^b clarinets, and because their tone quality is somewhat lacking in resonance and drive. While I would not suggest the expenditure of funds for an alto clarinet at the outset, I would plan to secure one or more when other and more pressing needs have been met.

In bands of 25 to 40 in number, I would not expect to find any alto clarinets unless the emphasis were placed on the development of a wind ensemble. In that case, and as the instrumentation approaches 40, an effort may be made to include one. In bands of 40 to 60 pieces, I would recommend having at least one alto clarinet, assuming that all other priorities had been met. In bands ranging in size from 60 to 80 I should include a pair of these, and in organizations having 80 to 100 three of these could be included in the process of achieving balance. In bands of 100 to 120 pieces, three and possibly four alto clarinets should be included to promote balance among woodwinds and in the band as a whole. It should be noted here that while the bass and alto clarinets may not be normally considered part of the marching band, players of these frequently play either B^b clarinet or saxophone which could serve to better effect in that organization.

Baritone saxophone

The baritone saxophone which can readily add support to the bass line of the music and to the sonority of the band in general should be among the first of the school-owned instruments. Since the fingering systems of all saxophones are alike, it is a simple matter to shift one of the alto saxophone players, usually found in abundance, to the baritone sax in an effort to promote improved sonority and balance in the band. It is important to select an individual of above-average size and breath capacity to adequately "fill" this instrument, and above-average strength and height to manage it.

Because of the part it plays in the band and the tone potential it possesses, I would include one baritone saxophone in small bands of 25 to 40 members. One such saxophone should also be adequate for bands of 40 to 60, while in groups ranging from 60 to 80 and 100 a pair of these could contribute effectively to achieving good balance. In view of the size and weight of this instrument, it is not normally pressed into service for marching band functions. While it may be included, it is quite heavy and awkward to carry and control, particularly for any distances or at quick cadences. Most often on these occasions the players resort to the use of either an alto or tenor sax, whichever they own or is available.

Tenor saxophone

Although many students own tenor saxophones, to assure having at least one available from the very beginning stages of the band building process one should be purchased by the school. In addition to covering a range of some two and a half octaves, the tenor sax frequently supports countermelodies written for baritone horns and trombones. Its size, although larger than an alto sax, does not exclude it from use in the marching band. For use in the school stage band, it would be considered to be highly essential.

In bands of 25 to 40 and up to 60 pieces, one tenor saxophone should be included. Depending upon the judgment of the director, the availability of other instruments covering similar parts, and the emphasis of the band's function, two might be needed in a 60 piece unit. Bands of 60 to 80 could afford to include two tenors, while those ranging from 80 to 100 could manage well with three. In bands of 100 to 120, three tenors would be considered to be adequate for most purposes; however, more could be pressed into service for outdoor marching events.

Alto saxophone

Instrument inventories of bands in their initial stages of development do not generally include alto saxophones which, because of their size and popularity, are usually owned by individuals.

In bands of 25 to 40 pieces, one would expect to include two altos, and in bands ranging in size from 40 to 60 at least one pair and possibly more would be included. For normal indoor playing purposes one pair of altos should be adequate. Again, for marching band services more could be used. Bands having 60 to 80 members could readily accommodate three or four alto saxes, while those having 80 to 100 should include two pairs, assigning two players each to the two separate parts that normally are provided. Bands of larger numbers would still find four altos to be adequate for most purposes except for outdoor appearances. As mentioned earlier, those playing baritone sax, bass clarinet, and alto clarinet frequently shift to either alto or tenor sax for marching band affairs.

Although it was not mentioned earlier, the inclusion of one or more string basses in the band is both a legitimate and effective practice, especially in the performance of certain types of music performed in concerts. Also, since the author has considered the subjects of band instrumentation and the development of an adequate instrument inventory for the school to be closely interwoven, he chose to deal with them in this light. Furthermore, while certain priorities should be attached to the accumulation of basic equipment, the process of developing a substantial inventory of school-owned instruments is rather extended and requires periodic evaluation as growth and changes occur. For those who find figures and charts to be of value, a summation is offered in the following chart, "Suggested Instrumentation for Bands."

SUGGESTED INSTRUMENTATION FOR BANDS

Size of Band	25	40	60	80	100	120
Flutes (Picc.)	2	3(1P)	6(1P)	8(2P)	10(2P)	12(3P)
E^b Sop. Clar.					1	1
B^b Clarinets	6	10	15	20	25	30
Oboes (Eng. Hn.)		1	2	2	3(1EH)	4(1EH)
Bassoons		1	2	2	3	3
Contra-Bsn.					1	1
Alto Clarinets			1	2	2	3
Bass Clarinets	1	1	2	3	3	3
Contra-Bass Clar.				1	1	2
Alto Saxes	1	2	2	3	3	4
Tenor Saxes	1	1	1	2	2	2
Baritone Saxes	1	1	1	1	1	2
French Horns	2	4	4	6	6	8
Cornets	4	6	6	8	10	12
Trumpets		1	2	2	2	4
Fluegelhorns					2	2
Trombones	2	3	5	7	9	10
Baritones	1	1	2	3	4	5
Basses (String Bass)	1	1	3(1StB)	4(1StB)	5(StB)	6(1StB)
Percussion	3	4	5	6	7	8

Note: Figures given in parenthesis indicate doubling within the section. It should also be understood that for marching purposes, these figures would vary.

It may be of some interest to the reader to compare the figures given in the second table. The percentages suggested may be used as a guide in developing a balanced instrumentation as well as a complete inventory of school-owned instruments as they relate to the high school band.

Variations in the figures suggested here will occur in accordance with the number and kinds of players available, the size of the budget allotted to the purchase of instruments, the number of years the program has been in existence, the director's personal tastes, the special demands of the music most frequently performed, and the evolutionary trends in bands and band literature. Beyond these factors, the nature and size of the pre-high school instrumental program will have a direct influence on the instrumentation of the band and upon the instrument inventory of the schools within the system.

SUGGESTED PERCENTAGES RELATING TO THE DISTRIBUTION
OF INSTRUMENTS

Woodwinds		Brass and Percussion	
Flutes (Picc.)	10%	French Horns	8%
B^b Clarinets	25%	Cornets and Trumpets	12%
Oboes (Eng. Hn.)	2½%	Trombones	9%
Bassoons	2½%	Baritones	4%
Alto Clarinets	2%	Basses	5%
Bass Clarinets	4%	Percussion	7%
Saxophones	9%		
	55%		45%

   In schools having an established program of instrumental music, certain provisions will exist in reference to supplying some of the basic instruments, including the large and more unusual brasses and woodwinds, as well as percussion equipment from the elementary grades upward. Beyond that, where an orchestral program is carried on, the school instrument inventory will include instruments such as string bass, 'cello, and viola, with some also providing violins of varying sizes to accommodate young beginners.

PIANOS IN THE SCHOOLS

   It should of course be understood that the school system will provide pianos at all levels and commensurate with changing needs. At the high school this generally includes at least one large grand piano and perhaps several studio pianos. The music director responsible for the procurement of pianos must be armed with specific knowledge of pianos in order to select wisely in terms of the needs of the school or schools under his jurisdiction. Leading manufacturers of pianos will supply detailed descriptions, including specifications of various type of pianos suitable for school use. These materials should be studied carefully with a view to comparing construction features, dimensions, the action, materials used, the casters, the make-up of the sounding board, ribs, and bridges, and the tone quality, as well as the cabinetwork and finish. Some of this would obviously require visits to piano dealers in the area for purposes of inspection and trial. Since schools function on the basis of budget allotments, it is the general practice to secure bids from several dealers in an effort to keep costs in line. Service policies and warranties should also be taken into consideration when making a final decision on the purchase of pianos for the school.

chapter 7

Using Effective Organizational Aids

The process of organizing the high school band has innumerable facets, the most important of which we shall deal with in some detail here. During this whole procedure the band director will have to be concerned, at different times, with matters such as the seating of the band, taking the attendance, the care and distribution of music, auditioning players, holding election of officers, appointing section leaders, establishing credit for band, developing a band handbook, setting up a point system, and constructing a system of awards—to mention but a few. While there are a number of approaches to each of these subjects, we shall attempt to offer some thoughts which may be of value in establishing guidelines.

SEATING ARRANGEMENTS

Seating arrangements of bands have undergone a number of changes since the day of bands such as those directed by Sousa, Pryer, Conway, Creatore, Simons, and others. School bands in those days, naturally influenced by these professional groups, tended to follow their example. A typical seating arrangement involved placing the B^b clarinets to the left of the conductor, similar to the location of the first violins in an orchestra, and the lower woodwinds and saxophones to his immediate right. Flutes and oboe together with one or more E^b clarinets were usually located directly in front of the conductor. The horns were located near the center and sometimes to the right of center. Cornets were sometimes found on the right side directly in front of the trombone section. Basses and baritones were often placed next to each other and at the rear close to the percussion section. Instrumentations were generally not as complete as bands of today, nor were bands as large for the most part. Over the past 30 to 40 years many different seating arrangements have been tried by directors of school, college, and professional bands, with a view to relating sections more closely and developing greater sonority.

Types of bands

The types of bands that have evolved over the years include the symphonic band, the concert band, the wind ensemble, and of course the marching band. While the seating arrangements of the first three may be similar, some adjustments have come about because of the size and makeup of these and due to personal tastes and judgments of individual directors. Regardless of the size of the band, there are certain relationships which need to be maintained in the interest of promoting a balanced band sound.

The symphonic band is usually the largest and most completely instrumentated indoor band. A membership of 90 or more is quite common in schools throughout the country today, and some have as many as 120 or more members. The matter of the instrumentation has been dealt with in some depth in Chapter 6, with recommendations for developing an acceptable balance in groups of various sizes.

In recent years, the seating of groups of this size has followed a pattern that has received general acceptance by band directors throughout the country. While the plan shown here is typical, it is by no means the only way to seat large bands. In fact, experimentation in seating should be encouraged in the process of trying to achieve the most satisfying band tone. It should be recognized that the acoustic qualities of both the rehearsal room and the stage will have some bearing upon the final decision, and it is frequently found necessary to alter the seating somewhat from rehearsal room to the stage. If the stage is equipped with acoustic reflectors overhead and behind the group it may not be necessary to make any adjustments in the seating of the band. Of course, another factor to consider when seating the group on stage is whether the number and placement of the portable risers is similar to the physical arrangement of the rehearsal room. If this is not the case, a number of changes may need to be made.

As mentioned earlier, certain relationships need to be maintained in developing a well balanced and sonorous band tone. These relationships involve numbers of instruments and their proximity to each other in view of the nature of the roles they play. Beyond that, some care should be taken in the placement of instruments within each section. For example, since the bell of the French horn is to the player's right side, it is common practice to seat the first hornist on the left side of the horn section so that those "teaming" with him will be better able to hear the first horn part. By the same token, since the bell of the trombone is on the left side of the player, one would expect to find the first trombonists seated to the right of others in that section. In the latter case, it might be effective to place the first player between those playing the second and third parts. Similarly, since saxophones are commonly held to the player's right, the lead alto sax player is usually found on the left side of the section.

Although some directors place their first cornet players on either the right or left end of the section for various reasons, I prefer to place them in the middle of the section so that players of the second and third parts, then located on either side of the firsts, are in a better position to hear the leading part. Since bass parts are of a rhythmic as well as harmonic nature, they are commonly located near the percussion section. There are also acoustic reasons why this plan is logical, particularly with the increasing use of tuned percussion instruments which can be more effectively synchronized both rhythmically and harmonically.

While some directors locate oboes and bassoons close together because they are both of the double reed family, I prefer to place them in relation to the parts they play. Since bassoon parts are often similar to those of the bass clarinets and baritone saxophone, I would locate them close to each other. Because of tone quality relationships, alto and bass clarinets should be next to each other, and in general, the entire clarinet family should be grouped fairly close together.

The French horn section of the symphonic band is most frequently located in the center of the band directly behind some of the high woodwinds, adjacent to instruments such as alto saxophone, which often relates tonally to the horn, and directly in front of the cornet section. In view of the fact that horns are often required to blend with certain woodwind passages, and because of their tonal focus or direction, they should be kept well forward in the seating arrangement of the whole band.

The cornet section, which in earlier days was found to be at the conductor's right, is now generally located in a semicircular fashion in the center of the band directly behind the horns and in front of the basses. In this position this leading section of the brasses can readily be heard by the vast majority of bandsmen. Furthermore, their parts can also be fused within the tonal structure of the whole band, and the need to project is also lessened. These factors can contribute to the development of improved intonation, better tone quality (since forcing of tones can be avoided), and better balance in general.

While the trombone section is usually found on the right side of the band on the top riser and behind the cornet section, some directors prefer to have it on the extreme left of the band in view of the location of the bell of the instrument. These directors like to have the first players on the outside toward the audience, and knowing that other players in the section can hear the first parts better when that part is located to their right, they place them in this manner. In some instances directors have placed the trombone section in front of the cornet section, realizing that cornets and trumpets, with their high parts, project more readily than trombones, which frequently play in the middle and lower registers. In cases such as this it may become necessary to experiment with the location of various sections to bring about the desired balance.

It should be pointed out that while instrument tonal relationships should generally be maintained regardless of the size of the band, some variance is bound to occur—particularly in view of stage considerations of symphonic groups having more than 100 players as compared to wind ensembles of approximately 40, where in many cases only one player is playing a particular part. Also the acoustic peculiarities of the hall or auditorium where public performances are given need to be observed in an effort to seat players most effectively. During this process care should be taken to locate instruments whose tones are easily projected in positions that will avoid having their sounds bounce off the side walls of the hall.

While the seating arrangement employed for concert bands of 60 or 70 or more players is generally similar to that used by large symphonic groups, the plan used by the small wind ensemble may differ to a greater extent. This is due in part to the total numbers which comprise these groups; however, as in the case of the small wind ensemble, the element of greater influence is likely to be the fact that a greater number of parts are being handled by individual players. The seating plans shown in Illustrations 7-1 and 7-2 are among those frequently used by high school bands.

As mentioned earlier, these are but two seating arrangements among the many that are used to good effect with large groups as well as the small selected units. Again, directors are reminded to engage in some experimentation in seating bands because of acoustic factors, the number of members in the group, and the kind of instrumentation balance (or imbalance) that exists.

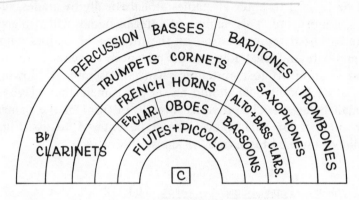

ILLUSTRATION 7-1

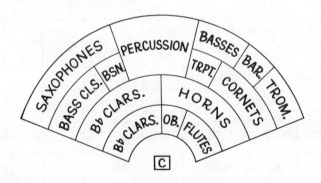

ILLUSTRATION 7-2

TAKING ATTENDANCE

Most schools require that attendance be taken in each class on a daily basis; therefore it behooves the band director to develop a technique which will be both accurate and swift. In the small band of some 40 members, such as would comprise a wind ensemble, this procedure is a relatively simple one since it can be done quickly with a visual sweep of each section. This may be done by the director himself or by an elected or appointed band secretary. The director's official school roll book with names listed alphabetically can serve to record those in attendance. To save time in this procedure it is suggested that no mark of any kind be placed next to the names of those present, while a straight vertical line be entered next to the names of those who are absent. With this technique, a late arrival would merely require that the straight line be made into the letter "L". In some instances, depending upon the marking system used, it might be helpful to enter all names alphabetically by grades, such as seniors, juniors, etc. This manner of entering names will also give the director a visual representation of the number of seniors who will soon graduate and what adjustments may need to be made from year to year in an effort to maintain a balanced ensemble. Following the names of each individual should be the instrument they play, and in the small box generally provided directly in front of the names the folder number of each player could be entered to assist in the handling of music. Illustration 7-3 shows this.

Folder #	Pupil's Name	Grade	Inst.	Week of Sept. 15				
				M	T	W	T	F
16	Adams, James	12	Cor.					
1	Gently, Ruth	12	Flute					
19	Cordas, Richard	12	Trom.					
12	Dalton, John	12	Horn					
5	Eltrom, Susan	12	Clar.					
26	Andrews, Wm.	11	Bass					
6	Barton, Dathie	11	Sax					
30	Chase, Gordon	11	Drum					
7	Dewey, Charles	11	Clar.					
3	Anderson, Peter	10	Oboe					
27	Benson, Louis	10	Bass					
4	Collins, Nancy	10	Bsn.					

ILLUSTRATION 7-3

For the band whose average membership numbers around 70 or 80, a similar procedure could be employed. However, to expedite the taking of attendance, whether by the director or a student, a seating chart could be effective. This device would require that each person occupy the same seat at each band rehearsal so that accuracy can be assured.

For the large symphonic band of 100 to 120 pieces, attendance procedures can be speeded by having each section leader responsible for reporting to the secretary any absences occurring within his immediate section. If a section is unusually large, such as might be the case with the B^b clarinet section of a band of this size, a section leader for first clarinets should be appointed, as should one for each of the remaining sections of the entire group. By the same token, if sections are small, as in an oboe or bassoon section, these may be combined. This technique might also be applied to basses and baritones.

Some directors prefer a technique involving a large piece of heavy cardboard superimposed upon another piece of similar size and thickness, with slots cut into the surface piece wherein small cards bearing band members' names are inserted. Daily attendance is noted on each card by the organization secretary who tallies this record at the end of the week or month, as the case may be, particularly if the organization functions under a point system. These cards need to be smaller than a playing card, yet large enough to include the student's name and instrument and to contain dates of the month which could then be circled to indicate absence. In this system, the secretary would need to mark an "X" over the circle, should the individual arrive after the attendance has been taken. While there are a number of other procedures used by directors for taking attendance at band rehearsals, those given here have proven to be effective. The prime considerations for this operation are accuracy and speed so that little time is consumed at the beginning of rehearsals. It should, of course, be noted that some systems require more secretarial time and assistance than others.

DISTRIBUTION AND HANDLING OF MUSIC

The whole process of handling music for the average high school band is vital to the success of the group and calls for the close cooperation of all members of the band. While it is the responsibility of the director to establish procedures in connection with the cataloging and handling of music from week to week, he must rely on volunteers in the band who will serve as librarians. In view of the vast amount of music handled during the course of a school year by these librarians, three or four individuals would be needed to serve in that capacity. One of these should be designated as head librarian to give leadership and direction to this all-important part of band organization. Periodic meetings between the director and his librarians should be held to assure the consistency in procedures established for the filing and distribution of music.

```
Title_____      Library
                                                     Number _____

                                              ☐ Band   ☐ Orchestra   ☐ Ensemble
_____        ☐ Quickstep ☐ Octavo   ☐ Concert

Composer and/or Arranger _____
Type of Number_____ (Classification Guide) _____
Publisher_____ Original Cost_____ Date Added_____
Playing Time:_____   Condensed Score _____ Full Score _____
                          (List performance dates below.)
_____




PEPPER LIBRARY SYSTEM CARD #10-1           J. W. PEPPER & SON, INC.      jwp
© 1965, J. W. PEPPER & SON, INC.           PHILADELPHIA · ATLANTA · DETROIT
```

ILLUSTRATION 7-4

Library procedures

In view of the amount of music generally found to be associated with the high school band, including its many classifications and the many different instrumental parts published for each separate number, it is vital that a specific system for handling this be established as early as possible and that it be followed with consistency from year to year as the library is expanded. From the very outset a master index should be established which would include all vital information concerning each selection. This information should include: the title, the composer and arranger, the type of number for classification purposes, the performing time, when purchased, its cost, whether both a full and condensed score are available, date of its performance, and, perhaps most important, a library number to aid in its speedy location. These cards which are generally 4" x 6" should be kept in a metal file drawer readily accessible to the director and librarians. Such a card is shown in Illustration 7-4.[1]

---

[1] By permission of J. W. Pepper & Son, Inc., 231 N. Third St., Philadelphia, Pennsylvania 19106

Title cards should be filed alphabetically to expedite locating individual selections. The specific library numbers associated with each selection are used to indicate its location in a particular file cabinet drawer or shelf, if the latter kind of storage is used. Some directors prefer to develop a dual card file system which is established alphabetically by composer's names. This technique is helpful at times since many directors remember the composer's name but forget the title.

A rubber stamp identifying the name of the school or organization should be made for stamping each part. Beyond that, a numbering device is also effective in helping to keep track of all the individual parts. Both the stamping and the numbering procedures should be continued with consistency once the library system is established.

The rubber stamp and numbering process should also be applied *folder* to band folders for easy identification when issuing new selections. Each folder should be clearly identified with an instrument label, and the user or users of each folder should be entered in the director's roll book. It might be well to place a complete list of band members with folder numbers on the band room tackboard or tape it to the door or wall in or near the band library or sorting rack, depending upon the procedures used in the distribution of music at rehearsals. Furthermore, each folder should contain a signout card which may be left in place when the folder is taken home for practice purposes. The signature of the player is required, together with the date the music is signed out. Upon its return, the librarian initials the card and places it back in the folder (Illustration 7-5).[2]

Since different methods are used in the daily handling of music, it will be the responsibility of the director with his librarians to develop specific handling procedures. Where a sorting rack exists in the rehearsal room, folders may be kept in a designated place to be picked up by players as they enter. If no such rack is available, it may be necessary to have the librarians distribute the folders at the beginning of each rehearsal. This process can be speeded up by using section leaders or individuals on a rotating basis. In some cases, music folders are placed in slots in the wall or in a cabinet, or on shelves in the music library room adjoining the large rehearsal room. Here it becomes the responsibility of each player to pick up and return his own folder. This physical setup can be speeded by designating certain individuals within each section to be responsible for a group of folders during a given week or month. Regardless of the type of

[2]Ibid.

Part **Cornet**   ORGANIZATIONAL STAMP   Band **Wind Ens.**

Desk **1st**   **L.H.H.S.**   Orchestra _____

This card removed   **MUSIC DEPT.**
from above folio.   (Other Ensemble)

INSTRUMENTAL REHEARSAL SIGN-OUT CARD

Your signature below constitutes an agreement that the entire folio of music
indicated above will be returned to the Librarian before the next regularly
scheduled rehearsal following take-out date.

DATE TAKEN OUT*	SIGNATURE OF PLAYER	DATE RETURNED**	DATE TAKEN OUT*	SIGNATURE OF PLAYER	DATE RETURNED**
9/15/	Adams, J	9/16/			

* Player complete   **Librarian complete   J. W. PEPPER & SON, INC.
PEPPER LIBRARY SYSTEM CARD #10-3   PHILADELPHIA · ATLANTA · DETROIT
c.1965, J. W. PEPPER & SON, INC.

ILLUSTRATION 7-5

storage used, it should be arranged in a numbered sequence to
expedite handling.

Another method used by directors to distribute and collect music
folders is through the use of a cart which contains two or more tiers
of slots whose dimensions are predetermined by the size of folders to
be used and the amount of music generally stored in them. This cart
is described in some detail in Chapter 5 under the heading "Music
Storage Areas."

As new music is purchased, stamped, and filed, librarians should
be alerted by the director as to when this music should be placed in

the folders for rehearsal purposes. This should be done by librarians during study periods and after school. At times like this it may be necessary for the director to make it clear to band members that folders are not to be taken out. Music to be recalled from the folders may be taken out at that time and new selections entered in their place. Before returning music to the files, librarians should arrange all parts according to a standardized procedure with the conductor scores on top, piccolo parts next, and so on with the percussion parts on the bottom. This will eliminate the need to do this when the music is required again. At this time, if any parts are torn or damaged, steps should be taken to make repairs. Furthermore, in connection with new acquisitions, each should be assigned a library number beyond those already given to identify its physical location in the music storage room.

For further clarification of different types and sizes of music, the director may wish to develop a code for identification purposes. This code may use numbers exclusively or letters in conjunction with numbers. For example, if the number *1* is used to identify with overtures, an overture in the library having the number *37* ascribed to it would be labeled *1-37*. Some directors use the letter *O* for overtures, which would require that the music be labeled *O-37*. In such a system the letter *S* might be associated with selections, the letters *SY* with symphonies, etc.

Marching band music

Music for the marching band has to be cared for somewhat differently than concert band folders. Music for this organization usually consists of a mixture of march books and single sheets, both containing a wide assortment of music such as is associated with the football band or the parade band. In addition, special music holders with transparent windows are issued to each player for use during the season. Since these, together with the music, represent a considerable outlay of money, many directors resort to the use of a March Folio Sign-Out Card such as is shown here to maintain a record of the kind and amount of music and materials issued to each member of the band. The signature of the student on the card signifies his willingness to assume the care of this equipment. On the back of the card is a place for the player's signature, the date when materials were issued, and the date this was returned. Folders of this type are frequently issued on a season basis and taken home by the student for the duration of the football season. While some of the music may be rotated from time to time, much of it remains in the individual's care for an extended period of time. In cases of this kind the employment of a separate sign-out card is invaluable (Illustration 7-6).[3]

FOLIO NO._____

MARCH FOLIO SIGN-OUT CARD

Name_____

Address _____

Phone _____

Home Room_____

Your signature on the reverse side constitutes an agreement to be responsible for the return of the above folio (valued at $_____), and its' contents, as of the date signed out. Lost or damaged parts will be charged to the signee, at the rate of   cents   per part.

PEPPER LIBRARY SYSTEM CARD #10-5   **J. W. PEPPER & SON, INC.**
© 1965, J. W. PEPPER & SON, INC.   **231 North Third Street, Philadelphia, Penna., 19106**

ILLUSTRATION 7-6

Library equipment

Certain equipment items are required by the librarians engaged in the task of handling the band's music. Among these would be the metal cabinet containing the drawers used for storing the 4" x 6" file cards, a sorting rack, paper cutter, a rubber stamp and pad, instrumentation labels, a music hinging machine, a typewriter, filing envelopes or boxes specially designed for music storage purposes, scotch tape (preferably the transparent type), a tape writing machine, special marking pencils, a notebook to contain the master index pages, and a supply of file cards and sign-out cards.

SELECTING SECTION LEADERS

Finding individuals with the necessary qualities to provide leadership from section to section within a large band is no easy task. While it is essential that these individuals exhibit superior ability on their respective instruments, it is also vital that they be respected by

---
[3]Ibid.

members of the section wherein they perform. The morale of the band can suffer from having certain individuals occupying a first chair position if it is felt by the membership that the position is not fully deserved. Beyond the morale factors involved are those concerning the musical leadership these individuals can supply by example if by no other means. In some school situations these individuals actively perform certain musical duties relating to sectional rehearsals and others which deal with non-musical or peripheral services. The manner in which they are chosen can have a decided effect upon the whole band.

In small schools having bands of limited size the manner of selecting section leaders may be fairly simple. In schools such as these we frequently find that all members of the band are given instrumental lessons by the school band director. Since he is aware of each individual's ability he can readily adjust the section in such a way as to provide the necessary sectional leadership. He must, of course, be sensitive to values beyond those relating only to performance technique. Even in situations like this, it might be well to have some student involvement in helping to select section leaders; this would certainly be more democratic, and would have a positive effect upon the band's morale.

In larger bands the process of selecting first chair players is quite demanding and time consuming since many more players have to be screened. While some of this activity may take place during regular band rehearsals, much of it could be done in sectional rehearsals held at times other than the band period, including after school. A common procedure used in determining first chair players is to select an audition piece to be prepared a few days or a week in advance of the audition. Beyond the prepared piece, which may be an excerpt from band literature or a solo associated with the particular instrument, the director should select some fitting material to use in connection with the sight-reading portion of the audition. This will give a more complete picture of each individual's ability.

At the time of the audition, it is expected that all members of the section interested in trying out for the position of section leader will be present and prepared. In some cases, the director may require the presence of the entire section to participate in the seating process, both as performers and as referees or judges. Some directors even require three or four players to go behind a screen or to an adjoining room to be judged by the balance of the section. During this procedure players are given a number to identify their position in the sequence of those being tested at the moment. Other directors hold periodic "challenge days" when members of a certain section may have the opportunity to match their ability against others in the section. In cases such as this, the director frequently employs the rest of the band to share in decision making.

During the process of screening players from section to section in

_____High School
Audition Form

Date:_____

Name:_____Grade:_____
Instrument:_____Organization:_____
Note: You are advised to judge on the basis of:
              1. Tone
                  a. Quality
                  b. Intonation
                  c. Dynamic control
              2. Technique
                  a. Facility
                  b. Articulation
                  c. Range
              3. Interpretation
                  a. Correct tempos
                  b. Rhythmic integrity
                  c. Phrasing

- -

A. *Rendition of Prepared selection:* (Grade by numbers from 1 to 10 for both the prepared selection and the sight reading.)
    Title of selection:_____
    Circle your estimated score: 1 2 3 4 5 6 7 8 9 10
    Comments:_____
    _____

B. *Rendition of Sight Reading piece:*
    Circle your estimated score: 1 2 3 4 5 6 7 8 9 10
    Comments:_____
    _____

    Please tabulate your total score for part A and B of the audition.
                                  Score: ☐
                   Audition judge:_____
                             signed

ILLUSTRATION 7-7

the early weeks of the new school year, or in the later weeks of the preceding spring if preferred, the alert band director will not only endeavor, with the aid of members of the band, to select the first chair players, but will look for alternates as well. Beyond that, he will make notations of the performances of all members of each section in an effort to achieve balance in the band by assigning a certain number of strong players to each part following the completion of the auditioning process.

In some schools where two, three, or more music staff members are available, the band director solicits the aid of these individuals in selecting first chair candidates. This may be carried on entirely by adult members of the music staff or in conjunction with student members of the band. For this procedure it might be advisable to develop a standardized audition form which will serve to promote a degree of consistency in arriving at decisions. The form shown in Illustration 7-7 might fit this need.

A form such as this could be used effectively in having players qualify for band membership as they leave junior high school and enter the senior high, and it could also serve to qualify band members desiring to move into a selected wind ensemble in schools where two bands exist. How the form is to serve would be up to the judgment of the band director or directors. Some might prefer to confine the use of such a device to staff members only, while others in more sophisticated situations would feel confident in having it used by students. Whether it would be applied in a general band rehearsal, at sectional rehearsals, or at special audition sessions held after school or on Saturdays would also need to be determined by the director in accordance with the needs that are to be met.

OFFICERS—ELECTIVE AND APPOINTED

Among the aims and purposes of band membership, aside from the musical elements, are those concerning the social and civic development of its members. Although the opportunities for independent expression by members of the band may be somewhat limited since its main function is to perform as a team, individuals in the band can develop singular talents by serving on the band council or executive board. Through participation in this group, they have the opportunity to develop qualities of leadership by sharing in the planning and execution of band activities. This council or board is generally made up of the elected and appointed officers of the band. The frequency of their meetings is usually determined jointly by the director and those holding office. If the band program is a highly active one with many special events throughout the year they may feel it necessary to meet on a regular basis. In the average school band these meetings would occur less often.

Elective offices generally include: President, Vice President,

Secretary-Treasurer, and perhaps Class Representatives. Although
some of the following offices may be elective, they are frequently
appointed by the director since they require certain specific interest
and talents: Manager, Librarians, Quartermasters, Drum Major, and a
Student Leader. The latter are usually found among volunteers and
those with special interest and talents in music.

The duties of the various offices are given here; however, it should
be understood that these might be expanded or diminished in the
light of the kind of band program carried on in the school.

President: Presides at all regular meetings of the Band Council,
annual elections, and special meetings, and partici-
pates in planning the concerts and other functions in
which the band engages.

Vice President: Assists the President and presides at meetings in
his absence.

Secretary-Treasurer: Records the minutes of council meetings,
takes the roll at all rehearsals, concerts, and other
functions, types special lists and forms pertaining to
band activities, and assists with the handling of ticket
sales and fund drives.

Class Representative: At least one member serving as a member
at large will represent each class level of the school
and actively participate in planning and carrying out
certain functions related to band appearances.

Manager: Supervises the physical set-up of the rehearsal room
through the use of a seating chart, assists in planning
field trips, presides at the recording equipment for
taping sessions, supervises the seating of the band on
certain occasions, takes charge of special equipment
used in connection with football and marching band
activities, and generally assists the director.

Librarians: Record, stamp, and file all new music. Issue music as
needed for rehearsals through distribution of same in
band folders, and collect and return to files all music
following its use. Additional duties include: daily
supervision of sign-out cards, typing music file cards
and maintaining the Master Index, and preparing and
distributing new folders when needed.

Quartermasters: Maintain numerical lists of uniforms assigned
to members, distribute and collect uniforms before
and after all functions requiring uniforming, inspect
uniforms and report damage, maintain the condition

of the uniform room, and report the need for repair and replacement of uniforms and accessories.

Drum Major: Leads the marching band, assists in planning of marching band appearances, assists in teaching routines, and assists in coordinating band and twirling corps activities.

Student Leader: Begins rehearsal warm-up procedures when the director is detained, assists in conducting the band on the field and in concert at the invitation of the director or his assistant, and stands ready to function with the "pep band" at rallies.

As mentioned earlier, these duties may be expanded or somewhat curtailed at the discretion of the director. While it is understood that at regular band rehearsals only a few of these officers function actively, all participate in the regular non-playing meetings of the Band Council. A band manager can be of inestimable assistance to the director during rehearsals, particularly if special equipment is needed or when engaged in recording the group. The most important functional office is likely to be that of the head librarian and the assistants. These individuals are busily engaged on a day to day basis in overseeing the sign-out card operation and in assisting with the distribution and collection of music and folders. In between rehearsals these individuals find themselves stamping new music, typing cards, labeling folders, and distributing and collecting music. The success of the whole music-handling operation depends upon the selection of interested and conscientious individuals.

USING A POINT SYSTEM

The use of a point system is felt by some directors to be a necessary step in organizing the high school band. Where it is used, it appears to be geared to methods of disciplining members of the band and for purposes of marking. In view of its designed purposes it is essential, if it is to work, to involve members of the band in its formulation. This may prove a worthy project for the Band Council and provide them with an opportunity to share in the responsibility of band citizenship. Since they are to be "measured" by the system, they should have something to say about its makeup. It would be an unwise move for the band director to arbitrarily design a system by himself.

It would seem at the outset that each band director would have to analyze his own situation before deciding to take further steps to initiate a point system. A system such as this might be helpful in developing new programs, or in programs in the early stages of development whereas in the long established program it may be unnecessary. Furthermore, in certain sections of the country it may work effectively, while in others where the level of sophistication is high it might be rejected. Unfortunately, too many of the point systems seem to accentuate the negative rather than the positive, with an obvious emphasis given to demerits rather than to meritorious action. For a point system to contribute effectively as an aid to the band director it must be based upon sound values and sound principles. Among the factors which should be included in evaluating an individual's membership performance, so to speak, are the following:

1. Regular attendance at rehearsals
2. Punctuality in connection with rehearsals
3. Evidence of advance preparation of the music
4. Responsiveness to director's suggestions in rehearsals
5. Attitude toward the band and its director
6. Attendance at functions requiring the services of the band
7. Holding an office, elected or appointed, and fulfilling the obligations of that office
8. Evidence of progress in performance
9. Holding a position such as section leader
10. Volunteering services for special tasks
11. Care in the use of school-owned equipment including instrument, uniform, and music
12. General behavior and attitudes as a citizen of the band

In assigning weighted values to each of these factors, the band director with the cooperation of the Band Council would have to determine which of these are essential to the band's successful operation and which may be considered less vital.

I have seen some point systems, developed to a high degree of precision by well meaning band directors, geared almost entirely to the negative with demerits for missing a rehearsal, coming in late, forgetting the music, forgetting an instrument, chewing gum, not having a reed, talking in rehearsal, and so on in a similar vein. To be sure, some of these things happen from time to time in all kinds of classes in the school, and in dealing with human nature one comes to expect a certain amount of behavioral eccentricities. While there are certain values in using a point system, it is finally up to each band director to weigh the pros and cons of such a system. Tabulating the demerits or merits, as the case may be, in a band of 75 or 100 players can become a task comsuming a great amount of time. The values of this procedure would need to be assessed with utmost care in view of other demands upon the band director's time. If all he does during a typical school week is conduct one band and teach a limited number of classes of instruments, perhaps he is in a position to carry on the secretarial work required under such a plan. The majority of band directors I know are among the busiest individuals in the school and their talents and services are put to many more substantial uses.

For the most part, since band is an elective subject and the large majority of its members enjoy and look forward to band rehearsals and activities, a detailed point system based on the many items just listed is not generally essential.

Pupil interest and the director's ability to work skillfully and enthusiastically with young people of this age level should be the basis of good organization in school bands. The 12 criteria listed several paragraphs ago could well form the foundation for evaluating each individual's contributions to the total band as a musical organization and as a social body.

While it is noted that some directors feel the need for a point system to provide certain guidelines for band membership, some of them engage in this practice as it relates to marking in general. Since school systems are geared to function according to a particular system of giving marks at the end of each quarter or semester, it is perhaps felt by some that the point system can be made to relate directly to the over-all school marking system. This, of course, would provide some justification for its inclusion in connection with the organization of the band. In this event, I would again point to the use of the 12 criteria suggested as the basis for developing a point system—and again suggest that where there is a felt need for such a system, it be initiated by the joint action of the band director and members of the band.

GIVING GRADES FOR BAND MEMBERSHIP

In the majority of high schools band is treated as an elective subject side by side with the many other electives offered in the secondary curriculum. The marking system in vogue in the school then becomes the one by which band members are also evaluated. In some schools grades are recorded on the basis of numbers, such as 90 for superior or high achievement, 80 for good achievement, 70 for average achievement, with 60 or less indicating failure. Other institutions use a letter system such as *A* for top achievers, *B* for those whose achievement is held to be good, a *C* to indicate an average or passing level, and a *D* for failure. In some cases an *F* is used to indicate the latter status.

Beyond the use of an alphabetical or numerical system, some schools require a separate evaluation of pupil effort as well, while still others include a mark for other factors such as attitude, school citizenship, etc. Furthermore, since many schools offer various levels of the same subject and function on the basis of a "track" system, it then becomes necessary to further refine the marking code by associating a "quality" point to the same letter grade at different levels. For example, assuming the school marking system is established on a four track system, the levels may be labeled by a number code to indicate to the teacher that one class in English is a "basic" group, another might be "general," another would then be identified as "academic," and the most comprehensive English course could be designated as "honors" division. On the basis of such a system, an A in honors English may be represented by ten quality points; an A on the academic level, nine; the general level A, eight; and an A in a basic class, seven.

The level at which the band mark is to function would normally be decided by the administration, perhaps with the cooperation or advice of the music faculty. Where the administration appreciates the intellectual, physical, emotional, and musical demands of performing on an instrument, the band would probably be listed among the academic level subject matter. In the advanced band programs in larger schools two bands may exist. The more advanced group, which in some cases is a small selective type of organization such as the wind ensemble, would perhaps be evaluated on an honors level, while the second band would be rated on the academic level.

Evaluating the individual

The problem of grading individual members of the band may prove to be rather difficult since they perform as a team for the most part. At this juncture, the skill and ingenuity of the director will be tested in an effort to arrive at a fair evaluation of each student's level of achievement and effort.

The director has a number of techniques at his disposal to help in arriving at a fair mark for each individual. These are more or less numerous according to the number of weekly rehearsals held, whether or not sectional rehearsals are conducted, whether band members are enrolled in the school instrumental lesson program, whether a challenge system is employed in determining the seating of sections, and whether the director devotes some time after school to checking the results of individual practice efforts.

In situations where the band meets four or five times per week, the director can obviously devote a portion of that time to hearing a certain amount of individual playing from section to section. He is thus in a better position to know more about the capabilities of each individual. If the band director is also engaged in teaching the various instruments of the band, as is often the case, he is in a unique position to judge individual effort without having to infringe upon band rehearsal time. Furthermore, this manner of evaluating the individual's achievement and effort is preferred since the experience of playing in front of the total band is much less traumatic. Over a period of weeks the director-teacher should be well able to make a fair judgment of each individual's playing ability and progress.

Some directors schedule weekly or bi-weekly sectional rehearsals, which give them further opportunities to observe individual effort and productivity and to make sound judgments. Beyond this, some directors employ a challenge system whereby individuals in each section are given an opportunity to challenge those holding the first chair position or to move up to another part in the section. Here again is another means for the director to observe and evaluate the progress of individual members of the band.

Still another technique used by directors is the after-school appointments with individuals in the band for purposes of checking their accomplishment in connection with the performance of the band literature in their band folders. This method may be more highly activated just prior to a major concert or festival appearance by the band. In addition to these techniques is the one which involves the use of the audition form introduced earlier in this chapter. Whether this form is applied in these after-school sessions, during sectional rehearsals, or during scheduled instrumental lessons would be up to the good judgment of the director, since band programs and time allotments vary from school to school. Beyond this, the emphasis placed upon the giving of marks in band would influence the need to apply these and other techniques to greater or lesser degrees. Where the periodic marking of band members is required and the method must conform to the over-all school marking system, band directors will be called upon to arrive at individual judgments that are both fair and defensible. The 12 criteria listed earlier in connection with the consideration of a point system might serve effectively as guidelines in this process.

AN AWARD SYSTEM IN BAND

At the high school level, it is a general practice to have a system of awards functioning in association with the various music groups, including the band. A number of different kinds of awards are used for the purpose of recognizing continuing membership, holding office, being a section leader, displaying outstanding performance ability, serving as drum major or student leader, and other similar attributes. Although letters or emblems are in use for music award purposes, pins, keys, cups, and plaques are more frequently associated with special musical attainments.

The establishment of an awards system for high school bands would lie well within the province of the Band Council, comprised of the officers, with the cooperation of the band director who normally would serve as its advisor. Whatever system is ultimately adopted should be based upon reasonable requirements which are attainable by those whose efforts, talents, and services are consistently of a high level. At the same time, the requirements should be realistic and within the grasp of a certain percent of the membership. It is also essential that once the system of awards is established it be carried on from year to year with as few changes as possible to give it meaning and substance. Furthermore, awards given for high achievement in band should be granted the same prestige as is attached to winnning a varsity letter in a major sport.

Types of awards

Awards given in connection with school bands come under a number of catagories and different kinds of articles are used to symbolize a particular type of award. The separate catagories would include: marching band membership, concert band, first musician (or first chair), festival solo and ensemble awards, Band Booster or Music Parents Award, and band scholarships. Membership awards are sometimes given out on an annual basis to recognize longevity in participation and service while other awards are generally more demanding and specific with reference to qualifying criteria. While it is appropriate to award a letter or emblem for marching band or in recognition of membership, keys, plaques, and cups are frequently used to signify other kinds of achievement in band. In some instances the Band Council functions in cooperation with the band director in determining those who are to receive certain awards based upon established prerequisites, while others are strictly confined to the determination of the music faculty. Where a music parents or band booster club exists, the governing board of that group together with the band director, serving as its advisor, determines who is to receive certain other awards. These could include a plaque, a savings bond, or an amount of money stipulated to represent a band scholarship.

Whatever the awards may be, or for whatever purpose, they should be determined on the basis of objectivity.

The following is offered as an example of the structuring that might be used in connection with issuing of band awards. It should be stated that this system would need to be fashioned according to both the general and specific needs of each band program.

Membership Emblem: For successful completion of two years of membership in the high school band the five-inch circular emblem in navy blue and white containing a music lyre, the letters L.H.H.S., and the name of the organization (Band, Orchestra, Choral). The emblem is made up in chenille and is presented at the annual awards assembly.

Marching Band Award: This award is given to members of the marching band who meet all requirements of membership including attendance at all football games, pep rallies, and parades in which the band is involved. The emblem is in the shape of a music lyre with the letters L.H.H.S. and the word "Marching" superimposed upon the design. The emblem is made up in chenille in school colors and is approximately 6" x 4" in size. It is presented at the annual awards assembly.

The Senior Honor Award: This award is a gold key presented to those seniors who have completed at least three years of band membership and have exemplified high standards of musical performance. Beyond that, they must be recommended for consideration to receive this award through the process of closed ballot voting by all seniors in the band. The award is based upon: (1) musicianship, (2) citizenship, (3) leadership, (4) attendance, and (5) service. The award is presented at the annual spring concert.

The Band Parents Award: This award is in the form of a scholarship, the specific amount of which will be determined by the state of the organization's finances. It shall be presented to that senior who has qualified for the Senior Honor Award and who plans to enter into the music field either as a teacher or performer. The final determination shall be based upon recommendations by the band director and music faculty of the school and the results of the closed ballot by senior members of the band with the final approval of the executive board of the Band Parents Association. The award shall be presented at the graduation exercises in June.

Again, it should be understood that this type of awards system would need to conform to the general makeup of the school music program. It may take a period of time to develop a system of awards which can give recognition to different kinds of participation and achievement. Obviously, if no Band Parents Association exists, other sources would have to be found for the sizable awards that could be sponsored by that kind of organization. In some communities civic groups, service organizations, and, on occasion, individuals volunteer to underwrite prizes of generous proportions.

Another type of award that has been used effectively in recognizing special efforts and abilities among band members is a system employing a series of ribbons of various colors and designs identifying specific positions in the band. These are worn on the upper left side of the band uniform coat or jacket and through the use of single, double, and triple base bars can indicate the class (sophomore, junior, etc.) of the individual, whether he holds office and if so which one, his position in band (first chair, etc.), and special honors including all-state festival participation, superior solo performance, and the like. These have proven to be helpful not only in recognizing special services or abilities of the individual, but also in stimulating and motivating greater effort for improvement in performance among members.

CREDITING BAND MEMBERSHIP

The practice of giving credit for band membership is a common one in the high schools of today. The amount of credit given, however, will be found to vary from place to place. Where band is scheduled during the school day, as is the practice in the majority of schools, it is treated as a curricular offering. Factors which determine the amount of credit for a given subject include (1) the number and length of weekly periods scheduled, and (2) whether or not outside preparation is required. Subjects which meet daily or for a specified and approved number of minutes per week and which require outside preparation generally carry one full unit of credit.

While it is recognized that students in high school music accumulate a certain number of credits to graduate and to qualify for college entrance, they usually have a fairly broad option in the choice of elective subjects. For many, the first elective may be band, while others elect courses in art, languages, home economics, business, or industrial arts. The number of units required for graduation may vary depending upon whether the institution is a three- or four-year one. Where a three-year senior high exists, the subjects taken during the final year of the junior high school may be taken into account in the process of evaluating the number and kind of credits gained. The following subject program is regarded as typical in senior high schools throughout the country:

4 units in English

3 units in history and social studies

2 units in mathematics

2 units in science

2 units in physical education

5 units or more in electives

It should, of course, be understood that these requirements will vary to some degree from state to state. It is further recognized that students planning on attending college will become familiar with the entrance requirements of the chosen institution to insure acceptance by that school. Since some have a specific language requirement for those entering certain fields, it behooves each one to know what these may be.

Although for many years membership in a high school band was accorded little or no credit, it has now attained a position of equality with other subjects in the curriculum, particularly since it has been scheduled as part of the school day. Formerly, the high school band was relegated to a position of an extra-curricular activity and was scheduled outside the framework of the school day. Bands existed for the most part on the basis of the interest and enthusiasm of a limited number of students, and were guided and directed by a member of the school faculty or an individual in the community who had a special flair for music and perhaps some prior training and experience. As the value of music became more fully recognized as an educational and cultural force in a democratic society, its position among the subjects offered at the high school level became more tenable. In due time, and with the mounting interest in music and the greater availability of trained personnel, it was provided for within the structure of the school schedule.

It is currently common practice to ascribe one full unit of credit to band members on a yearly basis where bands are scheduled to meet for four or five periods per week for a total of approximately 200 minutes. It is understood that membership in band calls for a certain amount of outside preparation of the music being studied or readied for public performance, and that members are also engaged in taking lessons on instruments as part of the school program or in private from a teacher in the area. On the basis of these factors, the awarding of a full credit for band is held to be entirely justified. In schools where fewer rehearsals are scheduled, the amount of credit allowed is reduced proportionately.

Some schools give consideration to the number of school and community services rendered by the band and ascribe a full credit to it even though the group may only meet three or four times a week. The hours that band members spend in drilling appearances at football games or rehearsing for performances in civic and patriotic holidays are held to be sufficient reason to justify crediting. Beyond that, it is also a practice in some schools to assess for credit the work accomplished by individual members of the band who are taking private lessons, perhaps from a member of a professional symphony orchestra. This practice would require careful evaluation by responsible music educators serving in the school system. Opportunities such as this are presently being encouraged and even sponsored by the government, particularly in connection with highly gifted individuals.

It is also gratifying to music educators to note that colleges are coming more and more to assess credits in music subjects and performance groups on a level commensurate with other subjects of the high school curriculum.

DEVELOPING A BAND HANDBOOK

The establishment of a handbook for members has been found to be an aid in organizing the high school band. While the director should put the booklet together, it would be both wise and helpful to involve members of the band in its formulation. Where a band council exists, this body should share in the production of this document. Others in the band having a special talent for writing and editing should also be invited to participate. Since a considerable amount of information needs to be gathered together and rules governing the band will have to be established, the production of a handbook will require many weeks and even months of concentrated effort on the part of all those engaged in its development.

Assuming the construction of a band handbook is a new venture, it will be necessary to devote a number of rehearsal periods to discussions as to the contents of the book. This process will also require a number of after-school meetings for those directly involved in writing the material to be contained therein. Depending upon the editorial skill of the director, he may wish to consult with the head of the English Department of the school, or the school yearbook advisor.

Contents of the band handbook

The nature, design, contents, and dimension of the handbook should be determined by the handbook production committee in the early meetings of the group. Its actual physical size and method of duplication or printing will also need to be determined at the very outset in consideration of the number needed and the period of time that particular edition is to serve before it may need to be revised or reprinted. It will be most economical to use a mimeographing process on paper of a standard size such as 8½" x 11" which is normally required for such purposes. The process of printing such a book could prove very costly, especially in consideration of its specialized and limited use. The inclusion of photographs should be weighed carefully in view of additional costs. A combination of processes could be used in the production of the handbook to save expense. Printed material could be done through the use of a mimeograph machine, while selected photographic plates could be prepared by a commercial printing firm. Obviously, specific methods of producing a band handbook should be thoroughly investigated before proceeding with such an undertaking.

While the organization or arrangement of materials may vary in accordance with individual tastes and philosophies which may lead to the emphasizing of one phase of band activity over another, certain basic items should be included. Furthermore, it would help to stimulate interest and creativity among band members to have an appropriate cover design made up by those in the group possessing some special talent along these lines. A table of contents should be included at the very beginning for obvious reasons. It is also recommended that a brief preface or foreword be formulated to describe the purpose of the book and the general philosophy of the band. An outline of the aims and objectives delineating the purposes and significance of band membership may follow.

The next section of the book could include the historical background of the band giving the date of its founding, if known, and something of the traditions of the organization. Mention could also be made here of the special events in which the band has participated, special honors won at state and regional festivals, appearances at music educator conferences, and special performances relating to visits by persons of note. Since the band should know something of its director's training and experience, a biographical sketch could be included also.

Following this, a list of band offices, both elective and appointive, might be added together with a brief description of the duties attached to each office. In this way, band members aspiring to certain posts will be better acquainted with the specific requirements of each office. One of the most important sections of the book, offering general information and guidance to all incoming band members, would logically be next in order. Contained in this material should be advice regarding the care of instrument, the care and handling of music, and the care and wearing of uniforms. Rules and regulations concerning the behavior expected of band members might be spelled out next with specifics concerning rehearsals, performances, and field trips.

The final sections of the handbook might include an explanation of a point system as well as the system of awards employed in band. A calendar of events in which the band is normally engaged on a year-to-year basis would be well to include to give incoming band members some idea of the number of services and performances given by the band.

As mentioned earlier, while the use of photographs would contribute to the visual interest of the handbook and vividly depict some of the highlight events involving the band, it may prove to be rather expensive. For the most part, band handbooks are issued to each new member of the band for the purpose of acquainting individuals with the patterns of organization and the rules which they are expected to observe when functioning as a member of the group. In general, the following outline is offered to serve as a guide in the development of a band handbook:

1. Table of contents
2. Preface or foreword
3. Aims and objectives of band membership
4. Historical background - Traditions - Honors
5. Biographical sketch of the director
6. Organization—Officers: duties outlined
7. General information and procedures relating to:
   a. care of instruments
   b. care and handling of music
   c. care and wearing of music
8. Rules and regulations
   a. in rehearsals
   b. in performance
   c. on field trips
9. Point system
10. The system of awards
11. The calendar of events
12. Miscellaneous

TAKING INVENTORY

Another element of good management in connection with school bands is the maintaining of an inventory of school-owned instruments and other equipment. This function is the responsibility of the band director and must be given regular attention to insure proper care of equipment and to aid in the assessment of future needs. Periodic inspection of school-owned instruments should be conducted by the director. Where he is involved in giving instrumental lessons to the majority of band members, as is often the case, he can carry on this operation during lesson periods rather than take time during band rehearsals. If he is not involved in an instructional program, he may need to resort to other techniques which might take a few minutes out of band rehearsals over a period of weeks so that no one rehearsal is completely taken up with this process. Beyond that, he may take time after school until this is accomplished, or he may send for students during one of their study periods. In some schools several music faculty members are engaged in the instrumental program. Here, the teacher of woodwinds could be responsible for checking the condition of all of these, while another staff member could check the brasses, etc.

A special form on which can be recorded all essential data concerning each school-owned instrument should be developed by the director along the lines of the form shown in Illustration 7-8.

In order to include all vital information in such a form, it will be necessary to use the long dimension of the paper. Also, whether a school number is assigned to each instrument would depend upon

_____High School Instrument Inventory										
Inst.	Make	Serial Number	School Number	Date of Purchase	Cost	Present Value	Name of User	When Issued	Returned	Repair Record

ILLUSTRATION 7-8

whether the inventory includes string instruments which normally do not have serial numbers and which may have to be assigned a specific school instrument number for cataloging purposes. For example, the first violin purchased by the school could be assigned a code number such as Vn I, while the first viola might be labeled Va I, etc. These identifying numbers could be applied to an inconspicuous place on the body of the instrument with a wood burner or other numbering device. In school systems where instruments are used on a system-wide basis the need for cataloging is even more pressing. A number of school suppliers have printed card forms for inventory purposes. These are usually printed on a standard 4" x 6" card and may be kept in a file box or drawer in the director's office.

While the maintenance of inventory records is a continuing process requiring attention throughout the year, there are two particular times when this procedure is especially necessary—at the end of the year when individuals using school instruments are about to graduate, and at the start of a new school year when incoming students may be issued certain school-owned instruments. Instruments being turned in by seniors should be inspected and cleaned before being reassigned, and note should be made of the condition in which the instrument was received. Before assigning instruments to incoming band members in the fall, the condition of each instrument should

---

FORM 7

INSTRUMENT RECORD CARD
(RENTAL OR LOAN RECORD CARD)

Instrument ....School No. ....

Make ....Factory Serial No. ....Value $ ....

Finish ....System ....Model ....

SUPPLIED WITH THE FOLLOWING ACCESSORIES

Case	Key	Lyre	Mouthpiece
Swab	Grease	Cap	Ligature
Reed Case	Strap	Oil	Screw Driver
Crooks	Sticks	Sling	Piston Wiper
Strings			Misc.

RENTAL OR LOAN AGREEMENT

Weekly Rental $ ....Monthly Rental $ ....Semester Rental $ ....

I acknowledge receipt of the above instrument and accessories. I agree to be responsible for any damage or loss that might occur while in my care. I also agree to return the instrument when requested to do so by the Superintendent or Director.

Approved:

             Pupil ....

             Parent ....

    Sup't or Director   Address .... Phone ....

This card will be surrendered when all rentals are paid in full and instrument and accessories returned to the superintendent or director in satisfactory condition.

P. O. BOX 329	SOUTHERN MUSIC CO.	SAN ANTONIO 6, TEXAS

ILLUSTRATION 7-9

be recorded on the inventory cards or list, whichever method is used. A record of repairs should also be kept to indicate when repair work was done. While minor repairs or traceable damage repair costs may justly be collected from individuals using school instruments, major overhauling costs should be covered by a portion of the school budget allotted for music needs. Taking steps to keep instruments in a state of good repair will not only insure their being available when needed, but will cut down appreciably on the total amount of money required for these needs. A card such as the one shown in Illustration 7-9[4] may be used for several purposes, including inventory and as a rental agreement form, if rental is charged. Notations about the condition of the instrument may be made on the back of the card.

INSTRUMENTAL INSTRUCTION INVENTORY

Another type of inventory which should be maintained from year to year to afford the high school band director with a quick visual account of the number of pupils engaged in the instrumental instructional program of the school system in order to assess needs is the type shown here. It provides a grade-by-grade tabulation of the number of pupils taking lessons on the various instruments included in the school instructional program, and enables the director to determine at a glance where increased effort may be required to promote balanced instrumentation. Summary forms such as shown in Illustration 7-10 are effective to include in the annual report to the board of education—particularly when seeking additional staff to meet expanding enrollments, not to mention equipment needs!

---

[4]By permission of Southern Music Co., P.O. Box 329, San Antonio, Texas 78206

Instrumental Instruction Inventory

Wallingford Public Schools

Department of Music Education

Spring 1966

INSTRUMENT Grade	5	6	7	8	9	10	11	12	Totals
Violin	27	25	18	5	10	5	5	3	95
Viola	2	1	1	1	1	1	1	0	8
Cello	3	3	8	3	0	2	1	0	20
St. Bass	0	0	1	1	0	0	2	0	4
Flute	28	20	10	13	8	4	1	3	87
Oboe	0	0	0	3	1	0	1	1	6
Clarinet	47	34	34	18	24	13	2	7	179
Alto Clarinet	0	0	0	2	0	0	2	0	4
Bass Clarinet	0	0	0	1	4	0	0	4	9
Alto Sax	6	2	4	7	5	2	6	0	32
Tenor Sax	1	1	1	4	0	2	0	0	9
Baritone Sax	0	0	0	1	2	1	0	0	4
Bassoon	0	0	1	0	0	1	1	2	5
French Horn	0	1	5	4	2	0	4	1	17
Cornet	26	23	22	24	9	6	1	6	117
Trombone	10	5	8	3	2	2	3	2	35
Baritone	0	0	2	2	3	3	0	1	11
Bass Horn	0	0	1	3	1	1	2	1	9
Percussion	39	25	29	7	12	3	3	2	120
Totals	189	140	145	102	84	46	33	32	771

ILLUSTRATION 7-10

chapter 8

Improving Rehearsal Techniques

A rehearsal may be said to be that period of time which is devoted to the private preparation of music that is to be presented formally in public. The main aim of the school band director should be to determine how this time can be used most effectively in obtaining steady growth and progress. To be most productive, band rehearsals at the senior high school level should be planned, organized, and conducted in a businesslike and professional manner with a view to achieving performance levels commensurate with the talent, ability, and maturity exemplified by senior high school students. The general aims of band rehearsal activity should be:

1. To develop a keener sensitivity to the elements of music.
2. To attain a deeper appreciation of music through the preparation of a wide variety of band literature.
3. To achieve a high level of performance through the attainment of technical skills.
4. To experience personal satisfaction through active participation.
5. To develop a greater awareness of the importance of others.
6. To provide opportunities for personal expression through music.
7. To foster the development of leadership qualities.
8. To promote experience in cooperative endeavors.

These and other related aims and objectives of band rehearsal activity can provide the framework upon which the successful high school band may be developed. Since membership in the high school band is generally established on an elective basis with pupils choosing to participate because of a particular interest, the chances of achieving the aims set forth here are highly favorable.

Band rehearsal activity at the senior high school level can be one of the most stimulating and exhilarating periods of the day for both the student and the director. It should be regarded with eagerness and enthusiasm as a time when the young performer may give vent to his feelings through the medium of musical sounds. The literature of the modern high school band encompasses a wide range of musical types and styles with many original works specifically scored for band and uniquely suited to its technical and tonal resources. The skills of the present day arranger and composer have provided a new color and rhythmic treatment which challenges the technical prowess and tonal range of the young musician as never before, and yet performances by the finest high school bands achieve a degree of polish generally associated only with professionals. This level of musical accomplishment can be achieved only through a carefully structured and planned series of meaningful rehearsals carried on throughout the school year with clearly defined goals in mind.

REHEARSAL PROCEDURES

If a rehearsal of the band is to be wholly profitable and productive for all concerned, it should start off on the right note. This implies that members arrive on time, that their instruments are readily accessible in individual lockers or group storage areas, that the music folders are picked up by members as they enter the rehearsal room or distributed by assigned personnel, and that the chairs and music stands are all in place to accommodate the membership. The roll should be taken with dispatch by the director or students assigned to assist in this routine but important procedure, according to methods described in Chapter 7. The selections to be rehearsed during the period may be posted on the bulletin board, listed on the blackboard, or announced at the beginning of the rehearsal by the director.

At the outset it is necessary to establish certain procedures in relation to the time allotted for warming up and tuning up by all band members. Some directors follow the practice of permitting individual members to warm up according to their own personal tastes, while others require all band members to be seated quietly and, when all are ready, to warm up and tune up as an entire ensemble. It would seem logical that the method used in connection with this important step in the rehearsal procedures would depend to

ILLUSTRATION 8-1

a great extent upon the musical experience and maturity of the group. While it may be preferable to have young and relatively inexperienced players resort entirely to the use of an ensemble approach to warming up and tuning, a mature and experienced band may engage in a more individualized procedure. In this connection, the most effective method would involve some of both procedures, including individual techniques according to the type of instrument played, and some ensemble activity such as unison scale and rhythm exercises together with the playing of one or more tuning chorales. (See Illustration 8-1.[1])

One thing is certain with reference to the beginning of the rehearsal period and that is the members should not be permitted to engage in loud and promiscuous blowing. Outside of the fact that this kind of indiscriminate blowing will have a very disquieting effect on the nervous systems of all those in the room, it is of no help in either warming up or tuning. If anything, it can lead to straining certain muscles and affect the playing stamina of the individual for that particular rehearsal period. Furthermore, instead of contributing to any unanimity of pitch from player to player and section to section, it is likely to result in wider disagreement with respect to the matter of intonation. Obviously, the best interests of students and director alike will be more productively served through the application of certain simple yet effective warm-up procedures involving some of the more common scale sequences and unison rhythm exercises. This will not only prepare the individual gradually for the more demanding playing that lies ahead in the rehearsal but will also help to foster the element of teamwork among members. The amount of time consumed at the beginning of the rehearsal for warm up and tune up procedures will depend upon the size of the band, the degree of musicianship represented in the band, the length of the rehearsal period, the number of rehearsals scheduled each week, the director's sense of judgment with respect to how much of this may be required, and the time of the school year when this takes place. (It is likely that early in the new school year it will be necessary to involve the whole ensemble in a greater amount of this activity as a group—particularly in view of the fact that a certain percent of new members are taken into the band each year and must become accustomed to the senior high school way of doing things.)

Tuning

One of the most important steps to be taken at each rehearsal is

---

[1]By permission of Southern Music Co., P.O. Box 329, San Antonio, Texas 78206.

that dealing with tuning. The amount of time allotted to this procedure will be determined by several factors, the most obvious of which are the size of the group and the degree of musical maturity existing among its members.

While the tuning process should take place early in the rehearsal, it will be more effective to first engage in a certain amount of individual and collective playing. This practice will enable players to warm up their instruments and to gradually bring into action those muscles involved in performing on a wind instrument before engaging in the finer aspects of tuning. The director should allow sufficient time for this process since the time requirements for warming up instruments will vary according to their size and the material of which they are made. Beyond these factors, the time of the year and the location of storage areas will influence the amount of time needed for this operation. For example, a bass horn stored in a closet located on an outside wall will require more time to warm up in the winter than will a small instrument, particularly if the latter is stored in a locker or other storage area.

Beyond the use of unison rhythm exercises, scales, and chorales, some directors like to have the band play a march or other short selection involving the whole band before proceeding further with the process of tuning. This step can prove helpful in preparing players for the more exacting requirements of fine tuning.

Some directors resort to the practice of using electronic devices in tuning with the band. In some cases players take their instruments out of their cases and go directly to the tuning device situated near the director's podium or stand and make a fast check on an agreed-upon tuning note before taking a seat in the rehearsal room. In addition to the fact that this is not a satisfactory method for tuning, it can cause a major traffic problem. Also, it does little to contribute to the improvement of intonation, since players and instruments are not sufficiently warmed up to make this practice worthwhile. Although such a device can be very beneficial in determining the degree of variation in tones selected for tuning purposes, it is essential that each player be led to develop a greater sensitivity to pitch by other than mechanical means if the total ensemble is to achieve a high degree of pitch integrity. Furthermore, it should be understood that while certain tones selected for tuning may agree among the majority of instruments, others will be found to disagree widely from instrument to instrument.

The practice of using an electronic device for tuning is most effective when used in connection with the instrumental instructional program, where it may be employed with one individual at a time or with small classes of like instruments. In this way, each player can become acquainted with the pitch discrepancies existing in his own instrument and learn how to make the necessary adjustments to overcome these disparities. Beyond these elements of tuning lie the problems of adjusting pitches of individual notes according to the melodic direction of the music, or the position of a given note as it relates to the harmonic structure of a particular chord. This problem then brings into focus the need to instruct each individual in the differences which exist between the "tempered" and the "untempered" scale and how a system of "true" or "just" intonation must be brought to bear in the playing of a band instrument in a sizable ensemble. From the very beginning, instrumentalists should be made aware of the imperfections which exist within and among instruments of the band, and of the fact that although instruments made by leading manufacturers today are generally superior to those made many years ago, the need to make slight adjustments still exists.

As mentioned earlier, the amount of time required for tuning in band rehearsals will depend upon the size and makeup of the group and the degree of musical maturity exhibited. Other factors which influence the amount of time allotted to tuning include the time of year, since more time is needed at the beginning of a new school year to acquaint new members with procedures, and public performances, just prior to which the director may want to stress intonation. Also, those directors who meet their bands daily will obviously be able to devote more time to certain rehearsal procedures than those whose bands meet but two or three times weekly.

Some directors follow the practice of having one instrument sound a tuning note which the band attempts to match as best they can. The instruments most frequently chosen to sound the tuning note include the oboe, clarinet, and cornet. The oboe is often used in the wind ensemble or concert band while the other two instruments are found to be more practical in large groups or in connection with marching band activity. This practice, regardless of which instrument is used, is more productive when the tuning follows a section-by-section pattern, since the problem of hearing the tuning note is then reduced.

The use of an electric tuner has been an effective aid in tuning the band since the tone emitted can be sustained for an indefinite period of time, thus eliminating the need to tax an individual player during this process. This device is especially helpful in bands which are composed of a large number of young players, since it is recognized that these individuals have great difficulty in sustaining a tone for any considerable length of time without varying the pitch. It is also more effective in large bands where a greater amount of time is required to assemble the group. Some directors, in the hopes of reducing tuning time, turn the electric tuner on while individual members are arriving at the rehearsal room and getting instruments out of cases in preparation for playing. The efficaciousness of this practice would depend in large measure upon the seriousness of purpose that band members attach to the whole tuning process.

Tuning in general can be very time consuming, particularly among players of limited experience, therefore directors should spend a certain amount of time in instrumental classes and in sectional rehearsals in demonstrating the most effective methods for tuning each type of instrument. Where a class, for example, consists of three or more individuals, a tuning technique involving the use of a major triad has proven to be helpful in making pupils aware of the need to make slight adjustments from note to note to achieve the desired state of "in tune-ness." Through this device, each player is required to play each tone of the selected triad in succession so that each may draw his own conclusions as to the need for adjusting certain tones. Specifically, let us assume that we have a class or section of three or more clarinets and we select third space "C" as the basis for this experiment. Begin by having each player sound this tone in an effort to establish a basis of common agreement. When this point of agreement has been reached by all in the class the next steps may be taken. This calls for one player to sound the "C" while a second player is requested to play the fourth space "E" and a third player is asked to sound the "G" in the space above the staff. The resultant triad may be in tune or one member of the triad may need some adjustment. Assuming that the bottom note is considered to be in tune following the preliminary step, the players themselves should determine whether the triad is in tune and if not, determine which tone is in need of adjustment and the direction in which this should be made. When this triad is considered to be in tune, the second player should sound the "C" or root of the triad, while the third player sounds the "E" or third of the triad, and the first player plays the "G" to complete the triad. As before, the determination of the need for adjustment should be made by the players, preferably without the help of the instructor. The next steps would require the third player to sound the "C" while the first player sounds the "E" and the second player supplies the "G" to complete the triad. Here again the members of the class, or section, should engage in the decision for the need to make adjustments to bring the triad in tune. This general procedure can also be applied in connection with the playing of seventh chords or more complicated harmonic arrangements. Furthermore, other members of the class or section should be actively involved in the decision making, as is required in this whole operation. Since this process is somewhat time consuming, it should be applied in full-band rehearsals on a limited basis only. In this connection it is effective in making all members of the band sensitive to the need for adjusting tones to achieve fine intonation within the entire ensemble.

Ear training

Another tuning technique that I have found to be effective in improving the general intonation of the band involves ear training, first through the use of the piano and then with the instruments of the band. Once this technique is understood by band members and properly applied by the band director, the resulting improvement in intonation can be quite remarkable.

In introducing this technique, it is necessary for the director to play a series of major triads in succession at a slow tempo and with the root of the triad in the top or "soprano" position. As these triads are played, members of the band are invited to hum what they think is the top tone. At this juncture it is always interesting to note how many band members hum a note other than the one in the soprano position. After this procedure is used for a minute or more, depending upon the ready grasp of this process by the band, they are then advised to sing a pattern from the top tone upward (in their own voice range), using the numbers "1, 3, 5" to identify the pitches of "do, mi, sol" and then returning down to "do" again. The pattern sung against a triad with the root in the top position then becomes the "1-3-5-3-1" which band members are urged to sing as a series of triads are played for them. In this way they become acquainted with a particular method of identifying the location of the root of the triad when it occurs in the soprano position. The next step would involve playing a series of triads, with the third appearing in the soprano position. The band is again invited to hum the top tones as a succession of triads of this sort are played. They are then asked to sing a pattern involving "mi" down to "do" and up to "sol," or by the numbers "3-1-5." Following this step, a series of triads with the third in the soprano position are played in succession at a slow tempo and with some spacing between to permit members to think through the pattern. They are then asked to sing the pattern "3-1-5" as each triad is played. When it is felt that they understand this pattern and can apply it readily, the next step is to play a series of triads intermixing the position of the soprano note between the two learned thus far.

The next step would logically involve the introduction of the fifth of the triad in the top or soprano position and the application of a pattern starting on the syllable "sol" and going down to "mi" and "do," or "5-3-1" by the numbers. A series of triads with the fifth in the soprano would then be played with the band responding as before. With a little practice they will soon come to apply this pattern as they hear a series of triads played in this position. After it is felt that the band has sufficient grasp of this pattern, the three positions may then be offered in mixed sequences. In addition to engaging in the singing of these patterns, the director may find it worthwhile to have members involved in writing down the answers on a piece of paper. If this is done, no more than three to five different triads should be played in a sequence until it is felt that the large majority are responding well. Furthermore, with short sequences members will be in a better position to recall the triads just played.

Once the band has gained some skill in applying these patterns and responds verbally or on paper, the director may wish to engage in some individual recitation activity. While individuals thus called upon to respond to the playing of a particular triad are directly involved, the band at large should be ready to respond in chorus in the event that the respondent is incorrect. In this way the entire group becomes involved in the process of judgment.

This whole process in band may be related to the playing of individual chords found in a warm-up chorale, or to the preparation of a specific piece of music by the entire band. Assuming the band is playing a chord, for example, the director would stop the band and ask, "All those playing the third of the chord, play!" While he might expect to hear all those having the third of the chord, he may at first hear others—and some may not respond at all because of uncertainty. It is at this juncture that the skilled band director will draw upon a quick review of the patterns learned earlier. A repeat playing of the chord should result in a more accurate response, whether he next calls for the root or the fifth. The director would then proceed to the next chord in the chorale or selection and inquire of members, individually or by sections, as to whether they are playing the root, the third, or the fifth. In their efforts to respond correctly, the band as a whole will have become more conscious of the position their individual notes occupy in the chord, and the whole process of playing in tune takes on a new face.

It should be understood by the band director that once this technique is learned and applied by the band with some skill it will prove a very effective aid in tuning up chords which frequently appear at transitional sections in selections being prepared for concert use. Although this technique may be used more frequently in the early part of the rehearsal, especially during the playing of specific warm-up and tuning chorales, it may be effectively applied at almost any point in a selection where the problem of intonation seems to be temporarily insurmountable. Furthermore, since a great many seventh chords are encountered in the band music of today, not to mention ninth chords and other tonalities, a procedure similar to the one described earlier should be used in acquainting band members with a method of identifying the note they are playing at a particular point in the music.

Since the dominant seventh chord is the most common of the species, it should be introduced first. The procedure for its introduction should be similar to the one described in detail earlier. It is recommended that the piano be used in the initial stages of presenting the dominant.

Band members should again be invited to hum the top tones in each case, and the following patterns should be demonstrated and repeated until the group as a whole has attained a fair amount of skill in applying the various patterns relating to the dominant seventh chord. As before, when the students respond vocally they will discover that one particular pattern will fit each of the four positions of the chord, and that the wrong one will result in a dissonance. It might be advisable during the teaching of this technique to spend a certain amount of time in singing the various patterns regardless of whether they fit or not. Through this procedure it will become clearer to band members why certain patterns work while others result in a dissonant effect. This practice should be applied in connection with all types of chords studied. It might be well to note here that minor triads would involve the same basic patterns used to identify soprano positions in major.

When the root of the dominant seventh chord is heard in the soprano position, the ascending pattern from 1 to 7, that is, "1-3-5-7," will be found to fit. As in the case of major triads, a series of seventh chords should be played in this position to promote its recognition by band members. When the third of the dominant seventh chord is in the soprano, a descending pattern from 3 down to 5, that is, "3-1-7-5," will be found appropriate. The pattern which applies when the fifth of the chord is in the topmost position would descend from 5 to 7, that is "5-3-1-7," while that involving the seventh of the chord in the soprano would descend directly from 7 to 1, that is, "7-5-3-1." As suggested earlier, each of these patterns should be played several times in successive rehearsals until it is felt that the band as a whole understands and applies them with a reasonable degree of accuracy.

Following the learning process which involves the use of the piano, the band director should have the band play warm-up chorales and other suitable tone studies which may further serve to improve the quality of the band's response to this procedure. The use of opening and closing chords and those which occur at transitional passages of music being prepared in rehearsal will also be found to contribute to the band's grasp of this process. It should be understood by the band director that while this procedure may take a little time, especially in the beginning, once it is grasped by the band as a whole the resultant improvement in intonation will be marked.

(Lest the reader be led to believe that I originated this system, involving a method for identifying the position of notes within each chord, may I hasten to give credit to Melville Smith and Max T. Krone, whose *Fundamentals of Musicianship* Book I and Book II, published by M. Witmark and Sons of New York, embraces this approach to training the ear. My only claim to fame may lie in the application of this system as a practical and productive method of achieving better intonation in school instrumental and choral groups.)

Beyond the use of chords as a means of improving the intonation of the band, the use of unisons and octaves is one of the most critical means of detecting shortcomings of individual members of the band. At this point a slightly clinical approach to the problem could be pursued to good advantage by the band director. In this connection the band director might choose an individual from the clarinet, cornet, or trombone section, for example, to demonstrate how to tune the instrument initially and how to make minor adjustments as required from one tone to another. In this way band members may be taught to listen for the beat, as the selected student and director attempt to match various tones. Whether or not the director is involved in this demonstration is unimportant, except for the fact that he will be able to do this more quickly since he knows what he is after. In addition to playing a number of unisons to arrive at the desired pitch agreement, the playing of tones an octave apart will further illustrate the need to listen very carefully and to be prepared to adjust tones slightly in an effort to achieve a perfect octave.

Another effective way to demonstrate the physical relationship of a given tone and its immediate octave above is through holding a piano key down, without causing it to sound, and then, with the sustaining pedal depressed, strike the key which is exactly one octave below. The band should be able to hear the upper tone of the octave which has become activated through sympathetic vibration with the tone that was sounded. This same effect can also be achieved by blowing a wind instrument into the sounding board of a piano with the sustaining pedal depressed. In fact, an arpeggio performed this way can produce an interesting effect.

Before moving on to other rehearsal techniques, I would like to offer the following suggestion to directors who prefer to achieve certain results with respect to intonation, balance, and blend through the direct use of specific band literature being prepared for consumption by an audience.

As an example, the introduction of the march shown in Illustration 8-2[2] can serve effectively as a tuning chorale by having all members of the band sustain the first note of each measure as a whole note and proceed from measure to measure this way until the first note of the first strain is reached. The latter can serve as a focal point of the chorale. This same procedure can be used to good effect by having the brasses play along, followed by a woodwind rendition of the same segment. Players in either section may be asked to identify the position of certain notes from measure to measure. This procedure demands greater alertness on the part of all members of the group and results in better tonal management, not only as it concerns pitch but also as it relates to balance and blend.

This general procedure can be applied to good effect in other sections of this and other marches, particularly at the Trio where the nature of the piece is usually more melodically oriented. While this approach to tuning and balancing the band is being used, the services of the percussion section can be dispensed with, at least temporarily, although their attention to what is going on should be required in the interest of what is to follow.

In retrospect, it should be understood that the whole matter of tuning as it relates to the band should involve a multi-approach by way of the individual, the section, and the entire ensemble—the last of these being the most complex because of its size and makeup. Furthermore, band members should be made to realize that the whole process of playing in tune does not end with the performance of a few unison exercises and chorales, but that these devices are just

---

[2]Used by permission of the publisher, Byron-Douglas, Phoenix, Arizona.

Captains and Kings

Conductor

Richard A. Otto
A.S.C.A.P.

ILLUSTRATION 8-2

the beginnings of learning to play in tune, and that the element of pitch management is an inseparable part of each tone that is sounded.

PLANNING OF REHEARSALS

To make band rehearsals a period of meaningful, productive, and yet enjoyable activity, it is necessary for the director to engage in a certain amount of preparation and planning. This implies a studied consideration of music felt to be worthy and within the musical and technical grasp of the band in a reasonable length of time; the preparation, by the conductor, of scores; and attention to a basic procedural pattern in rehearsal, as well as planned continuity from one rehearsal to another.

Obviously the band director must be familiar with the many details of each selection to be performed during the rehearsal period if this time is to be productive. Beyond this, a plan or pattern of procedure should be established in the rehearsal so that band members know what is expected of them from the time they enter the rehearsal room. This includes getting instruments out of storage facilities, obtaining music folders, being seated according to a prescribed plan, warming up and tuning up, getting music to be rehearsed out of the folders, and following an order of selections according to the posted or announced directions of the conductor. While the order in which music is taken up in rehearsal may vary from one rehearsal to another, there should be some planned organization of selections to be played during a given period. Such a plan for rehearsal might follow these lines:

1. Warm-up and tuning period.
2. Playing of a familiar piece, preferably one involving all members of the band (including the percussion section).
3. Sight reading for the purpose of improving the over-all reading ability of the band. (In some instances this may involve a piece of music merely to be "tasted" and not performed in public, while in others it may introduce a new selection to be performed in public.)
4. Detailed rehearsing on a major selection being prepared for a public performance.
5. Playing a less demanding piece which the band obviously enjoys.

It should be understood that while this plan could serve effectively in producing desired progress in rehearsal it might be altered to fit changing needs, particularly since there are many elements which influence a rehearsal and which require some alteration of a plan such as this. These influences include the following:

1. Number of rehearsals per week.
2. Length of rehearsal periods.
3. Time of the day when rehearsal is held.
4. Time of the year.
5. Scheduled music calendar event.
6. Unscheduled event requiring band services.

The director who meets the band on a daily basis is obviously in an advantageous position to cover more material and perform band literature of a more challenging nature than the director having only two or three rehearsals a week. Beyond that, the director who can schedule sectional rehearsals on a regular basis is able to devote more attention to the details of individual and sectional playing as it relates to the whole band, and therefore should be able to achieve at a higher level than those who are not so fortunate. Whether the rehearsal plan suggested earlier is followed or somewhat altered, the director who meets the band each day is in a good position to fulfill most, if not all, of its requirements. Furthermore, the director whose band meets daily can spend more time in tuning and in teaching the fundamentals of musicianship as applied to playing in a band. This amount of time permits the director to be more concerned with details and to attain a higher degree of polish in performance. The number of rehearsals held weekly also influences the amount, variety, and difficulty of the music that can be experienced by the band within a school year.

The length of band rehearsals also relates to the carrying out of a plan of rehearsal. The amount of time required for warming up and tuning the band will obviously impinge upon the time remaining to cover other phases of the rehearsal plan. The very size of the band will have some effect upon the plan of rehearsal, since a large group is likely to require more time for tuning than would a small wind ensemble, for example. It will be necessary for the director to decide in advance whether a given rehearsal period can include some time for sight reading for its own sake or how much time needs to be devoted to detailed rehearsing of a major selection being prepared for a forthcoming performance. The attention span of the average high school band member should also be taken into consideration when establishing the length of band rehearsals, since both their interest and ability to concentrate are limited. For the most part, the length of band rehearsals at the high school level will be determined by school administrators charged with the task of scheduling the whole school. In the majority of cases it will be found that these periods will run from 45 to 50 minutes in length.

It should also be pointed out that physical stamina plays an important role in determining the length of high school band rehearsals, since young players tend to tire rather rapidly. Naturally, the period of time it will take for a young player's stamina to fade will vary in accordance with the tonal and technical demands of the part being played and the physical resources that the individual has at his disposal.

The time of day will also have some effect upon the productivity of the band in rehearsal and can have some influence on the order of the rehearsal plan itself. In connection with this matter, schools operating on a rotating plan can provide schedule time advantages on a more equitable basis. Obviously, the least desired times of the day to hold band rehearsals would include the period immediately following the lunch period when wind instrument players will find their breath control to be at less than top capacity, and the last period of the day when mental and physical processes are at their lowest ebb. Band rehearsal activity and class participation throughout the school in general is most productive during the first hours of each day.

Another factor which influences the fulfillment of the desired goals of a complete band rehearsal is the time of the year when rehearsals are held. For example, at the beginning of each school year when new members have been added, more time will be needed for warm-up and tuning procedures and for working on fundamentals to rebuild a cohesive unit. At this time of year, the director may deem it wise to engage in a great deal of sight reading to evaluate the band as a whole, to promote their general sight reading ability, and to assess the kinds of materials which the group will be able to perform successfully. The obvious need for detailed rehearsal of one particular selection will be considerably reduced at this juncture. Instead, the band director will most likely be engrossed in the development of the marching band as it functions in relation to football activities throughout the fall. The requirements for marching band participation will vary a great deal from school to school and region to region. The amount of emphasis directed to marching band activities will have to be carefully weighed in consideration of the general policy of the school and the philosophy of the band director as a music educator. The fall of the year can be a trying one indeed for the band director faced with the dual task of rebuilding the band while attempting to field an acceptable marching unit.

As the year wears on, the director will find himself in a better position to follow a specific rehearsal plan such as the one suggested earlier in this chapter. Once again it should be understood that there may have to be a certain amount of latitude in the use of any rehearsal plan due to changing conditions, the variability of the time needed to solve problems as they arise, and the special attention needed for individual sections or certain parts of the music being prepared. As the time for the concert giving approaches, an increase in the rate of productivity in rehearsals will be evident as members of the band pay closer attention to the details of the music and tend to spend more time in the preparation of their individual parts. While the need to stress intonation will always be present in rehearsal, the need to develop a close teamwork among the various sections that comprise the band will become even more urgent than before. At this time of the year less emphasis will be placed upon sight reading since it is assumed that much of this will have taken place during the process of selecting suitable program material. Obviously, a certain amount of sight reading will be carried on through the year as new selections are chosen and prepared for subsequent concert and festival performances.

Much can be gained at times throughout the year by the use of a clinical approach to certain playing problems that are shared by the majority. This could involve demonstrations concerning breath control, tone matching, articulation, phrasing, and other elements of performance. Pupils eager to improve their own performance skills will be especially attentive at these sessions.

From time to time the service of the band is sought for an event which is unscheduled on the school music activity calendar. This service may take the form of a parade or a concert type appearance of the group in connection with a civic or service club in the community. Under the label of public relations, an event of this type may be approved by the school administration. While some of this kind of activity may be justified, it should be engaged in on a limited scale. (This subject will be elaborated upon in the next chapter.) This request for the band's appearance will obviously affect the daily rehearsal plan, since music other than that being rehearsed may be required. If a parade is involved, marching band materials must be reactivated. If it is an event with patriotic overtones, some special selections may need to be prepared. If the affair is out of town, some rehearsal time will have to be spent giving instructions to band members about their uniforms, the packing of music folders, the loading of large instruments and special equipment, and bus assignments. Temporarily the music being prepared for a scheduled forthcoming concert by the group will need to be set aside in preparation for this unscheduled event.

In establishing a plan for rehearsing the band, it should be understood that the order and amount of time devoted to certain aspects of rehearsing may vary somewhat according to the degree of musical maturity existing within the group. An experienced group will not only require less time for tuning, but can concentrate for longer periods of time on the challenging segments of major works being studied and prepared. On the other hand, a young and relatively inexperienced band will need more time for tuning and will require a musical menu of a greater number of selections whose technical and tonal elements are less demanding. In addition, the latter band will need continuing encouragement, particularly at the beginning of the year and when preparing for a public appearance. In view of their lack of experience, the director may need to focus more attention on the matter of building up their confidence as a unit as the year unfolds. He may also find it necessary to engage in a greater amount of demonstrating upon certain instruments to illustrate specific aspects of instrumental performance.

In summation, rehearsals that are properly planned and prepared by the conductor and structured along certain lines are not only more conducive to steady progress but also will result in musical experiences that are more meaningful, productive, and satisfying for all concerned.

APPROACHES TO REHEARSING INDIVIDUAL SELECTIONS

The approach to working on individual selections in band rehearsals may take one of several courses, depending in part upon the type of composition to be dealt with, the degree of its difficulty, and the purpose for which the number will be used. These approaches include:

1. Reading through the selection from beginning to end.
2. Starting at the closing section.
3. Using the "inside-out" method.
4. Dealing with isolated problems of a rhythmic or technical nature.
5. Using the sectional approach.
6. Playing of recordings.
7. Involving certain audio-visual aids.

Reading through the selection

The first approach, which involves the reading of a selection from beginning to end, is perhaps the most common. When used, it is generally prefaced by a few pertinent remarks by the director about the nature of the music, the tempo or tempos involved, key changes, and other special information that might be offered in the rehearsal notes to the conductor. It should be understood that regardless of the approach used for a given selection, a certain amount of "talking through" will be found necessary. Also, as mentioned at the outset, the approach that will prove most effective will vary from one selection to another in accordance with its nature, purpose, and difficulty.

One of the principal values derived from the so called "head-on" approach is that of improving the sight reading ability of the band as a whole. Obviously, school bands will be found to have among their membership those who are able to read readily at sight, while others in the group will find this process to be rather overwhelming. The periodic emphasis on the reading of new music, regardless of whether or not it will ever be programmed, should help to strengthen the reading ability of the band. Selections for this purpose should be chosen with great care since sight reading, especially by young bands, can be a demoralizing if not devastating experience. To build confidence in the group as a whole, it will be necessary for the director to select music that is not loaded with rhythmic and technical problems, especially at the very beginning of the new school year when engaged in the critical steps of rebuilding the band.

When this approach is used to rehearse a given selection, it will be necessary from time to time to stop the group, make corrections, and offer suggestions relating to the interpretation of the music. Undoubtedly, the number of pauses that occur during the course of the rehearsal will be influenced by the relative difficulty of the music together with the number of tempo, meter, and key changes encountered. The number of these interruptions required in rehearsal can be reduced if the director calls the attention of the band to these changes during the "talk through" prior to beginning the piece. Since transitional passages of a selection often call for a change of tempo which at times also involves a fermata, it may be necessary for the conductor to clearly illustrate the baton motions that will be used to negotiate such a section, especially if some parts are rhythmically subdivided and in motion under the fermata. Knowledge of this sort may also need to be imparted to band members when a change in the metric structure of the music is anticipated, as is frequently the case in an arrangement including the highlights of a Broadway musical or an opera. Music of this catagory usually includes several distinct changes of tempo and meter, thus time in rehearsals can be used to better effect if players are prepared for these in advance.

While this top to bottom approach may be applied with success more readily to numbers of short duration and with few, if any, tempo, meter, or key changes, it can also function effectively in connection with works of symphonic proportions. In fact, this approach may be more fitting, for example, when rehearsing such forms as the theme and variations, the prelude and fugue, and individual movements of symphonies where it is important to preserve the continuity of the thematic material.

Starting at the closing section

Another effective approach involves the playing of the closing section of the piece first before working out the details of earlier portions of the music. This technique tends to whet the appetite of the band, since the closing sections are frequently the most colorful and exciting and band members will look forward eagerly to reaching this part of the piece once again. Because of this desire to experience the excitement produced by the ending, band members will pay closer attention to directions concerning earlier sections of the work and will exhibit a higher level of concentration when it comes to performing some of the less attractive and perhaps more demanding segments. Beyond this, they will tend to exert additional effort in the individual preparation of parts outside of regular band rehearsals with a view to arriving at these climaxes with fewer interruptions in subsequent rehearsals. This approach to rehearsing a new selection may prove to be even more productive, depending upon the nature of the music, by having the brass and woodwind sections perform the closing segment separately. In this way, members of the band will come to a quicker understanding of the need to achieve and maintain good balance within their section and among sections throughout the band. This technique is also helpful in identifying pitch discrepancies in each section and, as a result, will contribute to the improvement of intonation throughout the band as a whole.

Using the "inside-out" method

The rehearsal approach which I refer to as the "inside-out" method is one where certain sections of the whole composition are attempted before starting at the beginning, as is frequently done with selections of an extended nature containing a large number of transitory sections. In one instance it may be a matter concerning the harmonic element where the change in tonality is observed to be somewhat unusual or abrupt. In another it may involve a change in the meter, where, for example, the music progresses from 2/2 to 4/4 meter and a change in the conducting pattern will be required. In still another case, distinct change in the style of the music may call for some special consideration.

This method is also effective in dealing with a segment of a selection that is "transparent" or thinly scored. This segment, unless dealt with directly, may later prove to be a stumbling block in rehearsal and result in time wasted. This approach is also helpful in connection with bands lacking a complete instrumentation, particularly where cross cuing or substituting one instrument for another may be required. Also, from time to time, the director will come across a selection containing a solo passage, the interpretation of which may need to be discussed briefly for the benefit of the solo player as well as the band as a whole in the interest of achieving the proper background or accompaniment. Having thus dealt with these kinds of problems in advance, the director can proceed with improved continuity and at a pace that will more readily retain the interest and attention of the members of the band.

Dealing with isolated problems

Another approach involves the isolation of certain rhythmic figures and dealing with them before attempting the whole piece. Since these will often be found to occur in a number of different individual parts, time in rehearsal can be saved by placing the selected examples on the blackboard, preferably prior to rehearsal, and analyzing them during rehearsal in a somewhat clinical fashion. This process may, at times, involve clapping, singing, or playing on a common pitch before performing the figures as written.

This method of approach is especially effective in connection with the preparation of Latin American dance forms which generally have an abundance of rhythm figures. While some of these rhythm patterns may serve to motivate the drive of the music, others will be found to relate to the melodic line. The former are more often associated with bass wind and percussion parts, while the latter occur more frequently in upper woodwind and brass parts, although these sections too contribute at different times to the motion of the music. Figures that are alike within a selection should be temporarily lifted out of context and dealt with separately before going on.

The portion of the score shown in Illustration 8-3[3] affords an opportunity for applying this approach in rehearsal. At letter "I," for example, there are five differing rhythm figures or patterns involved. One is identified with the melody, another relates to parts which somewhat parallel the melody, a third is a counterline in the upper woodwinds, another is associated with the counter-melody in trombone and certain low-voiced woodwinds, while a fifth is carried by the basses.

In dealing with this kind of situation, the director should first establish the desired tempo with the bass section for a block of from four to eight measures. Following this, the pattern involving the trombones, baritones, and low woodwinds should be handled briefly, after which the two might be joined. Next the rhythmic shape of the melody might be examined with care to articulate it as indicated. Then the accompanying harmony voices could be involved and, when felt to be satisfactorily played, rehearsed with the melodic lead. Finally the upper woodwind parts, which supply still another kind of counter melody, could be investigated for balance and rhythmic flow. As each part is being rehearsed, all those not playing at the moment should note how their parts relate to the one being played.

At different times during this process, it may be necessary to emphasize the proper placement of weight on certain notes and the need to articulate carefully to supply the rhythmic drive that should be accorded the particular number being rehearsed. Players should be urged to listen "across the band" in an effort to attain a high degree of cohesiveness throughout the entire ensemble. They should also be made aware of the obvious similarities which exist between certain brass and woodwind parts as they rehearse this and other kinds of music.

This approach can also be applied effectively in relation to problems of a technical nature, such as an unusual sequence of intervals, a peculiar grouping of notes, the management of a chromatic passage, or the actual speed required to meet the tempo demands of the music. The director should be sufficiently acquainted with the score to anticipate the possibility of having to deal with these kinds of problems during the course of the rehearsal period. Band rehearsals will then prove to be worthwhile educational experiences for all involved, and the pace of rehearsal can be maintained. If rehearsals have a tendency to bog down from time to

---

[3] The excerpt of the score of "Caribbean Holiday" by Richard A. Otto is used by permission of Shawnee Press, Inc. Copyright MCMLXIX, by Shawnee Press, Inc., Delaware Water Gap, Pennsylvania 18327

ILLUSTRATION 8-3

time, the director should reassess both his preparedness and his approaches, assuming of course that he has chosen music that lies within the capabilities of the band. The director must guard against the tendency to spend too much time working out the details of a particular problem since the attention and interest of those not directly involved will wane and may be difficult to recapture in rehearsal. It goes without saying that members will be expected to work out certain solutions to problems as individuals. Furthermore, some of the difficulties of the more challenging selections attempted by the band during the course of the year can be worked upon in music lessons and sectional rehearsals.

The sectional rehearsal approach

The band director who is able to schedule sectional rehearsals on a regular basis will find himself armed with another approach to rehearsing the band. In this way, parts of the music which are characteristic of the woodwinds, for example, can be dealt with in greater detail and at a more leisurely pace. Furthermore, specific technical, tonal, and physical problems can be dealt with since the instruments within each section will have more in common with each other. For example, problems relating to tonguing on brass instruments may be treated similarly, while tonguing on a woodwind is quite different because the involvement of a reed. Problems relating to fingering may also be gone into in greater detail from instrument to instrument, thus contributing to an increase in the rate of progress on the part of pupils involved in these sectionals.

In the event that one member of the staff is a woodwind specialist, he could carry on the rehearsing of this section while the brass section would come under the care of the specialist on brasses. This sectional approach to rehearsing will be found to be especially effective when preparing for a concert or festival, since a higher degree of polish can be achieved through the kind of detailed attention that can be devoted to the music involved. New music may also be introduced by way of the sectional approach from time to time in the interest of dealing with special problems more immediately and directly. Time should not be consumed in regular full band rehearsals for "sectionalizing," since those not involved will regard the time as being wasted.

Where sectional rehearsals are scheduled on a regular weekly basis, some of this time could well be devoted to certain clinic type activities, including the inviting of specialists on many different instruments into these meetings, perhaps on a monthly basis. This technique will prove beneficial in arousing new interest among members of the band and motivating them to greater individual efforts in practicing outside of school hours.

Playing recordings in rehearsal

An added approach suggested here and found to be helpful in stimulating band members to extra effort involves the playing of top quality recordings of selections performed by a fine band or wind ensemble, as they are frequently called. While band members will be impressed by performances by professional or college groups, they will be even more moved when the highly polished renditions of recorded selections are supplied by students of their own age.

The use of recordings is especially effective if the selections played are among those being rehearsed by the band. In this case, however, I would suggest withholding the playing of the recording until after the band has been given the opportunity to sight read the number in question and perhaps work on it for a time. In this way, they will not be playing the music "by ear." After they have the selection worked out in rehearsal, the playing of the recording can help to make them more aware of certain details which they may overlook. Furthermore, the use of recordings from time to time in rehearsal can effectively contribute to the development of desired concepts of playing in a band. These concepts include the following:

1. Unity within the whole ensemble
2. Tonal capabilities of the band (beauty, color, dynamic possibilities, etc.)
3. Technical cohesiveness
4. Balance and blend (both within and among sections)
5. Interpretation (shaping the phrase, varying tempos, changing volume levels, etc.)
6. Rhythmic elements (proper articulation and the use of accents related to weight, emphasis, pace, etc.)
7. Consistency in the management of tone (intonation, duration, dynamic shape of the music, etc.)

Beyond all of this, the use of recordings in rehearsals will provide listening experiences not otherwise available. Music of many styles and types and representing different schools of composition may be shared with band members. Among these should be included selections which lie beyond their immediate grasp to widen their musical horizons and broaden their taste and understanding.

Other audio-visual aids in rehearsal

A further approach to rehearsing the band involves the use of a tape recorder. This can be especially effective if an individual selection is recorded with planned continuity from the time it is first read at sight until a polished performance is attained. While time, facilities, and staff availability might place certain limitations on this kind of activity, it should be attempted for what it will reveal to members of the band not to mention the director. School performing groups have been known to develop the "halo" effect in regard to their own performance achievement level, and nothing will bring them back into focus more quickly than hearing a tape recording made in a rehearsal. Engaging in this practice from time to time will be helpful in detecting obvious mistakes or performance weaknesses.

At times in rehearsal it is effective to employ an overhead projector to show a few selected pages from the conductor's score to the whole band in an effort to illustrate and analyze certain elements of the music. At different times attention can be directed to a rhythmic figure shared by many in the band which may be especially difficult to play, or to passages of a technical nature that might prove troublesome. Displaying pages of either a condensed score or a full score is an effective way to have members of the band appreciate the complexity of such a score and come to a better understanding of the demand made upon the conductor. Also, the showing of a score on a screen as a recording of the number is being played can prove to be a real eye-opener for members of the band, most of whom have never seen a full score—much less attempted to read one!

In summation, regardless of the approach used in connection with rehearsing a given number, several basic elements need to be included in rehearsals of school bands to make these experiences musically enriching and educationally stimulating. Among the things essential to do are the following:

1. Establish a positive attitude toward rehearsals so that band members will look forward to the band period.
2. Develop a certain routine with respect to tuning and warming up individually and collectively at the beginning of the period and from time to time thereafter.
3. Establish and maintain a pace or tempo in rehearsals to hold the attention and interest of members throughout the period.
4. Include a wide variety of musical styles and types to appeal to the divergent tastes represented in a school band.
5. Include materials that are challenging and worthwhile, yet within the musical understanding and technical reach of young people.
6. Offer suggestions in a friendly and objective manner, avoiding sarcasm and remarks that tend to degrade.

7. Include the playing of music which all members can enjoy performing without the need for detailed rehearsing.
8. Develop a higher degree of discrimination and musicianship among members of the band.
9. End rehearsals on a positive note to foster a feeling of enjoyment, satisfaction, and accomplishment.
10. Develop a deeper sense of appreciation of music as a means of expression.
11. Aim rehearsal activity at worthy performance goals.
12. Develop and promote a desire among band members to continue their experiences with music beyond high school.

While all of these elements may not be present in each rehearsal, they should all, at one time or another, function to contribute to the attainment of desired goals in relation to performing in a high school band.

THE CHALLENGE SYSTEM

Many directors of high school bands throughout the country resort to the use of the challenge system to determine the position or chair each individual is to occupy in the band. The basic intent of this practice is to foster competition among its members and to stimulate increased effort and productivity. While some directors use this method for locating each member of the band from section to section, its main application is related to selecting individuals capable of occupying the first chair position in each section. In some instances, the director assigns specific solo literature for this purpose, although the majority tend to use excerpts from the literature of the band.

Generally each member of a section who is interested in trying out for the position is required to play the selected music in the presence of others in the band. In many cases, the non-participating members of the band are invited to assist in determining the results of the audition. To achieve objectivity in judging, band members may be asked to close their eyes or turn their seats around during this process while participants perform the required music. The latter would be assigned a number corresponding to the order in which they are auditioned; therefore, those judging would know them as participant #1, participant #2, etc. When all interested candidates have performed the required selection, chair assignments are allocated in accordance with the degree of success achieved by each.

While this procedure may be effective in motivating a certain amount of additional practicing on instruments by some in the band, others will regard this practice as distasteful and unnerving, even to the point where some of the better players will balk at participating. Although it may be felt necessary by some to conduct auditions for chair placement in this manner because of lack of time or staff, or because the director, who is not the individual's immediate teacher, may not be intimately acquainted with his ability, there are other ways of accomplishing the same end. One of these methods involves instituting a series of sectional rehearsals which will then permit the director to observe the contributions of each individual closely enough to draw some positive conclusions. Another method of selecting individuals for first chair is to invite a few interested members of various sections to remain after school or come to the director's office during a study period to perform without the benefit of an audience. Still another method, and perhaps the best, for determining individual capacities in relation to the position occupied, is that where the teacher and director are one and the same person and where individual or small class instrumental music lessons are carried on in direct association with membership in the school band. In this way, the director is in a strategic position to determine which individuals possess the necessary qualities for leading a section—particularly when these qualities go beyond performance ability.

Where it is deemed necessary or desirable to conduct some of this activity during the regular rehearsal, it should be done sparingly since those not directly involved may become bored and feel that the band period on such a day is wasted.

The use of the challenge system can prove beneficial beyond the selection of individuals to occupy the first chair in each section. Through its use, the director will be in a good position to assess the future leadership potential exhibited by all those who participate in these tryouts. Furthermore, this practice can also lead to a more strategic placement of band members in efforts to achieve better balance among parts. Some of the more competent individuals could thus be assigned to first chair second clarinet, for example, or first chair third clarinet, and in other sections to parts which need to be strengthened. For reasons relating to tone, technique, intonation, and balance, to mention the more obvious factors, it is unwise to place all of the most capable individuals on first parts throughout the band while assigning the least capable to third parts. By the same token, because of the register and range of certain parts, it would be equally unwise to have some in the band attempt to play the more demanding first parts.

While it may require some diplomacy on the part of the band director to achieve the desired balance through the distribution of strength, most of the band members, realizing the necessity for balance, will cooperate in this process. From time to time throughout the school year some shifting of parts should take place, especially in the larger sections, so that the experience gained by playing certain parts may be shared by several individuals. It should be understood that while this practice is desirable, certain limitations will be found to exist, particularly in relation to the first chair, since those occupying these positions should not only be capable of leading the section by virtue of superior musical ability and the possession of certain personal traits but also should be competent in the handling of solo passages, cadenzas, and the like.

HANDLING RHYTHM FIGURES IN REHEARSAL

I think most high school band directors will agree that more mistakes occur in rehearsal for reasons relating to the element of time and rhythm than for any other single factor. For that reason, band members should be given a thorough foundation in reading groups of notes as related rhythmic figures. The approach should be somewhat akin to that of building a vocabulary when studying a foreign language: that is, the figures should be taught with some degree of repetition and amid different settings to tax the individual's ability for recall. While these foundations should be laid in the early stages of instrumental study, it becomes necessary from time to time in band rehearsals to deal with problems relating to the element of rhythm. In some cases the problem will relate to a subtle point of interpretation, while in other instances the problem will be of a more fundamental nature.

Sustained tones

One of the most common problems found to exist among young players is that related to the sustaining of notes such as whole notes, dotted half notes, and half notes. While this is understandable, because of the recognized difficulty of playing long tones on wind instruments in general, the problem nevertheless is demanding of some special consideration.

Although the young performer may be knowledgeable in terms of the number of beats for which these notes should be held, he is frequently known to short change them. This practice may, at different times, be attributed to carelessness, underestimating their importance, or to a lack of breath control. The whole note, which requires the sustaining of tone throughout the measure and until the next measure is to begin, is frequently the victim of this practice. This is especially noticeable when several of these occur in a sequence, since obviously the performer must breathe at some point in any passage. This problem will be less evident in sections having a sufficient number of individuals, which will permit the introduction of staggered breathing. In general, however, young players must be coached in the proper techniques of breath taking so that a number of sustained tones can be managed in one breath. The practicing of measured or timed long tones in school and at home should contribute to building the capacity for playing sustained tones as they occur in the music. The young performer needs to become involved in learning how to use the breath sparingly while meeting the demands of the music. Since this is a physical process, the emphasis must be placed on the development of the diaphragm, lungs, and abdominal muscles engaged in the whole process of breath taking and control.

Similar situations arise in connection with the performance of dotted half notes and half notes, although to a lesser degree. Half notes performed by young musicians often dissolve into dotted quarter notes, thus: a 𝅗𝅥 becomes a ♩♪ or ♩. . This will be found to be especially true in phrases ending with a half note, when the half note occurs on the third and fourth beats of a 4/4 measure, and when the half note comes at the end of a rhythm figure as in the following example: 𝄽 ♩ ♪♩. ♪♪♩ ♪𝅗𝅥 | 𝄽 , etc. The band director may find it necessary to devote a considerable amount of time to this matter, particularly if it seems to reoccur frequently.

Other common rhythm faults

Another common fault found in the playing of high school bandsmen is that relating to the dotted quarter followed by an eighth note, thus: ♩. ♪𝅗𝅥 —especially in music of a moderate or slow tempo. All too often young instrumentalists tend to convert the eighth note into a sixteenth note, thereby failing to give it the full half count that it should have. Obviously, the nature and style of the music wherein this figure occurs will have some bearing on the exact length of time that it should be held. Accent and articulation marks affect the interpretation of note values.

The dotted eighth and sixteenth note figure ♪.♪♩ may also be included among the rhythm figures often misplayed by high school musicians. This figure, which I refer to as the "day-today" figure, too often deteriorates into the second form of the triplet♩♪, thus it loses its rhythmic identity. The dotted eighth and sixteenth figure must retain its snap and crispness so that it will not be mistaken for the more languid and lilting triplet figure.

I have found that teaching these two common figures, the dotted quarter followed by an eighth and the dotted eighth followed by a sixteenth, through the process of rhythmic augmentation, is very helpful. Through this method, pupils seem to grasp the relative values of the notes in each figure, as they relate proportionately to one another, more firmly. Thus the first figure ♩. ♪♩ becomes ♩. ♩ | o |, and the second figure ♫♩ is written as ♩. ♪♩ When it is felt that the proper relationship is understood, the tempo of each figure can be increased as it is applied by way of unison playing or in playing certain scales.

The triplet figure is also one that is frequently misinterpreted by high school musicians. This is especially noticeable when certain kinds of interval skips are involved in the playing of the triplet. For example, what may be played with a fair degree of evenness and equality of length on a unison basis will often lose its character when abrupt changes of pitch occur within the triplet; for example, ♫♩ may be found to become ♫♩ . Young performers, being anxious to negotiate the figure, will tend to rush the first two notes of the triplet and will therefore find it necessary to hold on to the third note a trifle longer. They need to be enlightened as to the nature and character of the triplet figure and come to understand that it is a somewhat lazy, rolling or circular figure having a distinct feeling of its own.

The second form of the triplet is another figure that is often played incorrectly. This deficiency may be most noticeable in the playing of a march written in 6/8 meter. Since the figure involving the quarter note followed by the eighth is so characteristic of the 6/8th march, it occurs very frequently. Here again, with certain technical considerations in mind, the figure often changes from ♩ ♪♩ ♪ to ♪♩ ♪♩, therefore the young bandsman may need to be reminded to sustain the first and third notes to provide the smoother, rolling effect more characteristic of the second form of the triplet.

Another figure that is troublesome for some is that involving the use of a tie between two notes of different lengths as in the following example: ♩ ♫♫|♩. ♪| . In his effort to fulfill the requirements of the tie, the young player finds that he has to rush the three remaining notes in order to arrive at the next down beat on time. He should be led to understand that the three moving tones following the sustained one must be played evenly and with full value, therefore the tied note must be somewhat shortened and spaced apart from that which follows, ie: ♩ ♪♫♩♩ | ♩. 𝄾 | . This spacing before the three moving eighth notes will also tend to give these three notes an added rhythmic drive as they lead to the following long tone.

Spacing is also required in the playing of figures such as this: ♫♫♫♩ to convey a feeling of lightness and movement. It should be interpreted as though it were written thus: 𝄾♫ 𝄾♫𝄾♫♩ , and the student should be taught to read it in this manner: 𝄾♫𝄾♫𝄾♫♩ —in other words, the eye training

process should involve learning to read by groups of notes and from the active to the less active as it were. Spacing is also demanded in the performance of syncopated figures where the emphasis or accent must be shifted to notes occurring on the off-beat. Furthermore, as mentioned earlier, the type of articulation required in the playing of any figure consisting of almost any number of notes (from one on upward) will significantly influence the manner in which the figure is played, especially concerning the weight of the accent felt to be appropriate and the amount of spacing that will be required. Other elements brought to bear here will be those relating to the tempo and the dynamics of the music.

While the band director will need to deal with these and many other problems relating to the interpretation of rhythm figures as they occur in the many selections he will rehearse during a typical school year, he will probably be led to the conclusion that as many, if not more, mistakes are committed because of the rests appearing intermittently in any given piece of music being studied. From time to time, therefore, it will be necessary for the director to isolate some of these problems and deal with each individually.

A practice or device that has proven to be helpful in the handling of unusual figures involving a mixture of notes and rests is that of penciling in the down beats in troublesome measures, as for example:

The lines drawn vertically above the staff will clearly mark each down beat so that there will be less chance for error in playing figures of this kind. This technique can save the young player the embarrassment of playing out at the wrong time. A somewhat similar practice is also used in playing selections where the meter changes frequently and suddenly during the course of the piece. For example, in going from a section of music in 2/2 meter, or "cut time" as it is often dubbed, to a section in 3/4 but with a feeling of "one in a bar," a single vertical stroke penciled in above the first note in each measure for a few measures will help to get things rhythmically aligned with little, if any, faltering.

It goes without saying that the band director should be familiar with all details of the score of each selection being prepared by the band in rehearsal. He will thus be prepared to deal with the various kinds of problems that arise in rehearsals involving young musicians. In this way, the positive pace of rehearsals can be maintained with the result that the time spent will be more satisfying and productive for all concerned.

SELECTION OF MUSIC

One of the most important keys to success in building a high school band is that which concerns the proper selection of music. In view of the many and diverse tastes and abilities represented in the average high school band, the process of selecting the right music may prove to be one of the director's most difficult assignments. Fortunately for the band director this task has been made easier through the cooperation of music publishers who are generous in their distribution of sample scores and through the use of recordings of these new works. This practice is a great time saver for the busy band director engaged in the periodic process of choosing new selections for the band. Beyond examining the score visually to determine its suitability for the band, the director is afforded the opportunity to hear a performance which can further substantiate his reasons for selecting or rejecting individual numbers. Obviously, where recordings are not available, the director will need to become involved in a visual examination of the score. During this process he will need to be concerned with the technical demands, the tonal requirements (particularly the harmonic idiom), the range factor, its rhythmic elements, and its over-all musical worth. Furthermore he will need to keep in mind the kinds of events at which the band will appear during the school year and select appropriate music.

In general, factors which will be most influential in the selection of music for the high school band will include the following:

1. Ability level of the band as a whole to meet the demands of the music with respect to its (a) length, (b) range, (c) tonal demands, (d) rhythmic complexity, and (e) technical requirements.

2. Appropriateness for educational purposes.

3. Diversity in period styles.
4. Degree of challenge and the potential of the band to meet the challenge in a reasonable number of rehearsals.
5. Appeal to the needs, interests, and tastes of band members.
6. Appeal to the kinds of audiences with which the music will be shared.

To choose music wisely for the high school band the director should have an intimate knowledge of the performing abilities of those who comprise the band. If the band director and the teacher of instrumental music is one and the same person, this problem will be infinitely easier to handle since he will be familiar with each one's capabilities. This places him in an advantageous position since he will have the knowledge required to determine the grade of difficulty of the music which his group will be able to manage within a reasonable span of rehearsal time. However, if the band director does not provide the instrumental instruction for a majority in the band, he may need to resort to other approaches in selecting music. Assuming other music staff members are involved in the instructional program, it may be necessary for the director to consult with these people to assess the ability level of the majority. He may also engage in a certain amount of experimental reading of different kinds of music to determine the general ability level of the group as a whole. The latter will be found more applicable in instances where the director is new to the position. Another helpful practice is to examine the contents of some of the printed programs of past performances—and of course one of the most obvious ways to judge the general level of music performed is to examine the band library!

Since performing in a high school band is primarily a learning experience, the music selected for it to rehearse and perform should be educationally worthwhile. Through its use band members should not only learn how to perform satisfactorily in a band, but should also grow in their ability to discriminate between music of lasting value and that of a passing fad. Music that is worthy will retain the interest of band members as they prepare it in rehearsal, and its real musical values will be recognized and understood as it takes shape prior to its performance. Examination of the lists of band publications by leading publishers of music will reveal a substantial number of challenging and worthwhile selections written by composers of national and world wide repute.

In choosing music for the band, the director should include a wide variety of types and styles to acquaint band members with the kind of music representative of different periods in the development of music in general. Through experiences with music of various ages, the student will not only come to a better understanding of the times in which that music was written, but also may recognize its relationship to and influence upon the music of today. During the Baroque and Classical periods, for example, a great amount of music was composed for the organ. Today a number of these have, rather logically I think, found their way into the literature of the band and to good effect, for in the hands of a skilled arranger and a sensitive conductor these compositions have provided enjoyment for bandsmen and audiences alike.

The music of certain composers of the Romantic period, particularly that of Wagner, Strauss, Tschaikowsky, and Berlioz, has lent itself quite effectively to being transcribed for use by bands. Most young people in high school bands will find enjoyment in the performance of the colorful and exciting works of these and other composers of the period. Since the majority of their works were composed for orchestra, although some were written originally for band, the director may be required to examine the transcriptions of these works very critically to determine their suitability. Some of the parts originally performed on string instruments, assigned to certain woodwinds in the transcriptions for band, tend to negate their use by other than the very finest high school and college bands. Furthermore, because of the nature of some of these selections with respect to the demands made upon wind instrument players, it would not be feasible to attempt performances except by large and fully instrumented groups which would permit the use of such techniques as staggered breathing by wind basses and the involvement of some alternate first chair players to temporarily share certain technical requirements.

Fortunately for the field of band literature, more gifted composers have contributed a number of significant works for bands in recent years. For the most part, these contemporary works are technically demanding and rhythmically sophisticated and are beyond the reach of the average high school band. They are programmed with good results by high school bands of advanced standing and by selected wind ensembles of both the high school and college levels. Names like Copland, Gould, Persichetti, Nehlybel, Dello Joio, Shostakovich, and the like are appearing with greater frequency on programs of band music. While music of these composers can and should be performed by high school musicians, it will lie within the province of the band director to determine how many of these works can be undertaken successfully in consideration of the number and variety of performance demands made upon the average high school band.

From time to time throughout the school year, the director should introduce works considered to be somewhat advanced for the group in order to motivate increased effort and growth among members of the band. Selecting music for which the band will have to put forth extra effort will be found to be rewarding since this kind of accomplishment can engender feelings of satisfaction and instill a desire to share further in experiences of this nature. Furthermore, the successful performance of more difficult works will promote marked growth among individuals and in the band as a whole. Beyond these benefits, a spirit of confidence will be kindled which will make subsequent experiences with difficult selections more tenable. In the process of selecting works of a more challenging nature, the director should be careful to choose music which the band will be able to perform satisfactorily within a reasonable amount of rehearsal time in consideration of all of its commitments for the entire year.

While works of an advanced level may be especially effective to include for festival purposes and, to some extent, in connection with major concert appearances, the bulk of the music prepared should be less demanding in the realization that the majority in the band are not about to become music majors! Therefore, the astute band director will select a wide variety of music representing many different types, styles, and levels of difficulty in order to appeal to the needs and interests of band members themselves. Beyond that, he should attempt to vary the pace of the rehearsal period itself by working on more than one number to hold the interest of the entire membership. Of course, it is understood that occasionally one work being prepared in rehearsal contains enough variety and interest to hold the attention and efforts of the group for the whole period.

Another factor that should be taken into consideration in the selection of music to be rehearsed and performed by the band in public is that of assessing the cultural level of the community and especially that of the immediate audiences of the school music performance groups. While many in this audience will be found to understand and appreciate some of the more sophisticated musical works contained in the program, many will expect to find music of an entertaining nature. It may, in fact, be safely said that some people will come to the high school band concert expecting a certain amount of color and exhibitionism to be included. Since the majority of school concert audiences are made up of parents and friends of the performers who would most likely attend regardless of the selections listed on the program, some thought and consideration should be given to including music having some special interest and appeal to these individuals. This consideration will be found to pay dividends in promoting and maintaining enthusiasm and support for the whole program of music in the schools.

In conclusion, the reader may note with some interest how these six factors, which have been suggested as influencing the selection of music, may also serve as general guidelines when it comes to dealing with the matter of program building itself! Most successful and complete programs by the many fine high school bands of our country will be found to incorporate the elements listed here.

DISCIPLINE IN THE BAND

A consideration of rehearsal techniques would not be quite complete without some reference to the matter of discipline. Since membership in high school bands throughout the country is most generally available on an elective basis, the aspects of discipline should not be expected to consume any considerable amount of time or energy on the part of the director. For the most part, I feel that the common interest of sharing in the performance of music tends to offset any appreciable amount of discipline. The very fact that music is in and of itself a disciplined art should allay the need for its added application in ways other than in pursuing a common goal through its performance.

A famous quotation attributed to Thomas Jefferson is felt to be apropos here. He said, "He who governs least, governs best!" Ideally, we should attempt to so organize and pace our groups that there will be little need for disciplinary measures. Rehearsal procedures and requirements should be made known to all members of the band from the outset so that they will understand the kind of behavior that is expected of them. Furthermore, they should be encouraged and guided in the development of self-discipline for their own benefit as well as that of the group. The greatest ally of the director in achieving a high degree of self control among members of the band is found in the music itself. Surely the morale building qualities of music which may be experienced by audiences can also be felt by the band members themselves!

Certain aspects of discipline in its broad sense can be instituted by the members of the band through electing officers to fulfill specific duties, through developing a band handbook which would contain rules and regulations, and through the development of a point system if such a need is felt. These steps were dealt with in some detail in Chapter 6 and need not be further amplified here.

Obviously the key to good discipline in the band is the ability, attitude, and behavior of the band director himself. To instill band members with proper attitudes, mature behavior, and enthusiasm, the director should serve as an example. He should be punctual at all rehearsals and be totally prepared to deal with all the details of the music being prepared as well as aspects of organization and administration. He should be friendly without becoming solicitous and should provide a stability and competence in leadership that will disseminate a feeling of security and confidence among the members of the band. His suggestions regarding the interpretation of the music or pertaining to the solution of a technical problem should be clear and objective. While his sense of industry should be self-evident as he attempts to achieve desired results, he should be aware of the diverse tastes and interests as well as the limitations of the young people that comprise the band. He will need to realize that their ability to concentrate in rehearsal may, at times, leave something to be desired, and therefore his sense of motivation and accomplishment may have to be tempered. His sense of enjoyment in working with young people through music should implant in them a desire to contribute to their fullest capacity to successful performances by the group. His serious efforts to develop a fine performing unit should be balanced with a sense of humor reflective of his understanding and humaneness.

As mentioned earlier, the students themselves can be brought into action with reference to the improvement of the musical and behavioral discipline of the band in a number of ways. Beyond those already discussed, the following suggestion is offered.

An approach that I have found to be particularly helpful in promoting a sense of involvement and responsibility is that requiring the use of a rehearsal evaluation form which is applied by individual members of the band. (Such a form is shown here in Illustration 8-4.) At each rehearsal one member of the band, selected in advance perhaps on a rotating basis, serves as an observer or adjudicator. This individual sits apart from the band during the rehearsal period and records his observations pertaining to the various aspects of discipline and performance as listed on the Rehearsal Observation Form. His observations and comments will be read to the band either at the end of the rehearsal period, at the beginning of the next rehearsal, or immediately after a certain selection is rehearsed.

There are a number of values inherent in this practice. In the first place, the individual member is afforded a different vantage point from which to view the band. As a result, he will be more sensitive to

DEPARTMENT OF MUSIC EDUCATION
WALLINGFORD PUBLIC SCHOOLS

REHEARSAL OBSERVATION FORM

Organization:_____Date:_____Time:_____

1. Rehearsal readiness:

2. Response to directions:

3. General Observations:
   a. Posture of members
   b. Position of instruments
   c. Tone quality
   d. Intonation
   e. Articulation
   f. Rhythm
   g. Technique
   h. Phrasing

4. Comments:

5. Suggestions:

Signed:_____

Observer

Illustration 8-4

the numerous facets of rehearsing such a group and will better understand the complexities involved in working out the details of any given number being prepared. Second, he will tend to be more critical of the posture of certain members and of the manner in which instruments are held. In turn, when he rejoins the group at the next rehearsal, he is likely to be more conscious of these elements as they relate to himself. Third, his attention can be channeled more objectively to certain aspects of performance such as tone quality, intonation, articulation, rhythm, technique, and phrasing. Since he will be called upon to pass judgment on these facets of musicianship, he will tend to pay more attention to these items in subsequent rehearsals. Fourth, he will grow in his awareness of the kinds of problems confronting the director as he attempts to forge a unified and cohesive group, and thereafter will be inclined to accept suggestions for improving performance more willingly. Finally, he will develop a greater sense of responsibility for his role as it relates to the band as a whole and will contribute more effectively to the attainment of success in performance experiences.

HELPFUL HINTS TO SUCCESS IN REHEARSALS

The following statements are offered as a series of suggestions in brief or digest form which may prove to be helpful in making rehearsals more productive and which also may assist in achieving better results in less time!

1. Get rehearsals started promptly!
2. Warm-up procedures should be brief and meaningful and involve exercises beneficial to woodwinds and brass alike.
3. Warm-up procedure should include the playing of unison rhythm patterns and scales in addition to chorales to activate the tongue and fingers.
4. Involve the band in a certain amount of singing on occasion to make them more conscious of pitch, blend, and balance.
5. In playing chorales, alternate the woodwind section with the brass section every two measures to make them aware of the need to match pitches across the band.
6. Use a clinic approach to handling certain problems affecting the band as a whole from time to time.
7. In using chorales for warm-up activity, do not play them too slowly as this kind of playing is very taxing, especially when players are not yet warmed up.
8. Work from strength in helping to solve rhythmic and technical problems, using section leaders to demonstrate on occasion.
9. Have percussion section stop playing from time to time to assess the intonation, blend, and balance of the winds.
10. Keep the score in your head—not your head in the score!
11. Stop conducting—and listen!
12. Periodically require the percussion section to play alone to determine their sensitivity to the music.
13. Rehearse the percussion parts along with the brasses to achieve agreement in the placing of accents, especially in certain selections where the rhythmic element is very prominent.
14. Think of a pryamid in working for balance. Few high-voiced instruments are needed to balance many low instruments!
15. Occasionally go out into an adjoining corridor as the band is playing in the rehearsal room. You will note that "distance

lends enchantment" in reverse. You can readily pick out pitch discrepancies, hesitation in rhythm, lack of precision in articulation and other weaknesses.

16. Concentrate more rehearsal time on working out the details in transitional sections and endings to insure solidity.

17. Be careful not to develop the "halo" effect in regard to your group's playing—remember, there's always room for improvement.

18. Be sure to include some music in rehearsals which you know they will be able to play satisfactorily in a short amount of rehearsal time, to promote confidence and enjoyment.

19. Intersperse your criticisms with compliments of their efforts —they will try harder to please you.

20. Rehearsals just prior to concerts should be held in the auditorium to aid the band in adjusting to the acoustical character of the stage and the seating arrangement.

21. During rehearsals in the auditorium, the director should go to various parts of the seating area to assess the visual and aural factors of performing there.

22. Pre-concert performances in school assemblies are helpful in providing the band with an opportunity to judge their readiness for a forthcoming public concert, and can also serve as a means of advertising it.

23. Spend some time in rehearsal away from the podium moving about the room to observe details of posture, position, and other mannerisms not otherwise noticed.

24. Keep the pace of the rehearsal moving!

chapter 9

Building Better Public
Relations

Public relations as it concerns the high school band director might better be termed "personal relations," since the nature of his position in the school and community is unique, bringing him into contact with individuals from all walks of life including students, teachers, other members of the music staff, school administrators, clerks, custodians, and music supply dealers. Beyond these individuals whom he sees quite regularly, he also comes to associate with civic leaders, service club members, members of the press, and parents of band members.

Because of the singular nature of his position in the school and community and the services he is able to provide, his influence for good can be far reaching. Whether by accident or design, he is frequently the link between the school and community and therefore carries a greater responsibility than the average faculty member in representing the school to various segments of the community. At different times he is in a position to attract the interest of the public and gain support for the schools in general—particularly since the public often judges the quality of the educational offerings by what it sees! All the more reason then for the band director to understand the sensitive implications of his position and to make special efforts to interpret and meet the needs of both the school and the many segments of the community.

RELATIONSHIPS WITH STUDENTS

Concerning the matter of public relations, the first responsibility of the band director lies with the members of the band with whom he comes in contact in music lessons and in band rehearsals. His primary goals should relate to meeting their needs individually and as a group. To do this successfully, the band director should take steps to meet with each member of the group on a regularly scheduled basis. In this way, he will be able to assess the abilities and needs of each individual and provide the necessary instruction, guidance, and motivation. These matters can be dealt with most readily within the framework of the instrumental instructional program where pupils are met on an individual or small group basis. Here the ability, needs, and progress of each can be observed closely and evaluated by the instructor with remedial steps being taken as and when necessary. This arrangement affords the director the opportunity to hear each player apart from the group and assign him to his proper place in the band with respect to his abilities and potential. Where this procedure cannot be instituted because of lack of staff or facilities, the director may organize a system on an appointment basis during study periods or after school.

The manner in which the band director attempts to meet the needs of each individual in the band will have a marked influence upon the morale of the group as a whole. The director who demonstrates genuine concern for the individual in the organization will have few problems to deal with relating to discipline, and pupils sharing in this kind of educational climate will become his best ambassadors when it comes to public relations in the broad sense.

The close personal relationships that can be afforded by meeting pupils on a weekly basis in a program of individual lessons or in small groups is not always possible because of lack of time, staff, facilities, or a combination of these. In such cases the director will be forced to deal with larger numbers on a more objective basis. Although he will have to forego the advantages available through individual and small group instruction, he can still achieve a good rapport with members of the band through a diplomatic handling of problems concerning the music or related to the behavior of individuals within the band. Comments and suggestions offered in group meetings, whether class, sectionals, or full band rehearsals, should be made in a friendly manner with the emphasis on criticism of a constructive nature. Being as sensitive as they are, young people of high school age will respond in more positive ways to this kind of treatment.

From time to time the band director should take the opportunity to encourage and recognize the progress and special accomplishments of individual members of the band. This can be done by way of a verbal pat on the back in rehearsal, by singling out an individual following a rehearsal, through the use of a citation of merit form such as is shown in Illustration 9-1 and which can be displayed on a bulletin board, or by arranging for awards and scholarships for the most deserving members.

Relationships with students can be further fostered by incorporating a number of special events in the annual band activities calendar. While these may be primarily musical in nature, the social overtones will be obvious. Exchange concerts with bands from high schools within the state or in nearby states are musically motivative and socially enriching. Attendance at state and regional music festivals is also effective in promoting a closer relationship between the band and its director as well as among members themselves. Sharing in performance experiences in general tends to generate an esprit de corps among those who participate in these activities. While this may be due in part to the effect that music has upon people, including the performers themselves, the emotional connotations of public performances contribute to the development of a closer feeling among all involved. Performances as part of the learning experiences of high school students will be dealt with in greater detail later in the current chapter.

Relationships established between the director and members of the band can be further enhanced by working together in the planning of marching band activity, in fund raising for special needs, and by arranging for such events as the annual band banquet and dance. Working directly with the elected and appointed officers of the band in planning the details of a forthcoming concert can also provide the director with an effective vehicle for building good relations with members of the band. Sharing in the creation of an awards system or in developing a band handbook can also be helpful in cementing relationships among those in the band and its director. Furthermore, these non-musical aspects of band organization can provide both the director and the student with new insights and understanding of each other's talents, aims, and contributions.

RELATIONSHIPS WITH OTHER STAFF MEMBERS

Since there are many occasions during the school year when music groups are called upon to provide special services, it is important that the band director establish and maintain compatible relations with other members of the faculty. Insofar as the band is concerned, these occasions may include: (1) appearances at football games, (2) performing at pep rallies, (3) providing music for other athletic

LYMAN HALL HIGH SCHOOL

Citation of Merit for Distinguished Achievement or Service

Activity_____Achievement_____

Project_____   or

Subject_____Service_____

    Be it known to all concerned that _____

of Grade _____ *has earned meritorious recognition in the aforementioned area above*
and beyond the standards of that area.

Date_____   Signature_____
                                     Teacher or Sponsor
Marking Period #_____

_____   _____
    Guidance Counselor   Principal

ILLUSTRATION 9-1

events, (4) performing at school assemblies, (5) participating in parades, (6) giving concerts in the school, (7) presenting concerts in other schools and communities, (8) participating in music festivals, (9) sponsoring exchange concerts, and (10) providing music for events of special significance in the school and community such as graduation, the dedication of a new school or civic building, etc.

In some of these instances, the services of the band are sought by members of the faculty responsible for a school assembly program. In other cases, it is the band director seeking teachers to serve as chaperones at a concert or on a bus traveling to a music festival or exchange concert. In the event that the band supplies music for graduation, the school principal or senior class advisor may approach the director for the services of the band. Where the band is called upon to perform at football games, it may be necessary for the director to contact the football coach or members of his staff to ascertain the time of the game or to make arrangements for the use of the field at certain times during the week for the purpose of preparing the half-time show. In the event that the band also performs at "away" games, it may be necessary to arrange for others on the faculty to assist in supervising students on school buses enroute to and from the neighboring community. In many schools, it is the practice of the principal to assign members of the faculty to duties such as this on a rotating basis. Present trends call for additional remuneration for these kinds of services supplied by staff members.

Also, from time to time the services of the high school band are needed at special events in the community such as civic and patriotic parades, the dedication of a new school or public building, or in commemoration of a community anniversary date such as a centennial. Unless there are several music staff members available to assist at these functions, it will be necessary to involve others on the faculty to insure the health and well-being of participating students. Where a band parents organization exists in association with the school music department, it is possible to solicit the help of parents to provide this service.

Relationships with other members of the staff involve a mutual realization that at certain times during the school year activities of one department of the school will need to take precedence over the others. For this reason, all members of the faculty need to be informed of the special demands made upon certain groups at particular times throughout the year. In smaller schools having limited student bodies, problems of this sort may become disproportionate since a few versatile individuals may become involved in a number of important activities running concurrently! To avoid such conflicts, it will be necessary to have an administrator or a member of the faculty in charge of coordinating all school events and to hold periodic meetings with heads of departments to insure the smooth operation of the school calendar. At best this is a difficult task because of the involvement of athletic teams with other schools, drama productions whose schedules depend upon the availability of the auditorium, science exhibits to be held in the school gymnasium, music festivals conducted on a local, state, or regional basis, and the innumerable other educational and social functions which are carried on as a regular part of the modern senior high school. This task is further complicated by the addition of previously unscheduled events for which special arrangements must be made!

It should be recognized that the relationship between the band director and other members of the faculty is a two-way street. While it is essential for the band director to understand the needs of others on the staff, especially at times of the year when a major testing program or an important exhibit is being prepared, it is equally important that they in turn come to some realization of the pressures and demands of his position. The emotional strain of performing for one event after another is considerable. Within each community there are a number of self-professed "experts" ready to criticize the latest performance by the band or the kind of music included on the program. Also, there are those on the faculty who claim that it is easy for the director of the band to display his efforts to good advantage while their subjects may catch the public eye on a limited scale. Although it is true that music lends itself readily to attracting the attention of the general public, it can equally be the subject of wide public criticism. What is sometimes not understood or is overlooked by others on the faculty is the fact that music personnel are required to have their groups perform in public at times when the director may have doubts about their state of readiness. At times like this the performance can produce rather traumatic side effects for both the director and the performer.

From time to time throughout the school year, conflicts may arise where certain school facilities are shared by several departments. The school auditorium and the gymnasium are among the most troublesome areas in this respect. The former may need to accommodate the rehearsals of both choral and instrumental groups unless there are specific and separate music rehearsal facilities. Where the auditorium must serve as a rehearsal area, there is bound to be some friction among staff members and the public to some extent also, since the high school auditorium, frequently the only large hall in the community, is pressed into service on many occasions. Among these are meetings by civic groups, drama productions by both school and community groups, concerts by school and community groups, performances by traveling professional musicians and theater companies, showing of films for school and community groups, teachers' meetings, town meetings, etc. The gymnasium also is often used by groups in the community, especially during the winter months, for holding dances, as an exhibit hall, and for evening school physical fitness programs. In schools where the gym must also serve as an auditorium, the possibilities for conflict are almost limitless!

In consideration of the many activities for which these areas are used, it is essential that adequate and separate facilities be provided for music classes and performance groups. Furthermore, no self-respecting band director should be pressed into the daily chore of setting the stage with chairs and stands in preparation for rehearsals. Beyond the fact that this procedure is physically taxing, it is wasteful of the training and talents of a music educator who presumably is being paid a professional salary for professional services.

RELATIONSHIPS AMONG MUSIC STAFF MEMBERS

The development of good relations within the music faculty itself is essential to the smooth operation of the department and to the attainment of desired educational goals. This condition can be brought about readily where the teaching assignments of staff members are clearly delineated by way of a job description, by the person responsible for hiring music personnel, or through mutual agreement among staff members themselves. In a high school music department consisting of two teachers, one is usually placed in charge of the instrumental groups, while the other is held responsible for the development of the choral program and the teaching of elective music subjects.

Since the nature of the preparation and training for these teaching assignments is quite different and the services for which each is sought varies to a great extent, the chances for a conflict of interests within the department should be minimal. Each staff member would soon come to recognize the singular talents and contributions of the other and an atmosphere of compatibility should be readily attainable. In providing performance services in the school or community, the nature of the event for which music is sought will usually determine the kind of group felt to be most appropriate for the occasion. On the other hand, concerts themselves frequently involve appearances by both choral and instrumental groups in the interest of providing continuing motivation for each performing unit and for the purpose of appealing to a wider segment of the community. In cases such as this, the members of the music staff will need to plan cooperatively with respect to the various aspects of concert giving. These include the nature of the program, the time of the year, the length of the performance of each group participating, the order of their appearance, the problems encountered in staging such an event, the possible inclusion of a massed chorus or grand finale involving a joint effort of both instrumental and choral units, and, of course, the business and managerial details including the handling of tickets, programs, ushers, stage crew, light crew, publicity, etc.

In large high schools having three or more music educators, the development of a smooth-working team will be more difficult by virtue of numbers if nothing else. However, here too, the compatible relations desired for those working with various music performance groups sharing the same facilities can also be achieved through the clear definition of the teaching responsibilities of each and through the development of mutual respect and understanding of one for the other. In a staff of this size, one member is usually placed in charge of the band and is given the concomitant responsibility of providing instrumental instruction on winds and percussion, conducting sectional rehearsals, and directing the band in all of its diverse capacities. Another staff member, usually a string major, is placed in charge of the school orchestra with an accompanying assignment of giving instruction on string instruments, conducting sectional rehearsals, and directing the group as it provides music at the school dramatic productions, the musical events, and at graduation. A third individual with a choral background and the ability to play keyboard instruments would be assigned to direct the rehearsals and performances of the glee clubs, the choir and small vocal ensemble, and elective music subjects. If he is qualified and the facilities permit, this individual might also be involved in giving instruction on piano, at least to the extent of developing competent accompanists, and on the organ if one is available.

In situations like this, staff members may plan joint concerts with one or more choral groups sharing the stage with one or more instrumental units during the course of the evening. Depending upon the size and character of the music program, it might be deemed advisable to conduct an all-choral concert at some point during the school year and an all-instrumental concert another time. From the standpoint of audience interest, however, it is generally advisable to include a mixture of choral and instrumental music at two or more concerts during the year. This type of program, while catering to a wider audience, may also serve to awaken the interest of some instrumentalists in joining one of the choral groups, assuming that they have the opportunity of hearing each other within the framework of the same concert or at a school assembly.

Relations among members of the music staff will be enhanced by scheduling joint meetings after school on a regular basis. These meetings will provide members with opportunities to keep each other informed of forthcoming events involving groups under their immediate direction. Furthermore, these meetings can serve as curriculum development sessions in which common aims and objectives can be crystalized with a view to improving and expanding the offerings of the music department. Through planning cooperatively, music staff members can coordinate certain facets of the program to promote a wider sharing of music performing and listening experiences. A team teaching approach to classes in music rudiment and appreciation can be helpful in stimulating greater interest in such courses and in providing greater depth in exploring the field of music in general. Beyond this, new insights can be gained by having music personnel conduct rehearsals of each other's groups from time to time. This process can be gainful to both students and staff members. By sharing in these procedures, members of the staff are likely to become more sympathetic of the problems confronting each.

Ultimately, good relations can be achieved among music personnel when each one comes to understand and respect the individual talents and abilities of the others and realizes that at various times throughout the year the services and activities of one will have to take precedence.

RELATIONSHIPS WITH ADMINISTRATORS

Administrators are responsible for all aspects of running the school. In view of this, the wise band director will communicate closely with the principal on all matters which in any way will relate to the music program. Again, the two-way street approach is necessary in this relationship, since the band director will need to be informed of events which may require the services of the band. The principal, on the other hand, must be aware of the special needs of the band since it is one of the most complex kinds of activities within the framework of the school curriculum. Band membership generally cuts across all class lines within the school; it also involves both boys and girls, and encompasses a wide range of abilities and tastes. Furthermore, since the raw material by which it functions is sound, it is necessary to consider the acoustical qualities of its meeting place for its own sake as well as for classes located nearby!

Since the school principal generally is charged with the responsibility of scheduling, he should come to understand some of the special problems related to the scheduling of the band and other music groups. Usually there is but one band in the high school. This, combined with the fact that the band is composed of pupils of both sexes and from all class levels and is frequently the largest "class" in the school, makes it necessary for the principal to account for its place in the schedule early in the process of scheduling the whole student body. To insure the inclusion of all those interested in joining the band, it will be necessary for the band director to submit complete lists arranged by classes early in the spring or prior to the time that the principal will begin to construct the schedule for the ensuing year.

Some administrators who are especially sensitive to the public relations aspect of the school in the community and aware of the exhibitive nature of performances by the high school band tend to call upon it to dress up certain school affairs involving attendance by the general public. These kinds of appearances are effective not only in improving relations with the public at large but also in gaining support for the music program itself.

Approval of the school head is generally required in connection with participation in local, state, and regional music festivals as well as exchange concert activity which involves transporting the band. In some schools, the principal is held responsible for making the necessary arrangements for buses, chaperones, and the like, while in others the band director assumes this responsibility. In the latter instance, the principal's approval is needed, although he may choose to leave the details regarding travel arrangements up to the band director. In all cases involving travel by common carrier such as bus, train, or plane, the band director should investigate insurance coverage supplied by both the local Board of Education and the carrying company. Administrators often require the development of special field trip permit forms giving the particulars of the event and signed by parents. (See Illustration 9-2.)

Since expenditure of funds for music and equipment frequently comes within the province of the school principal, it is prudent for the band director to be on good terms with this individual if for no other reason than to insure adequate funding of band needs. Although some schools operate on the basis of a formula which regulates the per pupil allotment of funds by departments, many are not required to maintain strict lines in this connection. In cases like this, the band director on good terms with the school head can manage to obtain certain desirable pieces of equipment somewhat earlier than originally hoped for.

As is frequently the case, the band director may find it necessary to augment funds allotted by the local school board by engaging in a certain amount of fund raising activity. In this event, he will need the advice and approval of the school principal since the latter is likely to be more familiar with general Board of Education policies regarding this practice. Because of their concern for public acceptance of certain fund raising approaches, the board will most likely have a set of policies regulating this kind of activity. While it is hoped that activity of this type can be kept to a minimum so that the band director can direct his main efforts to music education, some may occasionally be necessary to raise money for a trip or for the procurement of special equipment which the school budget is unable to provide. For contingencies of this nature, a band parents association can be of inestimable assistance to the band and its director. More will be said about this later.

From time to time throughout the school year letters are received inviting participation by the band in some event of importance in the immediate community, in a nearby city, or at a point some distance

Lyman Hall Field Trip Form
School Year 19-___ 19___

Name:_____ has my permission to go with the Lyman Hall Band to the: Eastern Division Convention of the Music Educators National Conference Jan. 30 to Feb. 2, 1969 in Washington, D.C. via licensed carriers arranged through the Thompson Tours, Inc.

Medical Information

The following information is required in the event of an emergency:
Name of family physician:_____
His office address:_____ Telephone:_____
His home address:_____ Telephone:_____
Is your child covered by any form of hospitalization or surgical insurance? If "yes" give name of company and membership number(s)
_____

Person to be informed in case of emergency: Name_____
Address_____ Telephone:_____
Relationship:_____ Is there any allergy or special disability that we should be made aware of? (Confidential—please note here)_____
_____

It is my understanding that expenses (including illness or accident) in connection with this trip are not the responsibility of the school. (It should be noted here that Thompson Tours, Inc. provides insurance amounting to $500.00 per person—accident and $500.00 —hospitalization.)
IT IS MY UNDERSTANDING THAT ALL RULES AND REGULATIONS CONCERNING ACCEPTABLE BEHAVIOR HAVE BEEN DISCUSSED WITH AND WILL BE ADHERED TO BY MY SON OR DAUGHTER IN FULL KNOWLEDGE THAT UNACCEPTABLE BEHAVIOR WILL BE DEALT WITH IMMEDIATELY WITH PUNISHMENT AS DEEMED NECESSARY BY THE CHAPERONES. (Signature of both parents is required below.)
Father:_____ Mother:_____
Dated:_____
(This form has been developed by and with the approval of the members of the Lyman Hall High School Music Parents Association.)

ILLUSTRATION 9-2

from the school. While some of these are addressed to the school principal, many are sent directly to the school band director because of his immediate involvement. In either case, the principal and band director should sit down together and cooperatively assess the educational worth of the event. These considerations should include the feasibility of participating, the significance of the event, the finances involved, the scheduled time of the event, the amount of time consumed, the amount of time required for preparation, and the general nature of the affair. Occasions for which the services of the band are sought include the following: parades commemorating special events, "Band Day" at a state university during the football season, pageants marking an important date, the dedication of a school or public building, a performance in honor of some dignitary of state, national, or world prominence, a performance for a service club hosting a state meeting of its members, programs marking patriotic holidays, local and state P.T.A. meetings, and many more. However, regardless of the kind of event for which the services of the band are sought, and particularly in view of their public relations values, it is vital that these requests be examined and weighed by the band director and school administrator cooperatively. It should be understood that these involvements are above and beyond the regularly scheduled events of the school music department calendar which includes a variety of performances and services throughout the year.

Although the band director in the average high school may deal frequently with the school principal, he may rarely come in contact with either the Superintendent of Schools or the Board of Education. For the most part, the principal charged with administering to the needs of all departments of the school will serve as intermediary in matters concerning the band. In special situations, however, the principal may wish to have the band director attend a meeting of the board with him for the purpose of supplying details of band participation in a particular event, in connection with the procurement of special equipment, or to brief them concerning plans for a trip or event of singular significance together with proposals for financing such a venture. Beyond meeting with these individuals on such rare occasions, the band director can maintain good relations with them in several ways. These include: (1) sending each one a pair of complimentary tickets to band concerts, (2) mailing advance copies of the program to each member, (3) listing the names of board members on programs of special significance, (4) sending each a copy of special news bulletins concerning band performances and services, and (5) sending the board an annual report of the activities of the band, including facts about its growth, procurement of new equipment, festival participation and ratings, and other information of special interest.

RELATIONSHIPS WITH SCHOOL CLERKS AND CUSTODIANS

In view of the nature of the band and its involvement in school and community affairs, it is necessary to deal with members of both the clerical staff and custodians on a rather continuing basis throughout the year. These individuals should be treated as members of the school family since they contribute important and valuable services to the successful operation of the entire school. While both of these groups render service to music personnel in the course of the daily routine of the school, they provide extra assistance at certain times of the year when concerts are given, when field trips occur, and when other performance activity is involved. Concert time requires the preparation of articles for news media, printing of programs, handling of ticket sales, etc. In some schools, members of the clerical staff voluntarily assist in these matters, while in others they may be assigned temporarily by the principal to aid in providing special services. Field trips, including attendance at festivals and performances at other school assemblies, often require the preparation of travel forms, bus lists, and even housing assignments where an overnight stay is anticipated. Here again, the assistance of qualified typists is invaluable. While some of these routine chores might be relegated to student help, others require the aid of more responsible and mature individuals.

Custodial cooperation is especially important at those times of the year when the installation of portable risers on stage is needed in connection with a formal concert. The moving of school pianos, particularly the large grand pianos, for example, usually requires the presence of several custodians to insure proper handling. While student assistance may be sought in connection with the handling of certain items of equipment, school policies will usually limit the involvement of students, especially in the case of large and costly pieces of equipment, to avoid possible law suits against the school. In connection with field trips of various types, the custodial staff may be enlisted to load heavy equipment such as timpani drums on school buses or trucks. Furthermore, unless the band director has a key to the building and one which permits access to certain areas of the building when evening rehearsals might be scheduled prior to a concert, or on Saturdays during the football season, he may have to rely upon a custodian for these services.

While some of these clerical and custodial services are supplied as a matter of course and are incorporated in employment agreements, some are provided voluntarily while others fall into the category of "extra pay for extra work." Where these individuals are particularly generous in providing services without special remuneration, the band director can show his appreciation by supplying them with complimentary tickets to paid performances by the band, by inviting them to the annual band banquet, or by a special note of thanks for their efforts in behalf of the band.

RELATIONSHIPS WITH MUSIC SUPPLY DEALERS

Relations with those in the community or area who deal in music merchandise should be established on a business-like basis from the outset. A band director coming into a community should take immediate steps to become acquainted with business people from whom he is likely to purchase music, instruments, and other equipment and materials. During this process, he should assess the kind, quality, and scope of the music supplies handled by various dealers and, at the same time, should investigate the service facilities and policies of each.

In buying music, unless the local dealer is in a position to stock a wide variety of band music, the band director will find it necessary to order music and perhaps other instructional materials by mail. While the average music store may carry a limited supply of methods books, few will provide much in the way of band music. Fortunately, many publishers engage in the practice of sending catalogs and other advertising materials through the mail to keep music educators informed of their latest publications. Others send sample copies of condensed scores to directors throughout the country, thus enabling them to evaluate various selections in terms of their fitness for use by their own band. Some include a small disc record containing all or portions of these new releases, which gives the band director the added advantage of being able to hear the finished product and therefore to determine with greater accuracy the suitability of the music for his purposes. This practice is not only a real time saver for the busy band director, but also offers guidance in the selection of proper tempos and in certain other facets of interpretation. If the disc contains a complete rendition of several selections, the director might find it helpful to play these for the band after they have had the initial experience of sight reading. Since many of these recordings are made by fine college, university, and professional bands, listening to them helps high school band members to understand what is expected of them in the way of balance, blend, phrasing, dynamics, and other aspects of good bandsmanship.

The director new to the field of school band music should write to leading publishers and request that he be included on their mailing list to receive certain educational music materials. There are also a number of large music supply houses throughout the country which carry music of many different publishers. These "jobbers," as they might be called, are usually in a position to provide rapid service by mail to most parts of the country. In addition, some employ educational music consultants ready to give advice and assistance, particularly to newcomers to the field, in the selection of music and other instructional material suited for school groups at different levels of advancement. One very effective method of getting on the mailing list of leading publishers and making contacts with educational service agencies is to attend a regional or national convention of music educators. Here the band director will be in a position to register at the exhibit area to indicate interest in and need for certain kinds of music, supplies, and equipment. Furthermore, he will meet educational consultants as well as sales personnel and can specifically indicate the level of music his group can perform and discuss other problems relating to his needs, including instruments, uniforms, risers, electronic devices associated with music performance, and the like. By attending exhibits on a national scale such as are afforded by these conventions, the band director will be in a good position to assess trends in music education and to take steps to keep pace with them.

The methods employed in ordering music and equipment vary widely from one school system to another. In general, the band director must abide by policies established by his own Board of Education. While some directors enjoy greater latitude in ordering material and equipment, all will undoubtedly be required to go through certain procedures in this connection. In most cases a portion of the over-all educational budget will be allotted for the purchase of music and equipment. This budget is usually divided into three or more catagories, for example: Budget "A," Instructional Materials, would include textbooks, music, and supplies; budget "B," Capital Outlay, would involve expenditures for instruments, uniforms, and heavy equipment; budget "C" would provide for the repair and maintenance of instruments and other music equipment.

Maintaining good relations with music dealers is essential if the band director desires good service. The director who is reasonable in his demands for service and supplies the dealer with the correct and detailed information when ordering music and instructional material, or in connection with repairs needed on both school-owned and privately owned instruments, will stand a good chance of having his needs met promptly and courteously. At times these needs may include borrowing an instrument from the dealer while one normally in use is undergoing repairs. The band director may also need the cooperation of the dealer when a display of instruments is required in connection with an instrumental orientation program or when the local school is serving as host for a state or regional meeting of band directors.

The alert band director will find that much knowledge about instruments in general can be gained from the experienced music dealer. By talking with a number of dealers, the director will become more knowledgeable about construction and design features felt to be important in the selection of instruments for the school band. The interested dealer will also be ready to pass on to the band director tips about the use and care of certain items of equipment about which the average school band director may not be fully informed. He will also be willing to have the director try out new models of instruments and other equipment as they appear on the market. Furthermore, through closer association with dealers and others in the music industry, the director will come to a fuller understanding of the problems confronting them and thus temper his own demands for service and supplies. From the dealer's point of view, maintaining good relations with the school band director and those on the instrumental staff is a worthy business practice since a prospering band program in the schools lends to an expanding clientele for him.

Band directors would normally be informed by school officials of the amount allotted for music and that provided for equipment and repairs. With this information, the director will then need to carefully assess his needs on a priority basis and proceed accordingly. In ordering music, a standard requisition form adopted by the school board is usually required to be filled out in triplicate. One copy will be retained by the school office, one forwarded to the dealer, and one will be returned to the director himself following approval of the order.

Ordering music

In the process of ordering music, supplies, or instruments and other equipment, the director should exert great care in describing the items being requisitioned. With respect to ordering music, this should include the following: (1) the title, (2) composer, (3) arranger, (4) publisher, (5) publisher's code number for the individual selection, if one is indicated, (6) instrumentation desired; that is, whether a symphonic band, full band or other combination is sought, (7) quantity, and (8) price of each selection and the total cost of the order. Beyond this, it will be necessary to indicate whether the music is to be ordered from a central supply house, or direct from the publisher. In either case, the address or addresses should be included on the form. Needless to say, requisition forms should be typed using carbon paper for duplicate and triplicate copies. If some or all of the music is ordered "on approval" to afford the director with an opportunity to make a more detailed evaluation of the music, this should be made clear on the order form to avoid duplication of the order or discrepancies in the rendering of the monthly statement by the dealer.

Ordering instruments

In ordering instruments and other equipment, the local board will usually require the band director to seek bids from merchants in the community and surrounding area to assure efficient expenditure of public funds for education. In this connection, it will be necessary for the director to write up the specifications of each item in some detail to insure that the bid prices will be based upon articles of similar quality. Specifications should include the following particulars: (1) materials of which the item is made, (2) its particular design features, (3) the kind of finish applied, (4) its servicability, (5) its musical characteristics or contributions, (6) special construction features, (7) construction of the case, if one is included, (8) number, type, and quality of accessories including mouthpiece dimensions, etc. (9) the weight of the item such as in the case of a sousaphone or other large items that may have to be carried, and (10) dimensions such as those relating to sizes of various types of drums or the number of octaves to be contained in a set of bells, xylophones, or related keyboard instrument.

Selecting uniforms

Similar procedures will probably be required in connection with the procurement of uniforms for the band. Here again, the director will benefit from attendance at regional or national music educators conferences where he will have the opportunity to visit exhibits by leading suppliers of school band uniforms and compare the various features and prices of each. Items which should be of particular concern to him would include the following: (1) weight of the cloth with respect to comfort to the wearer, (2) durability of the cloth, (3) its ability to resist wrinkling, (4) its ability to resist shrinking, (5) the stain-repellent qualities of the material, (6) the color-fast properties of the material, (7) appropriateness of the design for high school use, (8) tailoring features which will permit ready adjustment from one individual to another, (9) flexibility of use for both indoor and outdoor purposes, and (10) provision to add or replace uniforms with matching materials, design, and color.

RELATIONSHIPS WITH THE NEWS MEDIA

The news media, which constitute the general avenues of communication with the public, can be of immeasurable worth in interpreting the aims and objectives of the school band as an educational force in the community. Through the newspapers, radio, and television, the band director can transmit information about the purposes and activities of the band to the average taxpayer and stimulate his interest in and support for this part of the school curriculum. Obviously, since they are paying the bill, the public should be kept informed of the kinds of educational programs which they are supporting. In addition to articles about the band which should point up its educational benefits, an occasional performance over the air or an appearance on television is not only an excellent means of reaching the public, but also can be a source of community pride.

Since a performance by the band on radio or television is likely to be a unique experience for members and even for the director, special care should be taken in selecting the music to be shared with the average listening or viewing public to insure its appropriateness and general appeal. Furthermore, since the acoustic problems in each case will be quite different from those encountered in the school music rehearsal room or auditorium, it may be wise, if not necessary, to hold a rehearsal prior to the performance to accustom the group to these differences. In the event that the occasion is related to an appearance of the marching band at a televised football game of regional or national scope, a two- or three-hour rehearsal on the field before the game will be mandatory. The technical staff involved in an appearance of this magnitude will require a great deal of advance planning on the part of the band director and close cooperation with these individuals as they deal with camera angles, microphone placement, and other technical matters. With respect to performing on the radio, the requirements, although exacting, will be somewhat less complicated since the visual aspects will not be involved. Of particular importance in a radio broadcast, whether from the studio or the school, will be the seating arrangement of the players, the number of microphones used, and the location of these as they relate to certain sections of the band—especially the percussion group. Since percussion sounds emanate from media that are quite different from those of the wind instrument families and therefore tend to stand out more prominently, special attention will have to be given to the placement of this section.

Handling publicity

The band director will come to rely upon the various media in both the school and community in informing the general public of forthcoming events involving the school band. Whether these performances are regular concerts sponsored by the music department and held in the school auditorium or performances relating to special events in the community, a state or regional music festival, or other type of service provided by the school band, the director will want to notify the public of these activities by way of the school paper, the local press, the radio, and, if appropriate, a television newscast.

Articles submitted to these media should be carefully prepared from the point of view of interest to the general public with certain aspects of the performance being "highlighted." If the band director has had little or no training in journalism, he may wish to solicit the aid of the head of the English department or one of its staff in preparing materials to be released. From the mechanical aspect, the news item should be typed on standard typing paper of good quality with lines being double spaced.

With respect to publicizing an approaching concert by the band, the director should plan a series of articles which will be given to the local papers over a period of several weeks to assure continuing coverage. While the initial release may be of a general nature, subsequent articles should deal with some of the specific details of the concert such as the appearance of soloists, a guest conductor, or perhaps an announcement of a first performance of a new work, or the distribution of music awards. Articles should be designed to attract and hold the attention of the reader. In this regard, a headline which catches the imagination of the public can be effective in drawing his interest to reading the details of the article. This should be presented in a straightforward manner with the most pertinent information appearing first and less relevant material included later. A reporter suggested to me on an occasion when I submitted a notice of a forthcoming concert that the writeup should begin with the "five editorial w's," that is, the "what, when, where, who, and why" of the affair to secure and hold the interest of the reader from the outset.

For the most part, newspapers prefer not to include large group photos in relation to news articles about forthcoming concerts. Instead, they prefer to use one or two selected candid shots involving just a few participants or a soloist. On occasion they also run the picture of the band director himself. Photographs submitted should be glossy prints of good quality with sharp detail, and since newspaper columns are usually 1 3/4 inches wide, they prefer to have photos conform to certain dimensions. It should be understood that standard photo dimensions such as the 4" x 6", the 5" x 7", and others can readily be reduced by the news staff. If the director wishes these pictures to be returned to him following their use by the newspaper, he should lightly stamp the back of the photo with a rubber stamp identifying the school. It is also a good practice to date news releases in the interest of promoting continuity, assuming a sequence of articles are submitted.

Just prior to the concert itself, if not on the very day of the concert, it might be well to include a copy of the program with the final article, or at least to point up the highlights and special features of the evening's program. Acknowledgement of special assistance by members of the faculty, the administration, or the band parents association should be contained on the printed program and in at least one of the articles released to the news media. Brief summary type announcements should be prepared for radio and television newscasts and notification of broadcasting or rebroadcasting of the program should also be made available to all media.

As a gesture of courtesy and in appreciation for their cooperation in publicizing the concert, complimentary tickets might be sent to members of the press and to those associated with other news media. Their cooperation will be especially valuable in the event that the concert represents a special fund raising effort for a worthy cause in the school or community. The presence of a reporter, photographer, or both would be a desirable asset in helping to keep the general public informed of the educational values of the school music program. Events involving performances by the school music groups, including the band, are of special interest to a segment of the population of any community, just as reviews of sports events are to the local sports enthusiasts.

Where several newspapers serve the community, the band director will need to take special pains to distribute news releases at the same time or at least equitably and in accordance with their going-to-press deadlines—especially if one is published weekly and the others daily. Furthermore, efforts should be made by the band director to supply articles which are particularly newsworthy on a continuing basis throughout the year. Included among these should be items concerning special achievements, honors, or awards involving members of the band; similar accomplishments of members of the music faculty including the band director; appointments or elections of staff members to positions of responsibility in professional organizations; additions or changes in the staff or the curriculum itself; attendance by staff members at state, regional, or national music conferences; speeches by music faculty members including the band director; notice of publication of articles, books, or music by the director; professional performance experiences of members of the music staff; festival ratings received by the band; items of interest about former band members; summer travel, study, or performance activities of either the members of the band or its director; and invitations received by the director to serve as a guest conductor or adjudicator at a festival held in another state or region. In addition to keeping the news media supplied with information of this sort, he may also contribute items of interest to state, regional, and national publications as well as articles dealing with special phases of teaching and directing instrumental groups.

The prudent band director will also avail himself of space and facilities in connection with the school publication itself. In this practice, he may find it expedient to involve the secretary of the band or a member of the band who happens to be a member of the school publication staff as well. Bringing the attention of the student body to the activities of the band through this medium can prove to be of distinct value since many students read the school paper with greater interest than their local newspaper. Articles in the school publication should reflect the student point of view and recognize the contributions and accomplishments of individual members of the band. Announcements of forthcoming events in which the band will participate should be included, as should reviews in brief of recent engagements and performances. Special mention should be made of those in the band who attain positions in the All-State Band, along with those who receive special honors, awards, or scholarships.

From time to time, candid photos of individuals or groups in the band might be included in conjunction with an approaching concert or marching event. Pictures of band officers, the drum major, the twirlers, or flag squad in uniform are effective in attracting the reader's attention and should be inserted in the local paper at appropriate seasons of the year. In some communities, it is the practice of the local newspaper to devote a full page on a monthly basis to school news items submitted by students and prepared by members of the student press. This practice, in addition to improving relations between the school and community, affords unique exper-

iences in journalism for a portion of the student body—and inciden-
tally helps to stimulate the sale of the local paper on the appointed
days.

RELATIONSHIPS WITH PROFESSIONAL MUSICIANS

Within each community there are some who teach music privately,
play professionally, or, in some cases, do both. The band director
would do well to become acquainted with all or at least some of
these individuals for his own benefit as well as that of his band
members. Usually the band director will find some in his group who
would benefit from private study, and therefore his knowledge of
these resource people in the community can be valuable. While the
band director who may also be involved in giving instrumental
instruction to members of the band can guide these students in
developing an appreciable amount of skill and musicianship, he
cannot be expected to display a professional level of performance on
all the instruments he will be required to teach. Where the band
director is a major on brass instruments, he may seek the aid of a
woodwind or percussion specialist in the area to assist, especially
with the more advanced players of these instruments.

In the event that the band director should engage in farming out
some of his advanced players to private teachers in the community,
he should be careful not to single out one teacher over another lest
he be charged with undue discrimination. To handle situations like
this, he should prepare a typed or printed list of all private teachers
in the area and distribute this list to all interested pubils. Pupils and
parents in the community will soon find out on their own who the
really qualified private teachers are by word of mouth and by the
achievements of their "products."

In some communities the school may arrange credit for members
of the band studying privately with professionals in the area, while
others even go so far as to arrange for lessons by these individuals in
the school on Saturdays. This can more conveniently be instituted in
schools located near large cities or close to colleges and universities
having a sizable music faculty. In cases where the school attempts to
link up with private teachers and professional musicians, it may be
necessary for school authorities to engage in certain evaluative
procedures. These could include: (1) demonstration of performing
ability, (2) evidence of professional study, (3) record of performing
experience, (4) prior teaching experience, and (5) evidence of degree
held. Where credit is given for outside study, it will be necessary for

the private teachers to report periodically to the school on such matters as attendance, evidence of preparation, and the general progress of the individual.

Although for many years the private teacher as well as the professional musician eyed the school music program with mixed feelings of apprehension, suspicion, and even fear, in recent years they have come to realize that music educators, for the most part, are proficient performers in their own right. Also, they are generally better informed of the requirements of becoming a music educator. Furthermore, instead of the school music program detracting from their efforts to earn a living, it has stimulated interest and participation in music on a scale heretofore unheard of, resulting in increasing benefits to both the private teacher and professional alike. On the other side of the coin, the music educator should come to understand the position of these individuals in the community and their influence on public opinion as it relates to the school music program. He should realize that in small communities throughout the country, these individuals represent the voice of authority on music within the town whereas he, as a newcomer, may have to prove himself through his products to gain public confidence and support. The thoughtful and wise music educator will take special steps to make these individuals the allies of the school music program. The formation of a community music advisory board will be found effective in unifying the efforts of all those interested in fostering music activity.

RELATIONSHIPS WITH PARENTS

Next to the members of the band themselves, those in the community most directly concerned with the stature of the school music program and the calibre of the band in particular, are the parents of these individuals. Parents, more than the non-parent taxpayer in the community, are naturally interested in the quality of education which their sons and daughters will receive and are directly concerned with the growth and progress of their child. The role of the parent in relation to the music program of the school can contribute in many ways to the success of the groups organized in the school. As individuals, they can display their interest and support for the program by attending concerts involving the various music performance groups throughout the year. They can also assist members of the music faculty in their efforts to build a worthwhile music program by encouraging regular daily practice by their offspring. In addition, since they understand the values of music as an educational force, they can influence others in the community to rally to the support of the music program.

One of the most effective ways to enlist the interest and support of the parents is to organize a Music Parents Club, or, if felt to be desirable, a Band Parents Association. A group such as this can contribute to the growth and development of the music program and its constituent parts. Their very existence in the community will be symbolic of their interest in and support of this arm of the educational program. Furthermore, they can help the director to attain worthy educational goals and foster a closer relationship between the school and the community.

Organizing the Band Parents Club

There are several approaches that the band director may take in organizing a Band Parents Club. These include: (1) sending a form letter home to parents by way of the members of the band; (2) mailing a letter to the parents announcing the date, time, and place of an organizational meeting; (3) submitting articles to the local papers announcing the purposes of the proposed meeting; (4) announcements through other media such as radio, television, school publications, and newsletters to parents; and (5) meeting briefly with parents of band members immediately following a band concert and soliciting their interest and aid in forming such a group. Whichever method the band director chooses to pursue, the aims and purposes for which such an organization is to be formed should be clearly stated. Furthermore, before any steps are taken to organize a group such as this, the approval of the school administration and the Board of Education should be sought.

A first meeting of the Band Parents Club should include an explanation by the band director of the needs and purposes for forming such a group, the election of a temporary chairman, and the appointment of a nominating committee to select a slate of officers at a subsequent meeting. If possible, refreshments might be arranged for by the director through the cooperation of the school home economics department, or through volunteers from the mothers of band members. Membership cards could be arranged for in advance by the band director, as well as identification badges to be worn by parents at meetings to facilitate their becoming acquainted with each other. It might be appropriate to invite the school principal to speak briefly in welcoming the parents at the initial meeting. Also, through a consensus of those present, a time for regular meetings should be determined. In addition to selecting a temporary chairman, it may be felt necessary to have a temporary secretary to record the business of the meeting. Following the meeting, the band director should meet briefly with the temporary chairman, the temporary secretary, and the nominating committee to plan the business of the next meeting. It will also be necessary for those on the nominating committee to meet to prepare the slate of officers which would be presented at the next regular meeting of the club. During this process, they will be concerned with selecting individuals based on their qualities of leadership and special talents desirable for certain positions. Individuals having ability in shorthand and typing should be considered for the office of secretary, while for the office of treasurer, individuals with some experience in business or accounting should be sought. In organizing the slate of officers, the committee needs to contact prospective candidates personally or by telephone to ascertain their interest and willingness to serve in a particular capacity. The band director may also need to meet with the temporary officers in determining the best approach to formulating a constitution and by-laws for the organization. This could be done through the establishment of a special committee which would have the responsibility of creating such a document and presenting it for approval at an early meeting of the club. A sample Band Parents Club constitution and by-laws is available through the Educational Services Department of the Conn Corporation of Elkhart, Indiana.

Once regular officers of the club have been elected and installed and a constitution and by-laws have been adopted, a format of meetings should be decided upon by the Executive Board. Meetings should include programs of interest to parents, a business session, and a social period when refreshments may be served and parents can mingle. Programs can include at different times speeches about relevant music subjects or experiences by individuals in the community and surrounding area, performances by student soloists and ensembles with the band or other school music groups, the showing of films or slides relating to music, presentations by the band director himself, performances by adults in the community, and programs calling for the direct involvement of club members themselves, including discussions of subjects of immediate concern to the group. A type of program that I have found to create a good deal of interest among parents is the conducting of an open band rehearsal in the school music facilities in connection with one of their regular meetings. Through this procedure, parents come to a better understanding of the problems confronting the director as he attempts to work out the details of a certain piece of music. They will also sense the nature of the rapport that the director has with the band, and better appreciate the finished product when they hear these selections performed in a concert at a later date.

Between regular meetings of the club, members of the Executive Board should meet with the band director, who will function as the club advisor, to discuss ways and means of stimulating greater interest in and support for the program of music in the schools and in the band specifically. Discussion should also center about activities of the club and ways in which it can be of aid to the director.

Role of the Band Parents Club

While the main aims of the Band Parents Club are concerned with arrousing interest in and getting support for the band, there are a number of other services which they can help to provide for the band. Since it is one of the most active and perhaps the largest organization in the school and is composed of the members of both sexes, the band will need the help and cooperation of adults from time to time during the year. There are times when the services of chaperones will be needed, such as trips to football games in nearby towns, or in connection with an exchange concert trip or one to a state or regional music festival. If a concert by the band is sponsored directly by the Band Parents Club, as might be the case in an exchange concert where the cost of transportation may be assumed by the club, members of the club may be involved in handling the ticket sale, ushering, programs, publicity, and perhaps the provision of refreshments for both bands in the cafeteria following the concert. In addition, some of the mothers in the club skilled in the use of the needle and thread might periodically sew loose buttons back on uniforms, or make other minor repairs.

Although the basic equipment and uniforms of the band should be provided through funds administered by the top school authorities, it may become necessary for the Band Parents Club to engage in fund raising activities on occasion. In the event the band is invited to perform at an important music convention such as those held by the Music Educators National Conference on a regional or national basis, it is likely that the club will be pressed into rendering such a service if they wish their group to accept such an invitation. Board of education funds do not, as a rule, cover such contingencies. Since invitations of this dimension represent a certain honor for the school and community, fund raising projects are usually supported successfully and with some degree of enthusiasm. Also, such projects may be undertaken by the club to sponsor a trip or concert tour felt to be educationally worthwhile. Other special needs may arise from time to time which will require the assistance of this organization. These could include: (1) giving individual awards to band members in recognition of outstanding performance or service; (2) providing scholarship aid to one or more deserving members of the band; (3) supplying additional uniform accessories such as raincoats, etc.; (4) purchasing a large or unusual instrument to augment those provided by the Board of Education; (5) providing acoustic panels for a stage; (6) sponsoring a trip by the band to hear a fine service, professional, or university band; and (7) cooperating with other agencies and clubs in the community in providing for a band shell for summer concerts and other community affairs. Booklets containing fund raising ideas are available through the cooperation of manufacturers of band instruments and other music supply houses.

Once the Band Parents Club is well established in the school and community, it will have little trouble in perpetuating itself. It will, of course, require a continuing interest and planning of worthwhile activities and programs by the band director and club officers. Parents, observing the extra energy put forth by the band director in his effort to make band membership among the most memorable and worthwhile experiences of the high school years, will rally to his support regardless of whether their sons or daughters are still in school or have graduated. To cite an example of this—in connection with a special fund drive to purchase an electronic organ, a father of a band member graduated two years earlier raised nearly two thousand dollars by himself through selling items on a person-to-person and door-to-door basis!

As each new school year approaches and new officers are installed, the band director should meet with these individuals to plan for activities felt to be of interest and worth to the club membership. Two or three weeks before the first regular meeting is held a letter should be sent to all members including parents of newcomers to the band. This letter should be an invitation to participate in club activities, state something of the purpose of the organization, and contain other kinds of information that will stimulate the interest of all concerned. The date, time, and place of the meeting should be stated and the nature of the program included. (See Illustration 9-3.)

It might also be fitting to establish certain practices which will become traditional over the years. This might include listing all past presidents of the Band Parents Club on the back of the program at the final concert of the year, instituting a special award to recognize the leadership of its outgoing president, or through some other method showing appreciation to officers and members of the club.

Lyman Hall High School
Music Parents Association

Oct. 6, 1969

Dear Parent:

We wish to take this opportunity to extend a cordial invitation to you to participate in the activities of the Lyman Hall Music Parents Association.

This organization was formed in the spring of 1952 by a spirited group of parents interested in supporting the active program of music at the high school. Over these many years they have assumed a vital role in furthering the cause of music education in the school and community and have sponsored many worthwhile projects for members of the various instrumental and choral groups of the high school.

The main objectives of the organization are: (1) to arouse and maintain interest and support for Lyman Hall music groups; (2) to cooperate with members of the music faculty in achieving the desired educational goals of the department; and (3) to foster social activities during meetings and at other times to bring parents together in a closer relationship.

Many special events have been successfully sponsored by the Lyman Hall Music Parents Association including exchange concerts by the band, orchestra and choir, and state and regional music festivals. The exchange concerts which are especially broadening and enriching have included visits and performances in communities throughout the state and to neighboring states such as Massachusetts, Rhode Island, New York, and New Jersey. A most memorable high peak was achieved last year in sponsoring the Lyman Hall Band in its appearance at the National Music Educators Conference in Washington, D.C.

The Association meets on the third Thursday of each month from October to May with the exception of December when no meeting is scheduled. Meetings generally include a business session, a program of interest to all, and refreshments.

The first meeting will be held on Thursday, Oct. 16, 1969, at 8:00 P.M. in Room 6G of the music wing. The program which will deal with Music Aptitude will be presented by Dr. Richard A. Otto, Director of Music at Lyman Hall and Supervisor of Music for all schools in Wallingford.

We sincerely urge you to attend this meeting to get acquainted with others in the community who have sons and daughters in the various high school music units. Come and participate in the discussion about proposed activities for the year.

Sincerely yours,
William Andrews, President

ILLUSTRATION 9-3

PERFORMANCES

Public performances by the high school band can be an effective instrument for promoting good relations between the school and the community. Through these activities, the school is in a strategic position to demonstrate to the tax-paying public what is being accomplished by one or more departments of the school (others may well be involved depending upon the nature of the presentation). Obviously, before performing in public, the performing group should be thoroughly prepared to assure a successful presentation. A good performance can be decisive in gaining support for the band and for the school as a whole. The band is frequently found in the position of ambassador of good will because of its versatility in being able to perform outdoors as well as indoors and while seated, standing, or marching.

While performances of the band are both necessary and desirable to sustain the interest and development of its members, the number, length, and frequency of these appearances should be of concern to the director, the principal, and other school authorities. Although the majority of the performances by school bands will be directly related to school events, there is a tendency to involve this organization in a certain number of non-school affairs each year. It is the responsibility of school authorities to make certain that events requiring the services of the high school band are educationally worthwhile and constitute learning experiences. Later in this chapter I shall offer a set of policies regarding appearances by school bands which may serve as a guide to band directors and school administrators throughout the country.

Performances by the school band are effective in motivating members to improve in their ability to handle music that is more difficult, more colorful, and offers greater challenge. Experiences of this kind, when planned with care, spaced apart on the school calendar, and adequately prepared for, can be among the most satisfying and memorable experiences of one's high school career. It should also be recognized that while public performances by the band may constitute a kind of test for the group, they also provide a form of public examination of the director's efforts, ability, and productivity!

Concerts by the band can also contribute to the cultural climate of the community. While it will be necessary at the outset for the director to assess the cultural level of the community, the music selected for public sharing should be chosen with a view to raising the musical tastes of the community. It goes without saying that the music selected for indoor concert programs of the formal type will be musically more worthwhile than that performed outdoors in a less formal atmosphere. Although the educational and cultural values of concerts contribute more significantly to the musical growth and understanding of both the "producer and consumer," the values of certain outdoor performance services of the band cannot be denied. From a public relations point of view, if no other, performances by the marching band are likely to reach a larger portion of the community because of their very nature. Football games, parades, and pageants attract a segment of the community which might not otherwise see and hear the high school band.

Types of performances

Performance activity of the senior high school band is considerably more varied and extensive than that of bands at lower school levels. Beginning in the fall with appearances at football games, the high school band finds itself immersed in an on-rushing stream of continuing activity right up to the time of graduation.

Time was when the main function of the band at football games was to sit in the bleachers and arouse support for the team by playing spirited marches and perhaps forming in block band formation on the field at half time to play the school song, the fight song, and other music suited to the occasion. Marching maneuvers were relatively simple, with some emphasis on precision drills and block letter formations. Today the amount of time, energy, and imagination that goes into the planning, preparation, and execution of the weekly appearance of the high school band is, at least in some cases, staggering to the point where the efficacy of this practice in terms of its educational worth may be the subject of some debate. While there are benefits to be derived from this kind of activity for the band, the public, and the team, the emphasis given to this phase of the program of music education must be carefully weighed in the light of the educational philosophy of the school as a whole.

From time to time throughout the school year, the band is called upon to perform at pep rallies. Performance activity also includes appearances in assembly programs in other schools in the community for the purpose of promoting interest in instrumental music and in recruiting future band members. In schools not having an orchestra the services of the band may be sought in connection with a drama production or school musical. School bands are also called upon to supply appropriate music for seasonal events during the year and to perform for the kick-off of a school or community fund raising drive.

Also, on occasion the school band is invited to represent a local service club in a parade at a state convention of that organization, or they may be pressed into service in connection with the opening of a new super-market. While there is no doubt that these functions provide opportunities for additional playing experience and carry with them a certain concomitant public relations value, care should be taken to see that these peripheral activities are kept to a minimum.

Other performance activities of the senior high school band include the presentation of concerts for the student body in the school auditorium during the school day, evening concerts for the general public, exchange concerts involving a shared concert with another band, and performances at state and regional music festivals. It is from these kinds of experiences that the real values in and enjoyment of band membership come into proper focus. Preparing the variety of selections that comprise a concert or festival program constitutes a learning experience that is both stimulating and challenging at the outset and satisfying and rewarding in view of accomplished goals. While the many fundamentals of musicianship can be learned through the use of regular methods books, some of the finer points of interpretation are better illustrated and learned through the study and practice of literature to be performed in connection with events of this nature.

Exchange concerts

Exchange concert activity in its most popular form includes elements of motivation, progress, sharing, and pacing. These affairs are generally organized to provide each band with an opportunity to perform as a unit and then combine in the performance of several pre-determined selections. While some directors plan this event on the basis of one overnight stay, others extend it to include visiting classes in the host school on Friday and a visit to an industrial plant, museum, or other point of interest in the area. One or two rehearsals of the combined bands will be scheduled, as will a dance or other event of a social nature. The dimensions which the affair will assume will be determined by several factors, including: (1) traveling distance, (2) time of year in consideration of the weather, (3) costs involved, (4) availability of school facilities and housing, (5) availability of chaperones, (6) points of interest to visit, (7) amount of rehearsal time required for the combined numbers, (8) whether the affair is scheduled during a school vacation period or on a regular school weekend, and (9) the degree of emphasis the cooperating directors wish to place on this event.

Events of this kind will be found to motivate members to practice more diligently and with greater regularity in hopes of keeping pace with members of the visiting group as they jointly prepare the selections to be performed by the combined band. Furthermore, the opportunity to see, hear, and observe another band in rehearsal and in concert can be stimulating, enlightening, and broadening. The efforts of their own director to establish and maintain certain standards of performance will be better understood, and the experience of working under another director can be interesting and enriching. The social and public relations values of these exchanges can be far reaching, as young musicians share their common interests with each other and with the parents who supply the housing for the visiting bandsmen. The public at large will gain a fuller understanding of the benefits of an active program of music in the schools and will thereafter support the band and other music groups with greater enthusiasm.

Contests

As part of the performing activities of school bands of an earlier era and in an effort to elevate the performance of high school bands in general, contests among bands were devised and implemented on a local, state, regional, and even national level. Events of this type were obviously geared to pit one group against another in an effort to determine the winner. Classifications were established in accordance with the size of the student body, and lists of graded music were compiled to be used in these contests. While band directors were given the option of selecting a warm-up march, one or more selections were required in connection with each classification and one other selection included in the performance was to be chosen from among those selected by state and national committees. The latter selection was to be in keeping with the graded level of other music performed. During the day, for example, the audience would hear the same "required" selection performed several times by bands coming from what were classified as Class "A" schools, or those having a student population of over a certain number. This number underwent some changes over a period of years and varied somewhat from state to state; however, if a band qualified as a winner in a certain class at the state level and desired to compete in the national, it had to conform to the established classifications of the National Contest Association. Schools having fewer pupils were classified either as a Class "B" or Class "C" school in accordance with the population lines defined by the state or national committee. In those days, Class "D" was reserved for bands newly formed within the current school year.

While the warm-up march could be chosen by the director without restriction, the third or selected piece had to be included on the list of selections graded in accordance with the school population sizes established by the state or national governing groups. Eventually, sight reading was included as part of the contest and was figured into the total score of the band. Although bands had the option of competing in the next higher classification, none could choose a lower category. Winners were selected on the basis of elements of performance such as: (1) tone, (2) intonation, (3) balance, (4) interpretation, (5) musical effect, and (6) other factors including instrumentation, discipline, and appearance. Each of the main elements contained certain parenthetic sub-divisions. Scoring was based on a possible total of 1000 points.

Although there were many flaws in the early contests, they did serve to contribute to the growth and development of school bands and to the establishment of certain standards with regard to literature and expected performance levels. For many directors, these experiences served to underscore the need for more rehearsal time, better facilities, and improvement in the band's instrumentation

Festivals

While band contest of various types are still sponsored in different parts of the country, the contest as it was formerly carried on in affiliation with state and national music educator groups tended to evolve into a music festival which focused the emphasis on participation by groups rather than competition between them. These were developed on the basis of a bi-lateral plan. That is, bands could elect to perform music chosen without regard for categories or grade of difficulty and receive comments from the adjudicators without any rating whatsoever. They could, on the other hand, elect to try for a rating based upon the performance of music selected from prepared state lists. The most difficult music was labeled "Grade VI," with that of a less demanding nature labeled "Grade V," "Grade IV," and so on. Levels of performance were indicated by letters "A," "B," "C," "D" and so on. A top grade performance of selections chosen from the most difficult category thus would have an "A–VI" rating. While several bands at each festival may attempt music from the "VI" list, usually only one or two manage to provide an "A" performance in this category. Ratings usually were accompanied by

comments by the judges which, for the most part, offered suggestions for the improvement of the band from the standpoint of
intonation, tone, facility, instrumentation, discipline, appearance and
so on. Here again, the band director was afforded some support in his
requests for more time and better equipment for the band upon
returning to his home community.

Present trends in conducting music festivals, at least at the state
level, seem to follow along the lines of this bi-lateral type of festival.
This permits the director to select music freely from his library and
from current music publications and to decide on the merits of going
for a rating as compared with merely seeking comments and criticism
(constructive, we hope) by the adjudicators. Other types of festivals
are held on an area basis in many states with bands in adjoining
communities getting together on a less formal basis to hold a festival
where each group will have an opportunity to hear all the others.
Actually, there are many festivals involving large numbers of bands
which include the massing of these groups at the conclusion of the
day in either a concert type performance of pre-selected music or in
a parade through the host city. Obviously, festivals of this dimension
require superior facilities, a tremendous amount of planning, and the
involvement of many agencies in the school and community.

There are many values inherent in participating in festivals of these
kinds, since they not only motivate the individual to greater
achievement, afford enjoyment and enriching experiences, provide
opportunities for young bandsmen to hear performances by others,
stimulate support and interest in music, but also tend to arouse
public support for music, promote the social development of the
individual, and create an atmosphere of good public relations.

Although the types of performance activity will vary from place to
place with the emphasis adjusted according to the existing educational philosophy of the school, the kinds of activity described here
are among those most prevalent in high schools throughout the
country. Obviously, one type of performance activity is of greater
educational value than another, and it is the shared responsibility of
the band director, the school principal, and other school authorities
to emphasize those which contribute significantly to the intellectual,
emotional, and cultural maturation of the individual.

POLICIES GOVERNING PERFORMANCES BY SCHOOL BANDS

Since school bands are called upon to perform for events of
importance in the school, the community, and beyond, and decisions

need to be made regarding these appearances, it is essential that some code be established to provide reasonable guidelines to regulate this activity. In light of this, the following policies are offered:

1. The utilization of school pupils for musical performances in the school and community or beyond should be limited.
2. The occasion for which the services of the school band are required should be educationally defensible.
3. The nature of the environment and the type of performance required should be given careful consideration.
4. Provision for adequate health and safety measures should be made by school administrators in behalf of pupils and staff members involved.
5. Adequate advance notice should be forthcoming to allow for the proper preparation of the music and services to be rendered.
6. School administrators should consult with the band director before making any commitment for the appearance of a group for which he is directly responsible and which requires his presence.
7. An adequate number of adult chaperones should be provided for by administrators in proportion to the size of the group and the number of buses involved, with at least one adult of each sex available on each bus.
8. The musical demands of the event for which the band is to perform must be within the physical, mental, emotional, and musical grasp and capabilities of pupils of this age.
9. The element of time as it relates to the length of the performance and its place on the school calendar in consideration of other scheduled performances should be the concern of the director and school administrators.
10. Requests for the services of the school band by organizations or groups outside the school should be carefully screened to determine whether it is for a worthy cause or is commercially motivated.
11. Consideration needs to be given to whether the affair at which the band is to perform is school or community related and whether it is a scheduled or non-scheduled event.
12. Provision to underwrite the cost of transportation should be the responsibility of those requesting the services of the band.

13. Consideration should be given to the make-up of the band with respect to the instrumentation available in relation to the kind of event for which the services of the band are sought.

14. Determination for the use of a school band should be based on whether the affair for which the services of the band are required comes within the province of a school group, or infringes upon the rights of professional musicians as stated in the Code of Ethics of the Music Educators National Conference and the American Federation of Musicians.

15. Other considerations applying to appearances by school bands should include: (a) the time of day, (b) the time of year with special reference to the temperature if held outdoors, and (c) the amount of pupil and teacher time required to prepare for the event with respect to its importance to the school or community.

It is the hope of this author that these guidelines will prove to be sufficiently broad to cover all performance contingencies and will be of assistance to band directors and school administrators in determining the worth and validity of requests made for the appearance and services of school bands.

INDEX